GOURMET
in the
GALLEY

KATHARINE ROBINSON

GOURMET
IN THE
GALLEY

QUADRANGLE/
The New York Times Book Co.

Library of Congress Catalog Card Number: 72-83288

International Standard Book Number: 0-8129-0263-7

Book Design: Dorothy Upjohn Lewis

TO

The Skipper

VALIANT NAVIGATOR, STENTORIAN ORDER-BARKER,
SEVERE CRITIC, AND PATIENT RECIPE-TESTER,

AND TO *W. J.,*

WITHOUT EITHER OF WHOM
THIS BOOK WOULD NOT HAVE BEEN WRITTEN,
AND, NOT LEAST,

TO *P. Hall,*

THE FIRST TO ENCOURAGE AND URGE ME ONWARD

Contents

SECTION TWO

Menus & Recipes
for many
Winds & Waters

~

Appendix

Foreword

Though a galley is not a kitchen, and life afloat is very different from life ashore, people who like to eat well relish the pleasure of good food and drink, whatever the surroundings. Meals can be as wonderfully succulent in the open cockpit of a sloop or the comfortable cabin of a cruiser as they are in a twilit patio or vine-covered porch. For the cook who enjoys cooking and loves to eat and drink well, cooking in the galley of a boat that's any length from roughly twenty-two to forty-four feet can be a fascinating challenge to her skill and ingenuity. This book is written for her, and for all others who love life on the water and may not yet realize that they can make gourmet delights part of it.

Over the years, I have arrived at the firm opinion that cruising is not an endurance test whose purpose is to prove that human beings can take a lot of punishment and come out of it with nothing worse than frayed nerves, short tempers, and a general inclination to be glad it's all over. What's the point and where's the fun? The notion that cooking on a boat must be a cross between catch-as-catch-can picnicking and boy-scout camping is, to me, pure nonsense. Imaginative, soul-satisfying, and really elegant meals are well within reach, with moderate quickness, and without undue effort. Ingredients need not be esoteric. It is the combinations and blendings that lift things from the humdrum and these can be achieved in the simplest of ways. Radish roses, for example, have no place; crisp, fresh, well-scrubbed radishes do.

These days, cruising in any sort of craft is more and more a family activity. Though the racing-cruise fraternity remains, and even grows bigger year by year, it is the female cook with family or friends to feed for whom this book is chiefly intended: the wife who is part-time crew, part-time on galley duty; the mother with a raft of ravenous kids to feed, plus a skipper with tastes of his own; the lady who is chief cook in a group of adults; and for all who must adapt shoreside patterns of keeping everybody happy and well-fed to the confines and circumstances of living afloat.

My first experience with on-board cooking was on our own eighteen-foot Cape Cod knockabout which had no galley of course, so I rigged the semblance of one. It consisted of a folding one-burner Sterno stove and, as ice chest, a wooden box lined and covered with tarpaulin. Both were stowed under the foredeck, the stove when not in use, the "icebox" all the time, except when hauled into the big cockpit for filling. I found it less trouble to crawl forward under the deck to get out the necessaries than to lug the thing out and then shove it back again. I used the stove mostly for boiling water for coffee and for heating soup. The boat was a day-sailer, so for each day's sail I tended to carry aboard at the start an armful of quart-sized thermos bottles filled with hot and cold liquids and a couple of shopping bags loaded with beer, fruit, tomatoes, sandwich material, and whatever else I thought might be wanted in the way of provender. The "icebox" could hold no more than fifteen pounds of ice, but, what with martinis and all, this diminished fairly rapidly, making ample room for all the refrigerator-requiring food I might have brought along.

My second galley stint was diametrically the opposite. My husband and I signed on as chaperones for a ten-day cruise on a seventy-two-foot schooner, built during the latter days of the American Revolution and now in the Mystic museum. It fell to me to preside over the galley, wherefrom I fed thirteen hungry college students, having at my disposal two three-burner stoves (one with built-in oven) and two large ice chests, one each to port and starboard. There was fantastic stowage space and a fabulous complement of equipment. I'd collect the week's food ration money from each person on board and go through the nearest supermarket like a lady tornado.

Aside from these two poles-apart extremes, my years in the galley have been spent on boats chartered by my husband and myself for ten days to two weeks. Guests have been aboard from time to time, for varied lengths of stay, but mostly it's been just the two of us, which, to my way of thinking, is just dandy, even though, as sole crew, I do get yelled at a good deal of the time.

Chartering is a lot different from owning a boat of your own, especially from the cook's point of view. To be sure, even as owner, you may not at first have any choice as to galley layout, stowage space, and such vital matters. You may have to begin by making do with whatever has already been built into the boat. But, sooner or later, you may have the time and money to redo the galley as you'd like it. In chartering you're stuck with the layout that's there—period. In matters of equipment, however, I've learned to do something about the situation, or have the whole cruise a flop and everybody on board, most particularly the skipper, thoroughly down on me.

The phrase used in all the ads, "fully equipped for cruising," has been a big laugh to me, because practically never does it extend to housekeeping facilities. With a single exception, I have yet to come across a boat whose owner's idea of the meaning of this phrase remotely corresponds to mine, or whose pots, pans, dishes, drinking vessels, and all other cooking, food-keeping, and eating utensils seemed to me even practical, let alone sensible or at all efficient.

You can learn a lot about people from their boating artifacts. On one boat we recently chartered, the owner's idea of what is adequate for a two-week cruise was one frying pan and two saucepans (all three tiny), a quantity of extremely lightweight non-thermal tumblers, an equal number of three-partition plates and of soup bowls, all plastic. Obviously, this owner thought of boating as a recreation involving little, if any, cooking, and lots of having-people-on-board-for-a-cold-picnic. Another time, the galley was again stocked with plastic dishes, many of which were warped from home dishwasher heat. In contradistinction to the galley just described, there were, to be sure, at least a teakettle and a coffeepot (percolator). There were, as well, two frying pans (both tin, which rusts the minute you look at it) and two fair-sized aluminum saucepans.

Ever since my first experience of this sort, which necessitated a considerable advance outlay of money and a delay of more than a half-day's sailing time, a standard part of my gear is an ample bag in which I store (and leave ashore if not practical to stow aboard) all the nonsense in the way of galley accoutrements so "fully" provided by the owner. Another standard part of my gear is an equally ample bag packed with what I have found to be my own personal galley "musts," no matter what kind of stove, icebox, or stowage space is available. I've learned the hard way what's necessary and what isn't, and, finally, what's really useless and likely to become a downright nuisance.

Space is not necessary for good cooking, but organization is. You can't afford not to pursue the old adage "a place for everything and everything in its place." It's the little things you can't lay your hands on that can cause mealtime disasters. Planning, and painstaking care in meal preparation are terribly essential. And make sure there's a good, bright light placed so you can see what's going on in the bottom of your pans—plus another, if possible, shining on your work-surface. Even a strong flashlight or two, bracket-hung, can be a big help if there's no other way to acquire sufficient illumination.

The menus in this book are planned for family eating. You will know the additions and adjustments needed when there are children aboard, or when there are pronounced individual tastes to be considered. By and large, in most of the dinner menus, bread and butter are taken for granted and beverages are not mentioned, since individual preferences should reign in this area. Wines, where stowage space permits (and I think most of the time it does), are always desirable with lunch and dinner, beer, too, with some foods. Certain liqueurs, notably Kirsch and/or cognac, sherry or its cousins Madeira and Marsala, whiskey as well, all add much to many recipes. One of the best cooks I know says that all soups benefit from the addition of a spot of rye or bourbon, the only exception being onion soup.

Astute substitutions of all sorts can multiply the usefulness of this book. If, to take an example, thyme is called for in a recipe and you hate the taste of it, you can omit it altogether or substitute an herb you do like, with no harm to the end result. Scallions can substitute for chives, black olives for mushrooms, green olives for green peppers, water chestnuts for fresh celery. All of these may be for expediency *or* for preference. As for expediency pure and simple, I might mention that many a culinary triumph has come about because one bottle was full while another was empty. When it comes to economy, however, it's a matter of tightrope walking. Never substitute *ersatz* for the real thing just to save money, if you can help it. On the other hand, under the stringencies of offshore cruising, certain compromises may be forced on you. If they are made advisedly, not much mischief will be done.

It is my firm opinion that a cookbook is only as good as its index. I have tried to make mine as clear and helpful and complete as possible, and hope you will refer to it constantly. It should make planning your own menus easier, whether from scratch or to utilize a particular food you may have on hand. Another thing: the index will give you the key to the many "portmanteau" recipes. These are dishes based on one formula, in each of which the principal ingredient is different. You'll find separate listings for all of them.

Finally, all recipes are for four persons. For more, or fewer, increase or decrease proportionately, except for seasonings and sometimes cooking liquids. Generally, do not change either of these when decreasing from four to two, but when increasing from four to six or eight add one-third for six, one-half for eight.

Section One

A WELL-ORDERED GALLEY:
ITS TOOLS
&
ACCOUTREMENTS

Equipment

In furnishing a galley with the means necessary to turn out three gracious meals a day, you must have an eagle eye for absolute utility and space-saving, a keen awareness of the threat of rust, corrosion, and breakage, and a recognition of the importance of lightness in weight. Meeting these requirements will be a good test of your acumen and shopping ability.

Double-duty characteristics and nestability are basic to your choice of shapes and sizes, of galley utensils, because this not only shortens your equipment list considerably, but also furthers compactness of stowage as well as versatility.

While we're on this subject, I've recently found that I cannot, without inconvenience and difficulty, get along with fewer than three double boilers, the newest and most useful of which measures a full 8 inches across the top of its 2½-inch-deep upper part, and the bottom comfortably holds up to three quarts of water when used as a deep saucepan. I only wish I'd bought two, so as to have two lids whenever I use the lower part separately. One 1½-quart double boiler and one smaller one of 1½-pint capacity round off the group.

Other important double-duty pieces: bowls that can function as salad, serving, or mixing bowls; saucepans that can be used as frying pans; frying pans that can be used for boiling. To carry further the watchword of utility, make sure each cooking piece has a snug lid, to conserve fuel and water or liquids and to keep steam in, rather than have it escape all over the cabin, with consequent condensation. If your pots-and-pans cupboard has doors, or even a simple top-opening cover, see if the skipper can have rigged for you a combination of a lipped shelf and shock cords, behind which you can keep all your lids in one place.

The biggest double-duty boon to the ovenless galley is a heavy dome-lidded skillet a full twelve inches across, with a rack that fits into it. The skillet can be cast-iron, enameled iron, or aluminum. This piece of equipment, sometimes called a large chicken fryer, is much more than double-duty; it's multipurpose. In it you bake (biscuits, pies, and cakes), stew (ragouts and the like), sauté, fry, warm up bread and rolls, and even roast meat if the piece is not too tall for it. An eight-inch-square cake pan goes in nicely on top of the rack, as does an eight-inch pie pan.

All icebox jars should have airtight screw-top covers, and if you can acquire such jars in plastic, marvelous. If not, and you must turn to glass, view them as one permissible exception to the "no-breakage" rule because of their indispensability. They hold anything from tomorrow morning's fruit juice to this evening's canapé spread, sliced tomatoes for lunch, butter, cream, green pepper, leftover Beef Stroganoff, and bacon fat. If the icebox is crowded or if you want to conserve what ice there is by not demanding too much from it, these jars can sit in a bucket of melted ice water or cold water from overside.

Tin and aluminum have the virtues of lightness, but be warned that the former rusts and the latter eventually oxidizes in salt-damp. For most of your cooking equipment, stainless steel is the ideal material (except for food storage, where good strong plastic is best). Teflon coating is preferred by many, though I personally have never warmed to it. Some cooks feel that enamelware does not, in the long run, conduct heat as well as uncoated metal; others fear chipping and the rust-prone areas that follow. I have never had any trouble of this kind, and, much as I like stainless steel for certain utensils, such as pots, saucepans, and frying pans, for double boilers I much prefer enamel because it never imparts even the subtlest oddity of flavor to food, is easy to clean and cheaper than stainless. For a lightweight frying pan, coffeepot, or teakettle, stainless steel is, I think, the best. For bowls, it's a tossup among enamel, stainless, and strong plastic, with, for me, an edge toward the plastic, if it really is stout and rigid.

Two important exceptions to the above are one five-inch and one nine- or ten-inch cast-iron frying pan, and the twelve-inch dome-lidded heavy aluminum skillet afore mentioned. The iron pans are so useful they are well worth the comparatively small chore of keeping them rust-free, which is only a matter of proper cleaning and careful post-use protection with a small bit of oil or dab of bacon grease rubbed over the inside. Of course, enamel-coated cast-iron ware eliminates all this, if you think you can keep it from chipping—and can afford it.

All the tools you use for meal preparation and cooking, except when wooden, rubber, or plastic, should be stainless steel. There are, though, a few cooking accessories that I have never yet found rustproof versions of, but take along anyway because they are all essential to me as a cook. Show me a stainless steel flat grater, for instance—or ice pick or beer-can opener—and I'd make a beeline for the store offering them. Chrome-plated, perhaps, but at that hard to come by. For things like these I settle for what I can find.

In addition to the galley equipment that I consider absolutely necessary for cooking on a boat for any length of time beyond a two-week cruise, there is one piece of equipment that is nice to have, especially on a long passage, and that is a collapsible stove-top stainless-steel oven. If it's something that will turn your cuisine from mundane to inspired, fight for it; and above all, preplan its stowage nook. You can find them with built-in oven thermometers, but if the oven you wind up with does not have one, buy two of the little kind that need just be set on a rack in the oven, even though they are just two more things to find room for and keep track of. The time-honored brown-paper test for temperature is a last resort to fall back on—provided you have enough brown paper around to spare two or three pieces every time you light the oven. Stow your spare oven thermometer among your clothes or in some other protected place where you're sure you can lay your hands on it when needed.

If you or anybody aboard can't function without morning

toast, there are collapsible non-rust pyramidal stove top toasters, and also flat ones, though I've never found any of them sufficiently satisfactory to warrant the space they take up. If you do happen to carry a stove-top oven, and can spare the burner for it, toast bread in that if you prefer (three minutes each side at 350 degrees). However, all toast recipes in this book follow a process that I have found very acceptable: coat a large heavy skillet on the bottom with a little butter, put over a fairly high flame, and toast as many slices of bread as the skillet will accommodate in one layer; flip over and toast second side, then remove to the top of a heated double boiler, continuing until enough is done for four ravenous appetites, and that's that. Small dabs of additional butter may be needed before the process is completed.

The advocates of the pressure cooker are many and enthusiastic. I am not among them, having never used one with success. The food always seems to lack flavor, and coping with the pressure valve was too much for me. It's all child's play, I'm sure, but I have been badly burned more than once when the lid blew off or some similar disaster struck. "Thrice burned, forever shy" has been my motto ever since, though the fault was probably all mine. Anyhow, I don't hold with hurrying the cooking of anything that nature and the recipe's inventor intended to be cooked long and slowly. When you *are* short of time—or just plain don't feel like hovering much over a hot stove—there are enough recipes for good food, by tradition and definition quickly made, to keep you happy. So, though my opinion is purely personal, there are no pressure cooker recipes, as such, in this book. If you happen to be fond of one and quite familiar with using it, you probably know its ways well enough to adapt, whenever desired, the timing of my recipes to it.

One more personal predilection. I cook all green vegetables in a frying pan, or in a pot big enough to permit each stalk or slice or whole small vegetable to lie side by side, in one layer only. This is the easiest way to have vegetables reach the table cooked just to the right point—that is, a bit on the crisp side and not water-logged. It's the technique that's quickest, cooks each piece the most evenly, and, most important, needs the least amount of water—in fact, never more than half an inch, and frequently just enough to cover the bottom of the pan or pot. Even if the instructions on the frozen vegetable package say otherwise, and even if it looks like mighty little water, stick to my rule. Use a hot flame to bring it to a boil, turn the flame down to a simmer immediately thereafter, and don't cook a second longer than eight minutes (five, six, or seven for most green vegetables). This ensures your always taking the pan off the fire and draining it when the vegetable is not *quite* done; the heat of the pan itself will finish up for you. You'll notice I've been saying "green" vegetables. Potatoes, turnips, parsnips, and other non-green vegetables (except carrots) I always do the same way, covering with cold water, bringing quickly to a fast boil, turning to low heat, and timing for fifteen to twenty minutes, poking them with a fork to see if they are done and, if not, giving them five minutes more and poking again. When done, drain immediately.

On most boats, deep-fat frying is not advisable. Too much risk of a nasty flare-up of fat on fire. Abjure the thought of this type of cooking, much as we all love french-fried potatoes.

There may be some seagoing cooks who do not know what a flame-tamer is, and for these I will expatiate upon it. The name is now generic, there being many different manufacturers and countries of origin for the thing. Under whatever trademark they appear, they are widely distributed in hardware stores, large ten-cent and variety stores, and really comprehensive supermarkets. Basically, a flame-tamer is a circular metal plate, available in several sizes (the most common 6 inches in diameter), with a second matching plate, also metal, beneath it, and an air-space of $\frac{1}{2}$ to $\frac{3}{4}$ of an inch between the two plates. The two plates are held in their apart position by a vertical metal side with air vents placed at intervals around its circumference. Thus, heat and air escape from between the plates when the flame-tamer is put on direct flame, preventing too much heat being conducted from the fire to the pot, skillet or whatever set upon the burner. Not as effective for keeping heat low under any dish that requires it as are asbestos pads, I've found, flame-tamers do nevertheless have their uses, as many recipes in this book will attest.

An unmitigated boon discovered on our latest cruise—though widely used, I gather, throughout Europe—is called "Flint Fire

Lighter." It is a very simple grip-handled sticklike gadget with a thin piece of metal connecting the handle to the cigarette-lighter-type wheel at its end. The hollow stalk holds a supply of ordinary cigarette lighter flints. You prime and turn on the stove or oven (if you're one of the lucky ones whose "floating palace" possesses one), squeeze the handle, the wheel turns, sparks fly out, and the stove is lighted. It costs very little and you can find out where to send for one in the resource list, pages 312–322. After trying out this marvel, we threw away all our kitchen matches together with the metal Bandaid box we kept them in to preserve them from damp and all the extra emery boards we had carefully cut down to fit into the Bandaid box for use in striking recalcitrant matches, hung up our Fire Lighter on a hook handy to the stove, and were happy.

A final word before you take to the shops. Unless you are chartering in distant waters, or are about to equip a brand-new galley, go through all your cupboards and closets at home. You'd be surprised how many galley necessaries you already own and have only to pack sensibly. Nothing I've said is against your using your own favorite utensils, whose quirks you now know and understand, and whose special qualities you appreciate. By all means, keeping in mind the framework of scant space and pervading damp, take them aboard, use them, and cherish them.

CHECKLIST OF GALLEY EQUIPMENT

Pots and Pans
Pots:
Coffeepot, 10-cup capacity 1
(your preferred type)
Teakettle, 3-quart
capacity 1
Large double boiler,
8 inches across top,
3-quart capacity in
lower part 1
Medium double boiler,
1- to 1½-quart capacity 1

Small double boiler,
1½-pint capacity 1

Saucepans:
1-quart capacity 1
2-quart capacity 1
3-quart capacity 1
5-quart capacity, with
two handles 1

Skillets:
5-inch width, iron or

enameled iron 1
8-inch width, stainless
steel 1
9- to 10-inch width, iron
or heavy aluminum 1
12-inch heavy dome-
lidded piece, iron or
heavy aluminum or
enameled iron 1

Measurers and Mixers
Cups:
32-ounce (1 quart),
plastic 1
16-ounce (1 pint), plastic 1
8-ounce (1 cup), plastic 2
2-ounce (¼ cup), plastic 2

Spoons:
Graduated sets, non-rust 2

Bowls:
Mixing, sets of graduated
sizes—plastic, enamel,
or stainless, with
snap-on lids 2
Mixing, medium—plastic,
enamel, or stainless 1
Mixing, small—plastic,
enamel, or stainless,
usable for serving 6

Strainers:
8-inch, coarse mesh 1
5- or 6-inch, medium mesh 1
2-inch, fine mesh 1
Colander, standard size 1

Containers for Storage
Jars:
Assorted 6-ounce to
1-quart sizes, glass or
plastic 6–8

Boxes:
Assorted 1-pint to 1½-
quart sizes, plastic,
with tight covers 3–4

Tins:
Assorted sizes, square
or round, coated or
painted, with snug
lids 4–8

Bottles:
1- and 2-quart sizes, with
screw-on tops, plastic 4–6

Egg-tainers:
½-dozen capacity, plastic 4

Implements
Knives:
Paring, small, pointed 2
Chef, 7-inch blade 1
Serrated, for bread, etc. 1
Curved, for fruit 1
Peeler, floating-blade type 2

Forks:
Large, two-tined 2
Wooden, for salads 1

Spoons:
Wooden, for stirring 2
Wooden, for salads 1
Stainless, slotted 1
Stainless, solid 1
Ladle, for soups or stews 1
Narrow, for bottles 1

Openers:
Hand-type rotary can
openers 2

Beer-can openers 3
Corkscrews 2

Miscellaneous
Utensils:
Salad basket, wire,
   collapsible 1
Bread board 1
Asbestos pads, plain 6
Knife sharpener 1
Grater, flat (not square) 1
Juice extractor 1
Funnels, two sizes 2
Timer 1

Pepper grinder 1
Salt shaker 1
Pot holders, washable 4
"Imco" fire lighter 1

Implements:
Ice picks 3
Eggbeater, rotary 1
"Servespoon" slotted
   spatula 1
Spatula, regular size 1
Rubber scrapers 2
Pestle, small 1
Kitchen tongs 1

Tableware

Dishes

As important as lightness of weight is for almost everything else in your galley, it is not a virtue in tableware. In the cockpit, trying to absorb a little morale-lifting nourishment while braving wind and wave, the skipper will hardly be happy to see his meal, dish and all, blown overboard before he's had a chance at more than a bite or two. And if, on another day, the crew has joined him and is just settling down to a mug of hot soup or coffee, it's no fun when, thanks to a sudden pitch or roll, the mugs topple over into laps or onto seats, and go rolling over the deck or cockpit floor.

After participating in a few of these shenanigans, I am now an ardent supporter of good, heavy hash-house crockery. Its weight may make it a headache to lug aboard at the start of a cruise, but you'll never find it blowing away, and seldom tipping over. It holds heat very well, is easy to wash and dry, has a blunt, hearty air about it, comes in practical sizes and shapes, and is pretty nearly indestructible. In the years since I've owned some, I've never had a breakage, no matter how much things danced around belowdecks. What's more, it's fairly cheap. You can get it in any store that supplies short-order eateries and drugstore luncheonettes.

A good alternative seems to be the tableware put out by Corning. Though I've never had it aboard myself, I understand a lot of cruising cooks swear by it. Considerably more expensive than hash-house crockery, this ware doesn't seem to come in shapes and sizes quite as useful, nor is it quite as heavy, but it does appear to have nearly all the same practical advantages. And, to those whom prettiness is important, Corning ware may look a lot more tasteful, if not almost elegant.

Then there is "yacht china," emblazoned with your house or club burgee, or both, or with any other device you fancy. This can be of heavy Wedgwood or the like, with sturdy thick glass-ware engraving to match. It is obtainable from various stores that carry this sort of thing and are accustomed to special-order china-and-glass decorating, charging the usual arm and leg, of course.

There's a new tableware, launched at the 1972 New York Boat Show, on which I took home moderately explicit brochures, whose makers claim that the dishes are really un-tippable. Ac-cording to the literature, the non-tippability is due to the addi-tion of a special adhesive affixed in tiny strips on the bottom of all pieces. This adhesive, vinyl-based, is purported to cling to any and all surfaces—wet, dry, aslant, near-vertical or whatever. It is available in three patterns, of which I found one acceptable and the others too cottage-y. The ware is not cheap and I have not tried it, but it's worth knowing about at least. The manufacturer is listed in the appendix on resources and can be written to di-rectly, for information on outlets near your city where the table-ware is for sale.

Apart from these three types of tableware, ranging from the inexpensive to the grand-luxe, all others, being lightweight and heat-conducting, while certainly unbreakable, simply do not meet the demands of cruising conditions. Plastic holds heat moderately well, enamelware and stainless steel not well at all, their contents changing distressingly from scalding-hot one minute to unpalatably congealed the next. Although paper table-ware is cheap and labor saving, I find it unappetizing and totally impractical.

Cutlery

There are there choices of materials here: stainless steel, silverplate, and sterling. Whichever you decide upon, good heavy weight, simple design, and first-rate quality are absolutely necessary. In stainless, there are so many interesting styles nowadays (with more coming out constantly), and the price is such an appealing factor, it's no wonder most cruising cooks consider it the most practical. Still and all, it's good for many people's souls always to set the table (or cockpit seat or lap tray) with Silver (with a capital "S")—and there's no reason not to do so. In my own experience, cutlery does not seem to be among the myriad things that go overside or get lost somewhere on board (even in the bilge). So go ahead and use your best sterling if you want to and if you don't mind an occasional polishing session. Sterling and really good plate are among the materials least subject to the unending menaces of sea-damp and salt air.

Napery

Usually breakfast and lunch will tend to be extremely informal. If you're under way in a thrashing breeze and trying to make anchorage at a reasonable hour, dinner too may perforce be served with a mere nod to the table amenities. But on the average, during a coastwise cruise, one is at anchor for dinner and can break out suitable napery.

This may take the form of dinner outside under the stars, with placemats handed around to each person, followed by cutlery rolled in napkins; or of a tablecloth of plastic, oilcloth, cotton, or linen laid nicely over the cabin table. All of these can be stowed beneath a main-cabin bunk mattress between times, folded as flat as possible. Which ones you decide to ship aboard is your privilege, given your knowledge of the pros and cons of each.

For napkins, I have always used dinner-sized, heavy-duty paper napkins, either white or in clear, attractive colors and patterns, and found them very satisfactory, especially if put out in pairs, for double thickness. There may be other napkin materials you know of—or you may prefer napkins of linen, cotton, or other materials.

TABLEWARE CHECKLIST

Dishes (Crockery)
Per Person
Dinner plate 1
Butter plate 1
Soup and/or cereal bowl
(or equivalent) 1
Mug, flat-bottomed,
straight sides 2

General
Plates or flat dishes, for
serving 3
Bowl, deep, for serving
or ice 1
Platter, 10- or 12-inch 1

Drinking Vessels
Per Person
Tumbler, 8- or 10-ounce
(not glass) 1
Old-fashioned (not glass) 2

General
Pitcher (not glass or
crockery) 1
Cocktail Shaker, see-
through (not glass or
crockery) 1

Jiggers (glass only if
heavy) 2

Cutlery
Per Person
Steak knife 1
Forks 2
Soup and/or dessert spoon 1
Teaspoons 2

General
Tablespoons, for serving 3
Forks, for serving 3
Soup and/or dessert
spoons, extra 3
Knife, small, serrated, for
serving 1

Napery
Napkins, paper, dinner
size 1 box
Placemats, easy-care,
smooth surface, *per
person* 2
Tablecloths for cabin
table 3
Coasters, cup-shaped,
nonslip, sponge
rubber 8–12

Housekeeping

In a galley godliness isn't in it next to cleanliness, unless you're willing to have it turn into a floating pigsty. I keep three rules constantly in mind: clean up as I go, allow a minimum of debris, and economize on water, on soiling utensils, on detergents. Each was arrived at only after a harsh lesson in what can happen when the rule is ignored. I'll never forget the dawn hour after a glorious dinner celebrating a wedding anniversary. I had knocked myself out preparing the skipper's best-loved goodies, and tumbled into my bunk muttering that the morning was time enough for cleanup. The wind piping through the rigging awakened us both some time between three and four in the morning. One look told us we were not only dragging anchor but heading relentlessly toward a high sandy beach. By the time we'd coped and could safely consider having some fresh hot coffee, the cabin as well as the galley were what could only politely be described as a shambles—salad on the floor, steak bits on bunks, melon rinds and cake on the stove, and unidentifiable goo all over the work counter. Never since have I failed to clean up as I went, with especial reference to shipshapeliness after meals. I won't go into the equally hideous experiences that led me to the other two rules. Suffice it that they happened.

There's much more to cleanup than just cleaning. Begin meal preparations with newspapers—plenty of them. Lay them over your work counter and on the floor beneath your feet. Use them for any draining needed: bacon after frying, scallions after washing and peeling, fried fish, sausages. Wrap fresh-washed salad greens in them, too. Don't worry about the newsprint—it never comes off. Early on, set up a bowl, dish, or jar (preferably one already used), fill it with water from overside, add a smidge of detergent, and, as you finish with any paring knife, spoon, or whatever, drop it in. Half fill your galley bucket with overside water, and the minute you have a messy bowl or eggy dish, dip some water into it, and again add a spot of detergent to soften things and ease cleaning later.

Serve right from the cooking pot whenever possible. From course to course, try to wipe off "foody" plates and dishes immediately. Dunk other items into your water bucket to rinse off anything that might adhere and solidify. *And don't turn off the burners until you're positive* you have enough hot water for washing up all the dishes, using water from overside as often as you can to conserve the supply in your tank.

For washing up, stopper your sink for rinsing, use a plastic dishpan, big pot or bowl for sudsing. When there's space to stow it, a rubber-covered dish drainer is a lovely thing to have because, when not needed for dishes, it can hold so many little things, and is light to move around, completely non-prone to slide or tip over with contents. If not, a doubled-over terrycloth hand towel does a very good draining job. Nongreasy things should be washed first, then "foody" plates and dishes, pots and pans last. Here's where saved coffee-grounds can come in. Dump in enough to cover the bottom of the pan or pot, heat slightly, then rub around with newspaper, paper towel, or used paper napkin. Empty into garbage container or into small plastic bag, and wipe the utensil with fresh paper. Sozzle in leftover sudsy dishwater, rinse, and dry well. Saves scouring powder, not draining it down the sink to add to problems in that department. Be sure to dry *everything* thoroughly. I personally prefer good terrycloth dish towels for drying tableware and some pots and pans over paper towels. They do a better job. Dish-towel bars that are lightweight and fasten to most surfaces via suction cups or magnets are the best way to hang dish towels for drying out. They can be shifted from one area to another belowdecks, and even hung over the stove when it's not in use. The towels can also be hung over cabin porthole curtain rods.

The easiest and most efficient way I know of to cope with garbage, trash, and other debris is a double-bag arrangement set into the garbage container. A large brown supermarket food bag is lined with a plastic garbage bag and both are folded outward at the top to a depth of two inches or so and then fastened on each of the four sides with bulldog clips. Garbage that's likely to be smelly or somewhat moist should be put into small-sized plastic bags, closed tightly, and then put into the double bag. In the daytime, stowing this garbage setup is a bit of a problem. It must be convenient to the cook, yet not underfoot to trip somebody suddenly rushing forward to break out the anchor rode or fetch something needed from the forepeak. During the night, place it in the cockpit with its own lid or a plastic bag for a cover.

When the double bag is full, take it ashore if you are tied up, or going to be shortly. Considering the very real problem of water pollution, now of increasing concern to all sailors, not to mention the interests of common decency, it's a poor notion to toss your refuse overside in any anchorage. If you are in open water and well away from shore, then it is all right to drop it into the water to feed the fishes or dissolve into harmlessness. Be sure to remove the bulldog clips and leave the bag's mouth open wide enough to let water flow in and sink it, or find some other way to drown it.

Bottles, cans, empty boxes need not take up space in your garbage bag. Again, only when you're not in a populous harbor or anchorage. Cans with holes punctured in both top and bottom go under at once; filling a bottle at least half full with water from overside will have the same result, and boxes become waterlogged and submerge quickly as well when torn up into flat segments. Food peelings, coffee-grounds and tea-leaves, bits of meat fat, tobacco ashes and cigarette butts, small leftovers of food of most kinds can all go over—tossed out to leeward, of course, or you'll have it all back in your face and on the floor and deck. When you peel food onto newspaper, toss the peeling, not the paper; crumple that into the garbage bag. Paper neither sinks nor dissolves quickly.

It's a good idea to wash out the garbage container every so

often with hot water, detergent, and ammonia or bleach. About an inch and a half of the mix, sloshed around with a big sponge is all you need, followed by a thorough drying. The stove can stand cleaning and shining up from time to time, too, especially the burners. Don't be compulsive about these chores, but don't neglect them till the end of the cruise or the beginning of the next one, either.

HOUSEKEEPING CHECKLIST

Detergent	cold-water type, liquid
Scouring powder	pull off the stickum hole-cover; replace so that only half the holes are exposed (much less gets down the sink)
Washing soda	decanted into convenient plastic bottle with mouth big enough for pouring and tight lid
Cloudy ammonia	in plastic bottle
Bleach	in plastic bottle
Steel wool pads	soap-impregnated (to avoid rusting, rub into fresh moist soap after using, then store in screw-top plastic jar)
Soap	"Lava" brand, lathers in cold or salt water
Soap, laundry	
Scouring pads	"Scotch Brite" brand—invaluable
Copper sponge	"Chore Girl" or similar type
Sponges, 1 inch thick	2
Sponge, 1½ inches thick	1
Sponge, 2 inches thick	1 large
Brushes: vegetable	with hangup handle
scrubbing	oblong, with big stiff bristles
floor	horizontal or vertical, but saw the handle down to easy stowing length
Wax paper	
Aluminum foil	standard width
Plastic bags	sandwich size, boxed and on tear-off rolls
Plastic bags	food-wrap size, boxed and on tear-off roll
Plastic bags	heavy-duty, opaque, designated as garbage bags on package

Bulldog clips	at least 10. These are small versions of the clips on clipboards. Indispensable as substitute for cuphooks, as hangers for pot holders, asbestos pads, and small utensils in frequent use, for closing plastic bags tightly, and for many other uses you'll think of.
Rubber bands	assorted in size and thickness, separately kept
Paper towels	plenty
Dish towels	6, terrycloth
Soap dishes	4, all rubber: 2 with spiked inserts for soaps, 1 for hand sponge, 1 for copper sponge
Plastic basin	no more than 6 inches deep and with flat, broad base, for dishpan
Dish drainer	rubber-covered
Dish-towel bars	4, lightweight, fastened via suction or magnetism
Dustpan	1
Garbage container	plastic, capacious, with cover if possible
Plastic bucket	with bail handle, big enough for garbage container to nest into

Stowage

Stuffing things into the handiest nooks and crannies any old which way is certainly a quick and easy solution to the problem of getting rid of that pile of groceries and potables sitting on the dock, but it's not stowage. Stowage is storing goods in an orderly manner, making maximum use of every inch of available space, with some foresight as to their accessibility during the voyage and a due regard for the trim of the boat and the effect of metal on the compass.

Naturally, the first to be stowed are icebox perishables. But before stowing anything beyond these, measures must be taken against the pervading moisture. Cans must have their labels protected either by liquid varnish or plastic so they won't soak off or disintegrate. Cheaper and perhaps easier is to remove the labels entirely and identify the contents. This might be done with initials painted directly on the can or by crayon markings on waterproof tape. Any sailor who has been in the situation of having the labels wash off a quantity of cans is fervent on this point. Dry packaged foods should be emptied into heavy plastic bags, not forgetting to include any printed directions for their use. Drop in some desiccant crystals or a small package of silica gel as additional moisture protection.

Drawers are a lot better than lockers for storing food, though a waste of precious stowage space for canned goods, which can go anywhere provided they stay reasonably cool. Drawers don't spill their contents, if fitted with a proper latch. They are easier to get into and everything can be seen at a glance. Among the many surprise stowage areas that come to light are those behind, beneath, and to the sides of most under-bunk drawers. The head offers interstices that might be just right for wedging in booze, the hanging locker floor is another good place for stuff, and the forepeak is a notably commodious reception center for all manner of canned foods shoved under the boat-working gear residing there. In the bilge under the cabin sole are further stowage possibilities. Sometimes even the area around the engine may be pressed into service for canned items that withstand warmth.

Make a list of what's where and fasten it to the back of a convenient door. Then you won't have to wonder a week later where you've put something you need. It makes sense to group similar foods together whenever possible—for example, all canned fruits to port, vegetables to starboard, meats forward to port, soups forward to starboard, evaporated milk in the forepeak, and so on. A pad and pencil kept handy for jotting down items to get is a good idea.

The area near the stove and work counter is the place to keep the staples, condiments, spices, jams, jellies and such, that you use every day. Ideally, everything should be properly labeled, and in plastic containers with screw-on covers, but one-pound coffee cans with snap-on plastic lids and various similarly sized canisters that tea, candy, and biscuits are often packed in may also serve, though they may be noisy. If the shelf or work counter has no rail these provisions can be held by spaced lengths of elastic shock cord stretched tightly. Square containers make for a snug fit and save space. Another space-saver is putting spices in plastic shakers or pill bottles inside a larger receptacle. Eight can fit into one no more than four inches in diameter. Occasionally a glass jar is unavoidable; a sleeve, made by cutting off the ribbed top of an ordinary bobby sock, pulled over the body of the jar, and kept on firmly with a rubber band, will minimize breakage and cut down on bang-around noise.

If the staff of life is vital to your daily fare, have a good big box for it as well as for cake. Preferably this should be of stainless steel and have an airtight top—the more airtight, the longer the bread and cake will stay fresh and the less mould you'll have to contend with. Even at that, if a bit of mould does form, just slice it off and carry on. Rye and other nonwhite breads keep better than white, and unsliced bread better than presliced. If you can possibly make sure it's baked the very day you buy it, both bread and cake will last longer than ordinary stuff picked up casually in the market. If you can't buy it every five days or so, lay in some canned breads. Most of the standard varieties come canned as well as fresh; they're not quite as tasty as the fresh but will do. And there's always canned date-nut or Boston brown bread to fill the gap. Fruitcake, the old-time "holiday" kind, is a great addition to your ship's stores. It keeps excellently and stays with you when eaten, its rich flavor is a fine top-off to many a meal, and it's also a most satisfying between-meal snack—with milk, for instance. Moreover, it's usually packed in its own tight-topped tin. Cookies, crackers, and so on should be kept in canisters or in plastic refrigerator boxes.

Most fruits will stay fresh for a few days without refrigeration, some much longer. Citrus fruits, for example, in a ventilated open string bag or the equivalent, will keep nicely for as long as two weeks in a cool area. Apples and pears, as well, though a wrapper of tissue or something like it around each piece will help prevent bruising when the wind or waves knock things about. Bananas ripen pleasantly when bought green and stowed in a cool dark place. Once cut or peeled, however, any fruit should be put in a securely closed plastic bag and placed in the icebox. When lemons have been cut or the rind used for drinks, squeeze out the juice and pour into something unbreakable and small enough to stash in a corner of the icebox, to be hauled out and dipped from for many cooking occasions. But, unless your party is entirely mad for fresh fruit, take it a bit easy in this department. Fruit does take up a lot of space. Make the canned and dried varieties intriguing instead, as often as you can.

All vegetables go into the icebox, except for three roots— potatoes, carrots, and onions—which go into separate perforated plastic bags and are stowed where it's airy and moderately cool. Not too many of any vegetables should be bought at one time, the roots because they'll sprout and the others because of lack of icebox space. I have, now and then, taken aboard a few packages of specially favorite frozen vegetables, but they had to be consumed within twenty-four hours, since I've never had an electric refrigerator aboard. Frozen vegetables packed in plastic pouches that go directly into boiling water intact are more trouble than they're worth on a boat. Canned vegetables, which can be bought in terrific variety, are much less of a problem, and there are resources for fresh vegetables at most ports of call.

Fresh milk, cream, butter, and some cheeses must be kept in the coldest part of the icebox, as near the ice as possible. Fresh milk and cream stored in either screw-top plastic or glass bottles will last as long in a marine icebox as they do in an electric refrigerator. Butter stored in the same way will last as long as two weeks. Margarine need not even be kept in the icebox, provided it's put where it's cool enough not to melt. Most cheeses are so packaged that they can be kept in a cool place until opened. After that, either tie up in a plastic bag or wrap well in aluminum foil or pliofilm and put in the icebox. Processed cheeses keep without refrigeration, being chemically treated to do so, and some of them are delicious.

Soft cheeses such as Liederkranz, Limburger, Bel Paese, Camembert, Brie, and another wonderful but hard-to-find French cheese called Boursault must be kept in the icebox but should be taken out in time to ripen before eating. Cheeses like Muenster, Port Salut, Swiss, Roquefort, Gorgonzola, blue, cheddars, Wispride and similar products should stay in the icebox until the moment of actual use. Cream cheese, which I use a good deal for appetizers and sandwiches, I buy by the half-pound bar and store like butter.

The unfortunate thing about eggs is that you can seldom be sure that they are really fresh when you buy them, so that how long they'll keep is a question. However, stowing them so as to avoid breakage is not. For greatest safety, buy plastic "eggtainers" and, as an added precaution, line each cup with shredded paper. The cartons the eggs come in at the supermarket can also be utilized, provided they are also lined with shredded paper and then enclosed in a tightly tied plastic bag to keep out moisture. Eggs need not be refrigerated to keep fresh for two weeks or more if stowed in a cool place—the bilge, for instance. Powdered eggs are a good backstop in the event fresh eggs disappoint or you run out between ports, although they are a bit difficult to come by in less than hundred-pound lots.

Of course, meat and poultry must be refrigerated, but by all means take off the store wrappings and repackage them in fresh pliofilm or aluminum foil, all ends securely tucked under, folded in, and so on, to keep out both air and moisture. A further precaution—and a very sensible one—is to put the package into a plastic bag, tightly fastened. The meat will then stay fresh for a full four days at least. The one exception is chopped meat, which, as the old rule of thumb goes, must be cooked within twenty-four hours of purchase, refrigerated in the meantime as close to the ice as you can get it. Cooked fresh meat, either left over from a meal cooked in the galley or brought aboard precooked, will keep nicely in the icebox, but only there. I have had both a hunk of roast beef and a cut-up fried chicken in the icebox for up to a week, with no problems. Although I know that you can hang a whole salami or other well-cured sausage, or a smoked ham, indefinitely in a cool place without spoilage, I must confess that I personally would rather have such cooked meats in the icebox, even though it means buying in smaller quantities. There may be times, on a long trip, when you can't do this, of course; then, the other method is a smart one, much approved by our ancestors. Frozen meat dishes, cooked or uncooked, must stay as close to the ice as they can and used within twenty-four hours.

Booze is not a difficult stowage problem. If wine is bought in half- or full-gallon quantities, decant it into plastic bottles of suitable size and stow wherever convenient. Beer, mixers, and soft drinks are probably best stowed in the bilge, except for those put on ice. If you buy these in case lots, get rid of the cases and stow the cans themselves only. The space around and under the under-bunk drawers is ideal for liquor bottles; so is the forepeak, if they're well wedged in.

There will always come a time when you'll need a special set of supplies, due to emergencies of one sort or another. The size of the box or chest that constitutes your emergency locker has to be dictated by the size of your boat, as does where you keep it. In any case, it must be easy to reach, even if all you can manage is a wooden box wedged into a corner of the floor of a hanging locker. It should contain cans of instant coffee, evaporated milk, fruit juices, bacon, chicken, corned beef, potatoes, one other vegetable, soups, and fruits; also a folding Sterno stove (one burner) and a few cans of fuel for it, as well as some matches. And put in some hard candy and some cocoa, especially if there are children aboard. A spare can opener and beer-can opener are a help, as well as one good knife. Keep this box or locker at full capacity at all times. The minute you use up anything in it, replace it the very first chance you get—although you should really not have to go into it at all in the ordinary course of things.

The Icebox

There's a great quantity of humbug spoken and written about the importance of housewifely needs in boat design. With one exception—which nonetheless had its own built-in flaws—I have never yet struck a marine icebox that I could call really efficient. The odd thing is that no two are alike. I suppose this signifies that the designers are fumbling for a solution, but a tour of the latest Boat Show wasn't encouraging. I'm not thinking of the fancy equipment to be found on motor cruisers and on some auxiliaries, whose manufacturers had the little woman sufficiently in mind to try to give her pretty much what she is used to at home, but of the ice iceboxes so many cruising cooks must live with.

No matter what type of icebox you may have, it's wisest to get the bulk of your ice in block form, and some—say, ten pounds—in ice cubes. This is not too often possible, unfortunately. It's dismaying how many ports, marinas, town docks, and similar tie-up locales carry one sort of ice or the other, but not both. Cubes melt much faster and have far less cooling efficiency than block ice; therefore, you need many more of them to attain a sufficiently cool temperature in the icebox for all you have in it. This means less space for food, more space for ice. For four days between ports, at least four ten-pound bags will be needed. Leave the cubes in their bags, which are good insulation. If you have to take out some cubes in order to fit a bag in, strew them around in the box. If block ice is all that's available, try to get it in two pieces, one much smaller than the other—it's much easier to hack up a smaller piece for drinks. Put both pieces into the heaviest big plastic bag you can locate. This not only delays melting, but keeps the icebox itself drier. Besides, it's simple to dump out melted ice from a bag. If you have a separate plastic bag for each piece of ice, so much the better; the big piece can be undisturbed until the smaller one has been used up.

Cool the icebox before starting any trip, even if this seems like wasting good ice. Leave the ice in for anywhere from eight to twenty-four hours, and then replenish with fresh ice just before packing in the food. And try to have everything you put into the icebox as cold as possible to begin with. If you're bringing it from home, wrap each package, jar, or container in several layers of newspaper. It is excellent insulation and keeps cold things cold remarkably well. If you're returning to the boat fresh from market, ask the packer at the store to put perishables into double bags, or, better yet, into those special insulated bags usually reserved for ice cream.

Melted ice has its uses. An inch or two sloshing around in the bottom of the icebox never hurt any wet-proofed food, and does a neat cooling job on its own, thereby slowing down the melting of ice. When there's more than an inch or so, and the icebox is crowded, drain it into a bucket and let it be a short-term cooling agent for some of the icebox items.

This seems as good a time as any to talk about dry ice. Many are the cautions and reservations issued for its use, its so-called near-unavailability included. On one of our more recent two-week cruises I made up my mind that I was going to try some, to check out its pros and cons for myself. By the elementary process of looking up "Dry Ice" in the Yellow Pages of the medium-sized New England town where we were docked, I found three sources. Equipped with a styrofoam ice bucket, a pair of quilted mittens, and a number of small paper bags, we purchased all the ice bucket could hold, five pounds, at fifteen cents a pound. The store cut it into chunks about three inches thick and four inches square for us, and we brought it aboard. Gingerly, using the galley tongs, one by one I inserted a piece into a separate paper bag and when I had four or five individually bagged pieces of dry ice, I opened the icebox and placed them one by one alongside, on top of, and under the twenty-five-pound piece of block ice that we had just that morning taken aboard, stowing the balance, also individually bagged, in the styrofoam ice bucket.

The day was a scorcher, and I told myself the whole idea was a waste of time. After four days of very little shrinking of the block ice, in that weather, I was then a complete convert to dry ice. It's fabulous for keeping the icebox cold, for conserving block ice (often both difficult to come by and really expensive), and for its lasting qualities. I should have had a larger, picnic-sized styrofoam chest, bought twice as much dry ice, and spared myself several stints at emptying the icebox to make room for fresh ice, jockeying it in, rearranging the food in the icebox, and swabbing up melted ice. The dry ice also kept ice cubes much longer, and in general avoided dependence on the ice-dispensing machines at piers where we had no other reason to tie up. Even when those paper bags seemed empty, they continued cold enough to cling to, and keep from melting too much, our block ice. Since then, I have learned that the big boats customarily participating in the classic California-to-Hawaii "Transpac" race stock up before departure with as much as seventy-five pounds of dry ice.

As to availability, I'd like to mention two other sources, if at your point of departure or port of call no dry ice is listed as such in the local Yellow Pages. One: any local ice-cream plant uses dry ice for packing the ice cream and keeping it cold, and will maybe sell or give you some. Two: check with the manager of the local supermarket; frozen foods come from the suppliers packed in dry ice, which is generally discarded by the market when the foods are put into their cases. I've never cruised the Caribbean, where I understand ice is a continual problem, so I don't believe I can help you there, other than to recommend that you check with the manager of whatever frozen-food depots are in or near the town and explore for yourself.

Everything that goes into the icebox must be packed in with care and with prudent thought for the unpleasant possibilities that can eventuate from the shifting of its contents. Remember that under way a boat moves all the time, up and down or side to side or some of each. Since you will be continually using up and replacing things, you will find yourself repacking the icebox often. Bear in mind this constant motion every time you do, as it will affect placement of the contents.

A word about leftovers. Some cooks find them a creative challenge, even like to plan for them, and are geniuses at incorporating them into the most succulent dishes. I may not be the latter, but I do often plan on them, especially before starting off from home for a cruise. To accommodate them, I keep on hand some small and smallish containers, and treat these foods with the care they require until I've used them up. You may not be of the same persuasion—if not, you're much better off trying to have as few as possible, and giving the local fishes a good gorge with whatever you do wind up with after a meal. Dab-saver though I am, I'm by no means averse to stoking up the surrounding piscatorial population when it seems sensible to do so.

Open the icebox as seldom as possible, because, every time you do, you lose a boxful of chilling help. If you think it through, it's not difficult to map out all meal preparations to this end. Opening the icebox once for breakfast should do; ditto for lunch; for dinner, perhaps twice; and once or twice between times—period. The more times you aim to stick to this pattern, the more expert you'll get at following it.

About once a week, the icebox needs a really thorough cleaning to keep it smelling fresh as well as looking pristine. The best time to do this, of course, is when the ice is low, the food completely chilled, and the sun not heating up the box or its immediately adjacent area. First, take out the ice and place it in your bucket. Around it put the most perishable of the food. Cover entirely with newspapers, a folded-up blanket, or anything else that will serve as insulation. Next, remove everything else in the icebox—either to the work counter, to one of the main-cabin bunks, to the cabin table (if convenient), or even to the cabin sole. Put it all on spread-out newspapers. Drain the icebox as completely as you can, then sponge as dry as you can. Half fill the dishpan or a big cooking pot with water, fresh if feasible, if not, salt. Add three tablespoons washing soda, one tablespoon bleach, and stir to dissolve the soda. Dip your biggest sponge into the solution, squeeze moderately dry, and wipe the box from stem to stern, top to bottom, roof and floor especially. When the box is clean, sponge off the cleaning solution with fresh clear water. If the box has a drain, pour the clear water right into the box, splash it around with the sponge, and drain it. If you're taking on ice, now's the moment to put it in. On top of, or next to it, place the old ice; add the perishables next, snugged around the ice, and finally the balance of the icebox contents. Close the box immediately, with relief, and hope you have two or three hours before you have to open it again, so that some recooling of the food can take place.

The Night-Watch Kit

Every boat whose skipper contemplates more than one or two all-night passages should have a box or small locker, specially installed and securely anchored, located handily in the cockpit and designated for nonperishable and easy to ingest foods and drinks to help the helmsman and/or crew member keeping him company through the long night hours. Along about 2 A.M., the body reaches its lowest ebb of vitality and alertness, and hunger strikes those who are awake, cold, and frequently, wet. This is when one's weariness really asserts itself, and when blood sugar must be raised and energy revived. It is also when the wise galley executive might be able to catch some sleep, if she has kept fully stocked this night-watch kit—as important in its way as the ship's tool kit.

Into this saving grace for the graveyard shift should be put and kept:

Two nonspill mugs
Two thermos bottles filled with boiling water
Several 1½-ounce bottles of scotch, bourbon, brandy
Small packets of crackers in assorted flavors
Individual portions of wrapped cheeses
Wrapped cake and/or pie slices
Individual-sized boxes of raisins
Candy bars, assorted—including chocolates

Cans of nuts, mixed or of individual kinds
A good assortment of nongooey candies—sourballs, peppermints,
  coffee-flavored candies, etc.
Individual portions of instant breakfast mix
Instant coffee, tea, cocoa, and broths
Packets of sugar
Powdered cream

By remembering to fill the thermos bottles before retiring,
the worn-out cook can rest her bones and sleep uninterrupted by
captain or crew foraging for, and unable to find, this or that snack
or potable.

Ways to Make Life Easier

Anytime

~ During armchair cruising months, I start saving quart-sized and half-gallon-sized plastic bottles, and clean and air them well. Aboard, the quart-sized bottles will go into the icebox holding juice, milk, drinking water, or other liquids; the larger ones will be used to stow wine and extra drinking water wherever safe and handy.

~ Before embarking, save and cut off at the ankle a few pairs of runny stockings, fill the toes with damp-collecting crystals, and knot. Then tie to hangers of clothes in the hanging locker, tuck some anywhere dampness may collect in the cabin or head. Refill as needed.

~ Bedding grace note, if you're a home-sew type: Stitch up zippered bedding-roll covers out of stretch fabric in cabin-harmonizing colors, and you have neat bolsters into which to stuff each morning's complement of bedding and against which to lean during the daytime.

~ Ordinary blotting paper, used to line galley and cabin shelves, drawers, pot-and-pan bin, any shelves in the head, is another moisture-absorber, and nowadays comes in fantastic colors.

~ The best way to secure damp towels and bath linen when drying in the sun is to use enormous safety pins with bits of line strung through the hole at the bottom. Lifelines, handrails on cabin top, and standing rigging are candidates for the use of this idea.

~ Spring-type broom clips, screwed to any number of galley surfaces, will store all kinds of cooking gear snugly—the ice pick, a sieve, and cooking spoons, for example. Cover any vertical surface first with taped-on blotting paper, to keep banging at a minimum.

~ Clothes in the hanging locker, even on a two-week voyage, can turn out to have corroded zippers, rusty necklines, and plenty of wrinkles just when you have no iron on the boat. Plastic hangers, well padded (I know of one lady who sews ordinary shoulder pads on all hers), are the answer.

~ Even in well-sealed plastic bags, shore-going shoes in time can grow an unattractive green mould. Frequent inspecting and airing will solve this.

~ A foot-square piece of nylon netting beats both a brush and sponge for wiping off and then washing plates and bowls with food stuck on them. Besides, it dries in a moment and never goes rancid.

~ During thermos-bottle weather, save eggshells. Crush two or three, put into a thermos, add a small amount of detergent and some water, stopper and shake well, then rinse. All the guck from soups or stews will have gone down the drain with the eggshells.

~ Wet cleansing tissues or paper towels are the way to pick up bits of broken glass in galley or cabin.

~ Lemon or orange rind rubbed over any utensil in which fresh fish has been cooked will remove the fish odor.

~ Salt, and plenty of it, is the thing if you ever have the misfortune of having fat in a frying pan catch fire. It may ruin the food, but it will prevent a general conflagration.

~ Don't skimp on plastic bags, the heavier the better. They keep lettuce fresh, crackers crisp, and cake soft. Toss salads in them, mix batters in them, crush crumbs in them. Throughout this book you will see their use recommended again and again.

~ Instead of bringing on board and stowing the bulkiness of a large box of powdered milk, premeasure it at home into pint or quart amounts, tie up tightly in small plastic bags, and stow in a large plastic bag. Same goes for powdered eggs. These should be premeasured in one-egg amounts.

~ Washing dishes in seawater is fine, and the liquid dishwashing detergents are effective. Rinse thoroughly, also in salt water, then dry at once, or everything will have a cloudy look.

~ Many liquid shampoos bubble up grandly in salt water, and are also okay for a briny body-bath. What's more, they smell delightfully. Salt water never hurt skin or hair, if a fresh-water alternative is within, say, two or three weeks' reach.

~ Cheese will not dry out if kept in a covered container with a small bit of vinegar in the bottom.

~ Chocolate will not stick to any pan in which it is to be melted if the pan is first rubbed with butter.

~ Things to save, when space permits: any pickle juice (for pickling raw vegetables of any kind) ; green-olive juice (a small amount adds zest to any salad dressing) ; syrups from fruit cans (spiked with lemon juice, they make good breakfast drinks); liquids from any and all cans of vegetables (mixed with V-8 juice, they too help out the breakfast menu, or reduced by cooking slowly, enrich any dish where broth is called for) .

~ Fresh parsley will keep two to four weeks if pretreated this way: wash one bunch thoroughly. Holding by stems, shake off as much water as possible, and trim off stems. Roll parsley gently in a paper or cloth towel or clean rag to dry completely; then wrap, with towel or rag, in foil, loosely but well sealed, and store in icebox. If sprigs turn yellow after a time, sprinkle a few drops cold water over towel or rag, rewrap, and replace in icebox.

~ Gravy or cream sauce shortcut: at home, make a smooth paste of two cups each flour and softened butter, put into an air-tight container, and label clearly as follows: "per each cup liquid—thin, 2 tablespoons paste—medium, 2½ tablespoons paste—thick, 4 tablespoons paste."

~ To soften butter in a hurry for any reason, cut it up and pour over it a tablespoon or more of boiling water, then stir with a wooden spoon. Butter will soften in jig time; the water will separate from the butter, and can be poured off easily.

~ When you make sandwiches with sliced tomatoes in them, ashore or early in the day aboard, slip foil, clear plastic wrap, or two thicknesses wax paper between tomatoes and top slice of bread. Result: no sogginess.

~ Make it clear from the beginning that the galley supervisor is and must be as autocratic as the skipper where her area is concerned. A good way to emphasize this is to post a big sign in the cabin saying something like, "DO NOT HELP YOURSELVES. THE SANDWICH YOU MAKE NOW MAY BE YOUR DINNER." Or: "PLEASE DON'T HELP YOURSELF TO ANYTHING. CHECK WITH THE COOK FIRST." Such devices will guard against the disappearance of an important component of a forthcoming meal or two when there's no chance to go ashore and replace it. Better yet, post a sign in the cabin prominently headlined "SHORT ORDER PRIVILEGES" and list beneath the food, canned and in the ice-box, that may safely be raided to accommodate the hungry horde, together with the whereabouts of each item.

Rough Weather

~ Antislide devices for pots and pans and coffeepot, for food and cans and dishes on the work surface or cabin table or in the sink, are more than helpful—they are a necessity.

~ You should have at least one and preferably two large deep kettles with two handles so that the lid can be tied down with light and easily malleable wire, twisted once around the lid handle and again around each pot handle.

~ Ordinary screen-door springs, hooked over the stove railings and long enough to stretch around your largest pot, will secure it well if the hooks fit the rails snugly so that the spring doesn't pop off just when you least want it to, and yet can be disengaged without using every tool on board.

~ It's basic that you can't have too many sponges aboard, in sizes ranging from half-postcard to foot-square. In the galley, you need a dozen or so, and when damp (as they're sure to be), they make good cushioning around, under, and alongside noisy or breakable receptacles which should be laid on their sides in the sink, bottles especially.

~ In addition to a slide-in fiddleboard along the front of your work surface, you'd best cover the surface as fully as you can with two layers of damp turkish toweling. Depending on work surface sizes, a hand or bath towel folded in half crosswise has served me well.

~ When the boat is heeled sharply, dishes will not spill off the cabin table, and will stay reasonably level as well, if a piece of soft bread or roll is wedged under each.

~ They may be offensive to some, and, for sure, their colorings are awful, but weighted baby mugs with a sipping cover, which can be bought in infants' stores or departments, are guaranteed not to spill and to keep the contents hot. For liquids only, of course, but a godsend in the cockpit in a blow.

~ If coffee and lots of it, day and night, is a never-ending requirement of all on board, save yourself effort and constant coffee-ground disposal by copying the Mexican cowboys. Brew two full pots, double strength, one after the other, using exactly twice as much ground coffee as usual. Let it cool, then put into any airtight rigid receptacle (s) and keep anywhere handy. When you need one mugful or many, add an equal amount of cold water, heat to drinking temperature, and serve. If your antipathy to instant coffee matches ours, this idea could save the day (or night) .

~ Final note: never underestimate the fizz imparted by a chilled bottle of champagne. It's *the* pick-me-up, at breakfast or any time when life is dull, weary, dejected, becalmed, buffeted, or just plain in a "had-it" mood.

Menus and Methods

I believe that if you set up all menus with the basic idea of appealing to the eye and the appetite, the vitamins and minerals will take care of themselves. In the long run, if meals are interesting and satisfying, a good nutritional balance will generally be the outcome.

I have always enjoyed menu planning—the balancing of this food against that and making sure there's plenty of variety from day to day and week to week—browsing through recipe files and cookbooks to find new things to cook and new ways to cook old standbys. Since practically before the Ark, I've based each weekend's big marketing jaunt on a full week's chart of what to eat when, including plenty of scope for jockeying dishes around should desire arise. This predilection carries over *in toto* each time I prepare for a cruise, and is part of the enjoyment. Two weeks' food prognostication is enough, though. If a voyage is to be longer, it's better to begin at the beginning after the first fortnight, and plan anew or repeat.

This is not to advise sticking grimly to the letter of a plan, menu by menu and day by day. Breakfasts and lunches are movable feasts, and frequently you'll make choices among them, by virtue of your mood or the weather or the current contents of the larder. Dinners, usually more formal and the culinary high point of the day, might be considered less interchangeable, though here too mood, weather, or a necessary change of destination may easily bring about shifts, as can a fortuitous catch of beautiful fresh fish or local products suddenly come upon en route.

Be ready and, if possible, pleasant when the overlord, otherwise known as the skipper, makes one or more unpredicted decisions to change course, thus really fouling up your plans for forthcoming meals. These things happen and should never throw you, at least to all appearances. Keep outwardly calm and think rapidly how to surmount these charming challenges to your cooking reputation and your inventiveness. The same holds true when meteorological uglinesses intrude out of nowhere, or the overlord, quite unexpectedly, urgently needs extra crew above-deck and pulls you away from dinner preparations to man a winch or hang onto a sheet or glue your eyes to the compass to keep course while he performs some other equally important task elsewhere. On the other hand, if you yourself feel like stretching out on the foredeck or a cockpit seat to catch some sun, don't let your meal plans bother you. Switch them from here to there or change them completely to allow you to drink in the sunshine and acquire more tan or start that process.

Before working out any menus it might be a good idea, if you don't already know, to acquaint yourself with the eating quirks and quiddities of the members of your party. There are pickle-devourers, big-dessert types, seafood haters, and so on. Keep the children's special needs in mind, if one or more of them will be along.

Extremely important to menu-making is a thorough knowledge of both the versatilities and the limitations of every pot and pan you are going to have aboard. For every recipe you're considering for any menu, ask yourself whether you can accomplish it with what you'll have to work with, bearing in mind the cooking vessels needed for whatever else is on the agenda. With the usual two-burner stove, the art of pan-juggling really comes into its own, and takes some learning, calling for foresight in the cooking procedures you'll use for every meal, no two of which will be alike. If you happen to have three burners—the third possibly created by a single-burner Sterno stove hung in gimbals—you're way ahead of the game. Though all the recipes in this book are geared to two-burner cooking, often a keep-hot contraption is required. Fit a third pot or dish into the top of a double-boiler, thereby making it three-tier. Pile three or four asbestos pads on the work-counter close to the stove and shunt a double-boiler arrangement onto it, having the water in the lower part *just* off the boil; the food will stay perfectly hot till dished up. Make coffee first, before anything else goes on the stove, and put it into one or more quart-sized thermoses. Heat bread or rolls in the topmost part of a double or triple boiler. Warm dinner plates by cradling them in the inverted lid of a simmering pot, about ten minutes before serving.

Aim for truly abundant breakfasts. In nautical circumstances, the most confirmed juice-and-coffee people suddenly find pancakes, French toast, and a lot of other filling fare to be just the ticket with which to start the day. At lunch time, you'll notice the same phenomenon. Grownups who ordinarily gulp a hot dog or hamburger and call it lunch often develop, even earlier than noon, what is known as a "coming appetite," to be appeased only by three times that amount of food. In planning these meals, you need go no further than to note that there'll be x number of each between marketing stops, and more or less arbitrarily divide them into so many of one general type, so many of another, and so many of a third. Say there'll be, roughly, one-third "eggs-and-" breakfasts, another third "pancakes-and-" breakfasts, and a final third "cereal-and-hot-bread" breakfasts. The same with lunches: one-third may be hot dish and fruit; another third, sandwiches with or without hot or cold soup; the final third, perhaps, salad and cold meat.

Dinner, on the other hand, should be painstakingly thought out, even if the plan is deviated from. Start by choosing the main dish, then build around it, selecting the satellite dishes equally for compatibility and for contrast in texture, color, and flavor. One dish cooked with wine is enough for one meal. No more than one creamy dish. Not everything pale, or green, or brown. Crisp married to smooth, bland alternating with spicy, colorless with colorful. It's almost like composing a painting, with the palette limited to the equipment and larder of your boat.

Good cooking takes time. Even though the longest-cooking

recipe of a meal may take a mere twenty minutes, figure on a minimum of a flat hour for the full meal. Oddly though, a group of much more complicated dishes ought to take no more than two hours at the most. This excepts, of course, the long, slow cooking for stews, ragouts, and pot roasts of one sort or another. These do have to go onto the fire much earlier, with the key target to have everything come out even at serving time.

My own practice is what I call "consecutive cooking." First of all, I make one big foray into the icebox to get out *everything* I'm going to need for the meal. This is after determining from thorough study absolutely everything I'm going to require for the meal from that repository. Second, I do all the peeling, chopping, slicing, dicing, and measuring needed for the main dish, then set it all aside, together or separately, depending on the order in which called for by the recipe. Next, I get peripheral foods out of the way by doing the coffee, fixing the dessert, the salad, preparing and even cooking the vegetables, double-boilering them and thus freeing the stove burners for the main dish by removing the double-boiler edifices to asbestos pads. Last of all, I take on the main dish. It usually calls for the greatest concentration, and often for both burners. If the chef d'oeuvre utilizes only one burner, start heating the dishwater on the other.

Working in this somewhat loosely planned-out manner, one doesn't need any real timetable, mental or written. On the whole, my feeling is that an experienced cook has only to calculate how long the longest-cooking dish on the menu will take, and how long the most complicated one, picking the longer of the two as hour and minute for starting the meal. It will follow almost invariably that she'll come out even every time.

It's astonishing how much galley time you can save by bringing aboard for weekend trips, quick overnight hops, or at the start of a cruise planned for two weeks or longer, a sufficiently copious quantity of pre-cooked stuff, guided always, naturally, by the needs and duration of the trip.

The Transpac people have taught us all a lot on this one. That annual classic takes place, to be sure, on big boats, but, as in any racing, minimum displacement is of prime consideration and, pound for pound, pre-cooked comestibles brought aboard from home base have it all over cans. Styrofoam icechests, weighing next to nothing and often discarded when emptied (inexpensive as they are nowadays) fill the portage bill neatly. If yours is to be as long a passage as the California-to-Hawaii Transpac, for instance, have the blessing of two or three styrofoam icechests specifically for stowage of dry ice. They come in all shapes and sizes; remember, though, that squared-off receptacles are always easier to stow than those formed in-the-round.

You needn't feel you have to schedule a month-long cooking stint before you embark on a lengthy cruise. Explore all your local or nearby food stores and you'll uncover several who will cook for you and, needless to say, charge you accordingly. You decide which prospect you'd rather face: a jag of cooking or a near-astronomical food bill. Suggestions for such a supply: 5 or 6 appetizers, snugly containered; roast beef or lamb or ham; meat loaf (of which more later) ; roast, fried or sautéed chicken, with or without sauce or with sauce in a separate container; boiled potatoes, rice, and legumes; hard-boiled eggs; desserts; cakes; cookies; candies (if you're the type to make candy at home) . Be guided by a realistic knowledge of your craft's refrigeration capacities and the keepability of the food.

If you think about it, there's a lot of meal preparation that can be done topside, provided you're excused from crew duty. In sunshine or cloudiness, you can peel, slice, dice; you can stir and mix—batters and other combinations; make sandwiches, desserts, and actually put together a number of dishes. Don't cheat yourself, therefore, of one of cruising's great pleasures. Use the cockpit, whenever feasible, as a galley annex.

Provisioning

Ages before sailing time comes around, one of my more pleasant occupations is to wander through every food store I find myself near, whenever I have the time to do so, and make notes of new products and of ideas that strike me as I poke around. Any time something seems to have real boat possibilities, I try it at home, check it out. It may wind up on my tick-list for the big final prevoyage marketing, it may not. Other sources for products and ideas are the catalogues from the big food distributing houses. You can get them just by writing for them.

It seems childishly elementary to point out that before you go food shopping in preparation for any cruise, you must begin with some sort of comprehensive list. Buy higgledy-piggledy and, when you're days from shore, you'll be minus some pretty important articles. The most substantial part of your list should come from planned menus covering the duration of the trip, and the more clear-cut the better. From that menu plan, make up your marketing list by categories: perishables, staples, canned foods, and so on. And don't forget to include supplies for the emergency locker, as well as those extras you'll need in a pinch when your planned menu goes out the porthole, whether it's foul weather you have to cope with or unexpected guests. Common sense, stowage space, your itinerary, and the length of your voyage will all affect the scope of your marketing list. For two weeks' coastwise cruising between fairly well-populated harbors, you can fill in on ship's stores every few days if you want to, and consequently start out with shorter supplies. On the other hand, if stowage permits, it might be less bother to stock up on everything except perishables for the entire trip. Of the latter, buy enough to last two days beyond your first charted port of call, in case circumstances compel a longer run before you have access to a market. If you're going to be at sea for more than two weeks between provisionings, and in waters where only the basics are likely to be obtainable, cut down on these and instead take on more of the canned rarities that make the difference between exciting and so-so meals.

Whatever sort of trip you're getting ready for, stretch your mind a little. Try new jam and preserve flavors, canned fruits you've never tasted before, vegetables you never thought you'd like, canned stews, and so on. Test them all at home, for likes and dislikes. Doctor them, if they seem to need it, as they often do, with spices, wine, or whiskey—or even a bit of gin. Improvise boldly. But do it all before you get yourself out on the briny. Don't rule out carrying such things as water chestnuts, bamboo shoots, *marrons glacés* and the more esoteric condiments and sauces. Consider the "babies" among canned vegetables—shoepeg baby corn, *petits pois,* baby carrots imported from Europe, baby beets, tiny whole string beans, celery hearts. They are tastier and better looking than the regular size. There are any number of gratifying discoveries to be made if you put your mind and eye to it.

Admittedly, dehydrated foods are a temptation because they save space so dramatically, but, to my mind, most of them lack flavor just as dramatically. Dehydrated celery and green pepper flakes, to take but two examples, do not remotely resemble the fresh equivalent. However, there are exceptions that should definitely be on your shopping list: instant coffee, instant tea, powdered puddings; mixes for muffins, pancakes, biscuits; dried fruits, to be eaten either as sweets or snacks without water and cooking, or, cooked, as breakfast or dinner fruits; instant minced garlic, instant minced onion, parsley flakes. Dried mushrooms are something else. Their flavor is really not as good as that of canned mushrooms; still, because they keep well, it might be wise to have them on hand just in case you run out of the canned ones. Powdered milk and eggs should not be overlooked, especially if your group is more than ordinarily hungry for these foods. Four people can, if they've a mind to, easily run through a dozen eggs and a half-gallon of milk in one day. Powdered broths I find indispensable. I used them frequently in cooking vegetables, in strengthening the chicken flavor of diluted canned chicken broth, or when poaching meats of many kinds. They enrich the taste of canned beef gravy; solo, they are very good to drink after dissolving in the suitable amount of hot water. And they are, of course, miraculous space-savers, being packaged in small envelopes, whose contents, by the way, I often use double, or one-and-a-half, strength. I never go sailing without an assortment of all three of these—vegetable, chicken, and beef—stowed together in a largish canister. Every flavor's printed label being of a different color, it's a cinch to pull out the envelopes I need, as I need them.

As to quantities, you'd best count on appetites notably heartier than at home. There's something about the outdoor air and the activity of working a boat that makes people eat more than they do on shore. Even picky, eat-like-a-bird types will astonish you. This seems to be particularly true of sweets, so buy even more desserts and candies than you'd think ample. If your people are big on milk, you'll not only have to buy more fresh milk at the start and save it only for drinking, but lay in more evaporated milk to use for all cooking and, at times, no doubt, fall back on powdered milk for both purposes. So take factors like this into full consideration when deciding on quantities to buy of each and everything on your pre–cast-off shopping list.

Food cooked ahead at home deserves a special note, because it is so important in smoothing the cook's path the first week or so of a voyage. You can prepare such things as a batch of long-lasting cookies, a spicy cake that keeps, a three- to four-pound piece of boneless rare roast beef, a dozen or more unpeeled cold boiled potatoes in a tightly closed plastic bag, cooked rice in another bag, a dozen hard-boiled eggs, two fried chickens cut into quarters or eighths before frying, a two-pound meat loaf, enough ragout for one dinner. The cookies and cake are stowed with others of their ilk—all the other foods go into the icebox, where they will keep well. With the exception of the ragout, all are extremely versatile. In addition, you might fill as many as six or seven little jars or containers with a variety of appetizer spreads to take on board, counting on the emptied vessels for storage of leftovers later.

Section Two

MENUS & RECIPES
for many
WINDS & WATERS

A Sixteen-Day Warm-Weather Coastwise Cruise

These menus and recipes are based on a certain amount of pre-cooking before the trip starts, and on only three good opportunities to go ashore for marketing, spaced about five days apart. These marketing days are indicated in the right-hand margin. Breakfasts and lunches are categorized by main dish rather than allocated to specific days. Throughout, recipes immediately follow each menu and are cross-referenced in the index. Pre-cooked foods are asterisked and the recipes for them appear in a separate chapter.

SIXTEEN BREAKFASTS

SIX "EGG-AND-" BREAKFASTS
(Coffee, tea, milk, or cocoa is assumed for each, according to preference.)

CANTALOUPE
POACHED EGGS ON WHOLE WHEAT TOAST
CANADIAN BACON
GOOSEBERRY JAM

Cantaloupe

Cut a nicely ripened melon into four wedges. Squeeze lime juice over wedges before serving.

Poached Eggs on Whole Wheat Toast

Butter each egg cup of an egg poacher thoroughly before dropping the egg into it. Have half your toast done, buttered, and keep warm wrapped in paper napkins before you start the eggs. They cook quickly. With enough toast to overturn them onto, you can continue making toast on which to put the jam.

If the gang may call for two eggs each, do not turn off flame after poaching four. Serve the first four eggs, re-butter the cups (without washing) and poach four more eggs.

SEEDLESS GREEN GRAPES

CHEESE OMELET

RYE TOAST

Seedless Green Grapes

A pound and a half will serve four tidily but have some sugar handy for those who like to dip them in sugar.

Cheese Omelet

Break 6 eggs into a bowl, add 2 ounces of milk or water, and stir the mixture well with a fork. Set aside. Dice very finely enough sharp or mild cheddar or processed American cheese to make ¾ cup. Melt 4 tablespoons butter in a big heavy frying pan and pour in the egg mixture. Cook over medium heat, using a narrow spatula to loosen the edges from the sides of the pan and pushing them gently toward the middle as it cooks. Just when the eggs are "set" underneath, strew the cheese in a narrow row down the center. Allow to cook a little longer, then with the spatula fold over in half or in thirds, turn off the fire, loosen from the pan and slide onto a plate or a heated platter.

JUICE (SUIT YOURSELF)
FRIED EGGS WITH HAM
TOASTED ENGLISH MUFFINS
MARMALADE

Toasted English Muffins

Split and toast all of these before starting the ham and eggs, buttering them as fast as toasted, unless you are toasting them in a frying pan. In that case, butter them first and toast with buttered side down, ignoring the other side.

Keep hot in the top of a double boiler with boiling water in the bottom, placed over two asbestos pads, unless you are toasting them in a frying pan. In that case, butter them first and toast with buttered side down, ignoring the other slice, cover pan and remove to keep hot over two heated asbestos pads.

Fried Eggs with Ham

You will need two burners for this. Fry thin-sliced boiled or Virginia ham gently over moderate heat. While it is cooking, fry 2 eggs per person, to order, since preferences in this department are so pronounced.

A WHOLE ORANGE APIECE
POACHED EGGS WITH TOMATOES AND SAUCE
BUTTERED WHITE TOAST

Poached Eggs with Tomatoes and Sauce

Though the title doesn't say so, this involves bacon, too. Allow 2 strips per person, and cook over a slow fire, turning over often; when crisp, remove with tongs and drain on paper towel or newspaper. Meantime, slice 2 tomatoes, or 1 big one, good and thick; dredge each slice with flour shaken in a fine-mesh sieve over the tomato, season with salt and pepper. When the bacon is out of the pan, fry the tomatoes in the bacon fat for about 4 minutes on each side, or till they turn a good deep tan. All this time, you're busily toasting slices of white bread on the other burner, with four plates laid out side by side in readiness. Place a slice of unbuttered toast on each plate, two strips of bacon on top of that, and a slice of fried tomato on top of the bacon. With your first burner now free, poach an egg per person while, into the pan in which bacon and tomatoes were cooked, put 1 teaspoon Escoffier Sauce Diable per person, and 1 teaspoon Worcestershire sauce over all. Stir well, heat, and when you've slid an egg on top of the tomato-bacon-toast pile on each plate, pour a little sauce over each.

Buttered White Toast

Once the eggs are served, both burners of the stove will be unoccupied. Toast more bread on one; put on a pot of water to heat for dishwashing on the other.

BLUEBERRIES AND CREAM
CHIPPED BEEF OMELET
CHEESE BREAD TOAST
STRAWBERRY JAM

Chipped Beef Omelet

Proceed as for Cheese Omelet (page 52), but instead of cheese use ¾ cup shredded chipped beef, sautéed very briefly, with 1 tablespoon heavy cream or undiluted evaporated milk stirred into it. Add to half-done omelet just as you would if you were using cheese.

JUICE (SUIT YOURSELF)
SCRAMBLED EGGS
HAM BISCUITS

Ham Biscuits

Into a stout plastic bag empty 2 cups readymade baking powder biscuit mix, add ¾ cup undiluted evaporated milk or light cream. Close bag tightly and squeeze and knead to form a stiff dough. Add the contents of two 3-ounce cans deviled ham, re-close bag and squeeze and knead again to distribute ham evenly through the dough, then chill in the icebox for ½ hour. With floured fingers, shape into fairly flat biscuits 2 inches in diameter. Melt 1 tablespoon butter in a large skillet over low fire. Lay biscuits in it, with room to spare between each. Don't cover. Turn fire up to moderate. Cook for about 6 minutes; lift with spatula and turn, adding more butter at this point if it seems needed. As first batch is done, remove to top of double boiler whose lower chamber holds water just off the boil, cover, to keep hot till you're ready to eat, then add a tablespoon of butter to the pan and cook the next batch. Continue until all dough is cooked.

Scrambled Eggs

Break 8 eggs into any suitable container, add 1 cup undiluted evaporated milk or light cream and with rotary beater beat rapidly till somewhat bubbly. Over high heat, in a heavy frying pan, melt quickly 2 tablespoons butter but do not let it brown. Pour in the eggs, stir well, and keep stirring till eggs are cooked to your taste. Remove immediately to heated plates.

FIVE CEREAL-AND-HOT-BREAD BREAKFASTS

GRAPEFRUIT

WHEATENA WITH MILK AND SUGAR

SKILLET BISCUITS I WITH HONEY

Skillet Biscuits I

These are made in the same way as Ham Biscuits in the breakfast menu just preceding, omitting the ham. When done, split, dollop with butter, and urge everybody to be lavish with the honey.

Grapefruit

For each person, carefully section ½ grapefruit. Have sugar available for the sweet-tooth characters, but suggest trying fruit preserves instead.

Wheatena

Cook as directed on the box, using undiluted evaporated milk, for a richer taste, and offer brown sugar to put on it instead of white. Serve really hot.

STEWED PRUNES
COCOA KRISPIES WITH MILK, SUGAR,
AND CINNAMON
BRIOCHES AND BUTTER

Stewed Prunes

Allow 5 prunes per person, and add 1 slice lemon for each three prunes when you put them on to cook. Don't overcook; they should never be mushy. Cool quickly.

Brioches

Buy these in a bakery the day—or at most two days—before you serve them. If you buy the brown-and-serve variety because you have an oven or Dutch oven, cook according to directions on the box. Otherwise, set up the largest double-boiler facsimile you possibly can and heat them in that over simmering water. If you can't fit them all in at first, add unwarmed ones as you remove heated ones, in ratio of one to one. Allow 20 minutes to heat through.

JUICE (SUIT YOURSELF)
OATMEAL WITH CREAM AND BROWN SUGAR
HEATED CANNED DATE-NUT BREAD

Heated Canned Date-Nut Bread

Half-fill your biggest pot with water and bring to a boil. Puncture each can of bread to let steam escape as it heats. Two cans should be ample for four persons. Place cans in boiling water and heat for 15 minutes. After opening, slide out the loaf intact, slice moderately thin, and serve. You'll want plenty of softened butter to spread on it.

STEWED APRICOTS
RICE CHEX WITH MILK AND SUGAR
HOT COFFEE CAKE

Stewed Apricots

Buy the non–soak-ahead-of-time kind. Cook the night before, after the dinner dishes are done and while everybody (except the children) is sitting around in the cockpit enjoying the evening and discussing the day's passage. Drain well before turning in, put into plastic bag, and refrigerate if there's room; otherwise, stick in a cool place.

Hot Coffee Cake

Another shore-purchased goodie, which keeps for three days in its bakery package in a relatively galley-temperature location. Cut into serving pieces before placing in the top of the largest double-boiler arrangement you can contrive, with 2 inches water in the bottom; over moderate flame, heat for 15 minutes. If you have a stovetop oven along, you're in clover. Heat therein for 6 to 8 minutes, tops, at 350°.

SLICED PEELED ORANGES

MAYPO WITH MILK AND SUGAR

CINNAMON TOAST

Sliced Peeled Oranges

Peel 1 orange per person and slice into small bowls while the coffee is "working." Refrigeration is not needed, if the oranges are good quality.

Maypo

This is a recently formulated dry cereal that contains maple syrup as well as sugar; therefore little or no sugar need be added, depending upon the sweet tooth of each of your group. Milk, reconstituted powdered, diluted evaporated, or fresh, is essential, however.

FIVE BREAKFASTS, MISCELLANEOUS

PINEAPPLE CHUNKS I

MY OWN FRENCH TOAST WITH SYRUP

FRIZZLED HAM

Pineapple Chunks I

One 16-ounce can will serve four persons. Be judicious about the amount of juice added from the can to each individual bowl, and, to cut the oversweetness present even in the variety labeled "unsweetened," add a teaspoon of crème de menthe or lemon juice to each serving.

My Own French Toast

These proportions are for 8 slices of bread, which should be at least a day old. To 1 egg, beaten just enough to mix white and yolk, add 1 cup undiluted evaporated milk, and stir with a spoon. Add ½ teaspoon each ground cloves, ginger, and cinnamon. Stir again to blend in the spices. Turn mixture into shallow dish, and shake ½ teaspoon salt over it. Slice by slice, dip the bread in the mixture, first one side and then the other. While the first slice is absorbing the batter, heat a big cast-iron frying pan over medium heat and put in 1 tablespoon butter, swishing it around with a spoon till melted. Lift a slice of bread at a time from the batter with the fingers, holding it over the dish to drain off excess batter, place in frying pan, and put a second bread slice in the batter. Cook till brown on one side, turn over, and brown the other side, adding dabs of butter as pan begins to look dry. There should be a good coating of melted butter all over the bottom of the frying pan at all times. As each slice is done, slide onto a heated plate and pass over to the breakfaster. Continue dipping, draining, cooking, and serving till everybody but yourself has had full measure. Then serve yourself, while the others go on deck to attend to boat-working duties.

Frizzled Ham

Use any kind of sliced ham, from a ham steak cooked as a unit and then cut in pieces for each person to delicatessen ham slices. Put in butter over a low fire in a medium-sized frying pan and turned over as often as you turn bacon, using the hand not occupied with the French toast. If ready for eating before the French toast is done, keep it hot on three asbestos pads over a very low flame.

STEWED RHUBARB
RICE* GRIDDLECAKES WITH JAM
SAUSAGE PATTIES

Stewed Rhubarb

Use 2 bunches of fresh rhubarb or 2 boxes of frozen (the latter is preferable because it is far less work to prepare and takes up far less space in the icebox). Cook the night before you plan to eat it, cool, drain, and refrigerate in a plastic bag.

Rice* Griddlecakes

Into a plastic bag sift 1 cup flour with ¾ teaspoon baking soda; stir in 1 cup cold cooked rice.* In another vessel beat 1 egg slightly; stir into it 1½ cups sour cream, 2 tablespoons melted butter or vegetable oil, and 1 tablespoon salt. Add to dry ingredients, knead and squeeze till well blended. Heat a heavy frying pan, big enough to hold five cakes at once, moderately hot, melt 1 tablespoon butter in it, and drop batter by spoonfuls onto butter. Turn up heat if not browning fast enough, but don't brown too fast to cook batter thoroughly. Turn and brown on the other side. Keep buttering the pan and dropping batter in until all the batter is used. Any fruit preserve is good spread over these.

Sausage Patties

Shape 1 pound sausage meat into fairly flat 2-inch patties. On the second burner, over a moderate flame heat a medium-sized frying pan; put in the patties, then turn fire quite low and cook the meat slowly, turning it often, until brown. This will take about as long as to cook two pans of griddlecakes, so time yourself accordingly.

MELON
WHOLE-WHEAT PANCAKES AND SYRUP
BACON

Melon

Use cantaloupe or casaba or honeydew, whichever is plentiful or suits your taste. For any of them, a good squeeze of lime juice over each portion is a flavor improvement.

Whole-Wheat Pancakes

Into a stout plastic bag, empty 2 cups whole-wheat muffin mix, add 1⅓ cups evaporated milk diluted half-and-half with water, 2 tablespoons molasses, and 1 tablespoon melted butter or vegetable oil. Close bag tightly and squeeze and knead to blend into a batter the consistency of heavy cream. If needed to achieve this, add a little more milk, undiluted. Heat a big heavy frying pan medium hot, put in 1 tablespoon butter, allow to melt, then spoon batter into pan to make cakes about 2½ inches across. Cook till the bubbles on top are quite big, then turn and cook the other side. While the pancakes are cooking, heat 1½ cups syrup in the top of a small double boiler with ¾ inch water in the bottom. As soon as hot, remove from fire and keep warm on asbestos pads, to free the burner for the bacon.

Bacon

A cold frying pan to begin with, a low fire, frequent turning, and very slow cooking is my rule for bacon. As each piece is cooked to taste (rubbery, crisp, or in between), remove it and drain on newspaper or paper towels.

GRAPEFRUIT JUICE

CORNED BEEF HASH MAISON

FRIED TOMATOES, GREEN OR RIPE

RYE TOAST

Rye Toast

This should be done before putting either the hash or the tomatoes on the fire, and kept warm till they are ready.

Corned Beef Hash Maison

Open 2 cans corned beef hash by cutting off both ends of each can. Empty into a bowl. Stir in ¼ teaspoon garlic salt, ½ teaspoon onion salt, ½ teaspoon celery salt, ½ teaspoon salt, and ¼ teaspoon black pepper. Open a 3-ounce can of broiled-in-butter sliced mushrooms, and drain, leaving mushrooms in can. Chop 1 green pepper, pith and seeds removed. Grate medium-fine enough Swiss cheese to make ¼ cup. Measure out 2 tablespoons

(1 ounce) sherry or Madeira or Marsala. Heat a heavy frying pan to medium hot and melt in it 1½ tablespoons butter. Add mushrooms and sauté 2 minutes. Add green pepper, stirring well through mushrooms. Sauté 3 minutes more. Add corned beef hash and wine, stirring to mix everything well. Cook 6 or 7 minutes, to heat through but not brown very much.

Fried Tomatoes, Green or Ripe

Allow 1 fairly large tomato per person. Slice crosswise into thirds. Spread the slices on newspaper on work counter and shake flour over them through a fine-mesh sieve. Season with salt and pepper. Turn the slices and repeat. Heat frying pan moderately hot, melt in it a little more than 1 tablespoon butter, and sauté tomatoes till brown on both sides. Serve as slices are cooked, to make room for more to go into the pan.

BLUEBERRIES AND CREAM
CORNMEAL CAKES WITH APPLE JELLY
CANADIAN BACON

Canadian Bacon

Cook before cornmeal cakes, to acquire fat in which to fry the cakes; it imparts a special flavor. Keep hot in top of double boiler on second burner while cakes are cooking.

Cornmeal Cakes

Use either white or yellow cornmeal. In a stout plastic bag, place 1 cup meal, 1 cup flour, 1 teaspoon salt, 1½ teaspoons baking soda. Close bag tightly and shake and squeeze until well mixed. In another vessel, beat 2 eggs well, add 1½ cups sour milk or buttermilk. Pour into dry ingredients, re-close bag tightly and squeeze and knead to form a smooth batter. Knead in 2 tablespoons molasses and 3 tablespoons melted butter or vegetable oil. Heat a heavy frying pan quite hot, rub the pan well with fat from cooking Canadian bacon, and drop batter by spoonfuls into pan. When batter surface is covered with little holes, turn and brown other side. Serve with apple jelly.

SIXTEEN LUNCHES
FIVE HOT-DISH-AND-FRUIT LUNCHES

FRANKFURTERS AND SAUERKRAUT
HOT-DOG ROLLS
RAW APPLES

Frankfurters and Sauerkraut

Plan on 3 franks per person; cook them in an uncovered frying pan over low fire, turning frequently, until browned all over. According to whether or not you are going to toast the hot-dog rolls, heat the contents of one 16-ounce can of sauerkraut in either the bottom or the top of the largest double-boiler arrangement you can contrive. If you're merely warming the rolls, put the sauerkraut in the bottom of the double boiler and the rolls in the top. If you're toasting the rolls, use the top of the double boiler for the sauerkraut, heat it over boiling water, remove to a pile of three asbestos pads, and toast the rolls, split and buttered lightly, split side down, in a medium-sized frying pan over a low fire. Use one burner for these, the other for the frankfurters. Watch the rolls, so that they don't burn; in fact, they should be just tanned.

CURRIED CRABMEAT AND ROBINSON RICE
CURRY ACCOMPANIMENTS
PINEAPPLE SLICES

Curried Crabmeat

This is a short-cut way of making curry that is delicious. Set up a largish double boiler on one burner. Measure out into a small bowl or cup 2½ tablespoons curry powder; add to it a rounded ¼ teaspoon each ground ginger, cinnamon, and cloves, 1 teaspoon salt, and 1 envelope powdered chicken broth. Stir well, then add ⅔ cup undiluted evaporated milk or light cream. Open and drain three 7¾-ounce cans crabmeat. Pick over the meat to remove all bones and sinew, and stir into it the strained juice of 1 lemon or 2 tablespoons bottled lemon juice. Set aside. Into the top of the double boiler, empty 2 cans undiluted condensed cream of mushroom soup. Add the spices-and-cream mixture and mix well. Stir in the crabmeat. Heat over boiling water for 10 minutes, or up to 20 minutes if desired. Serve over rice.

Robinson Rice

Fill a 3-quart saucepan to within 1 inch of the top with water. Pour a tablespoon or so of vegetable or olive oil into the water. Cover and bring to a rolling boil. Pour in ⅔ cup raw long-grain white rice, and stir with wooden spoon till water reboils and rice is well in motion with none sticking to the bottom of the pan. Boil hard, for 9 minutes only. Drain into colander and rinse with cold water. Put about an inch of fresh water into the saucepan rice was cooked in, lower colander with rice into the pot, cover, and put back on low fire to steam. It can stay this way for up to ½ hour, and needs a minimum of 10 minutes.

Curry Accompaniments

I believe six of these are enough: canned coconut; peanuts or cashews; diced banana or apple; diced celery or green pepper; chutney, garden relish, or diced candied ginger; chopped hard-boiled eggs (two for four people). Set each in a separate small bowl and place in center of table for people to help themselves.

Pineapple Slices

Chill one No. 2 (16-ounce) can sliced pineapple from breakfast till lunch. When ready to serve, open and drain off half the juice. Fork the slices into saucers or bowls. Add 1 tablespoon rum or bourbon to each portion. Pour reserved juice evenly over all.

CROQUES MATELOTS

GREEN GRAPES

Croques Matelots

Trim crusts from 16 thin slices rye bread, spread one side of each slice lightly with soft butter, and lay out, open, in pairs, buttered side down. Grate Swiss, cheddar, Gruyère, or Emmenthal cheese medium fine till there is ¾ cup. Turn into any suitable receptacle and add enough undiluted evaporated milk or heavy cream to make a thick paste, then rum or bourbon to thin to consistency of mayonnaise. Spread on one of each pair of bread slices. On the other, lay a thin slice of ham, boiled or Virginia. Put the pairs together. Beat 3 eggs till blended, add 3 tablespoons any kind of liquid milk. Put a large heavy frying pan, with 2½ tablespoons butter in it, over moderate heat. While butter is melting, dip each sandwich quickly in egg-milk mixture, then sauté, ham side down, as many sandwiches as will fit into the pan. Turn and brown cheese side. Repeat till all sandwiches are cooked. Serve sandwiches at once, as they become done.

TUNA AND HARD-BOILED EGGS

PUMPERNICKEL

CANNED PEARS

Tuna and Hard-boiled Eggs

Hard-boil 4 eggs and let cool. When ready to cook, set up a medium-sized double-boiler with 1½ inches water in the bottom. Into the upper part put the contents of two 7-ounce cans tuna fish, ⅓ cup each sliced green and black olives, salt and pepper to taste, and half a white onion, coarsely chopped. Mix together well. Open and mix together 1 can each undiluted condensed cheese soup and condensed cream of mushroom soup. Add ½ can each chicken broth and undiluted evaporated milk, stirring in thoroughly. Add to the fish mixture. Stir together well. Cut the eggs lengthwise into eighths and add, stirring as little as possible in order not to break them. Cover; keep hot. On the other burner lightly toast 2 slices pumpernickel, black bread, or Boston brown bread per person. Serve fish mixture over half the toast, serving balance to eat separately.

Canned Pears

Open one No. 2 (16-ounce) can halved Bartlett pears, drain off about half the juice. Season each serving with a little crème de menthe or a drop or two of peppermint extract.

CHICKEN* WITH TOMATOES AND SOUR CREAM
TOAST
GREENGAGE PLUMS

Chicken* with Tomatoes and Sour Cream

Remove from bones the equivalent of ½ cooked chicken*; cut up and set aside. Or use two 5½-ounce cans chicken. Melt 4 tablespoons butter in a heavy frying pan. Put in half a small white onion finely chopped, 1 clove garlic chopped or a generous ¼ teaspoon garlic salt, and 3 medium-sized tomatoes, skinned and sliced medium thin. Cook, stirring, over moderate fire for about 5 minutes or until tomatoes have lost some of their shape. Remove from fire and add 4 tablespoons flour to butter remaining; stir till smooth. Pour on ¾ cup chicken broth mixed with ⅓ cup dry white wine. Put sauce back on fire and stir until it comes to a boil. Add ¼ cup shredded almonds, half a bay leaf, salt and pepper to taste, and the chicken pieces. Simmer 15 minutes Remove bay leaf. Add ½ cup sour cream, 1 tablespoon grated Swiss, Gruyère, or Parmesan cheese, and 1 more medium-sized tomato, skinned and sliced. Simmer a couple of minutes more. Serve on toast or split hard rolls.

SIX SOUP-AND-COLD-SANDWICH LUNCHES

(All soups are good hot or cold,
according to weather and taste.)

OXTAIL GUMBO
HARD-BOILED EGG* AND RELISH SANDWICHES ON
BLACK BREAD

Oxtail Gumbo

Open and mix together in a saucepan 1 can each undiluted condensed oxtail soup and condensed mock turtle soup. Add 1 can undiluted condensed chicken gumbo and 11 ounces chicken broth. Put over medium fire to heat. While soup is heating, chop 1 green pepper and ⅓ cup green olives; add to soup along with contents of one 7-ounce can shrimp, ½ teaspoon curry, and salt and pepper to taste. Simmer 10 minutes.

Hardboiled Egg* and Relish Sandwiches

Butter one side of each of 8 slices black bread. Chop fine 4 shelled hard-boiled eggs* and put into a bowl. Add 4 tablespoons each garden relish or chow-chow and chopped white onion. Season with salt, cayenne, and paprika. Add 6 to 8 tablespoons sour cream, or enough to make mixture of spreading consistency, and stir thoroughly. Spread on 8 unbuttered slices black bread, covering with buttered slices. Cut in half if desired.

SHRIMP AND OYSTER SOUP
TONGUE AND BLACK OLIVE SANDWICHES ON
LIGHT RYE BREAD

Shrimp and Oyster Soup

Into the top of a medium-sized double boiler with $1\frac{1}{2}$ inches water in the bottom, empty 1 can each shrimp bisque and oyster stew, one 13-ounce can undiluted evaporated milk, and 7 ounces chicken broth. Add $\frac{1}{2}$ cup chopped celery or green olives, 3 tablespoons chopped white onion or 1 teaspoon instant minced onion, 1 tablespoon parsley flakes or chopped fresh parsley, salt and white pepper to taste. Heat for 15 minutes.

Tongue and Black Olive Sandwiches

Butter one side each of 8 thin slices light rye bread. In any convenient container mix contents of two 3-ounce cans minced tongue, $\frac{1}{2}$ cup chopped walnuts and $\frac{1}{2}$ cup chopped black olives. Bind with mayonnaise; season with salt. Spread 8 slices unbuttered light rye bread with this mixture and cover with buttered slices. Cut in half if desired.

CRÈME SÉNÉGALESE WITH APPLE
CRABMEAT SALAD SANDWICHES ON
WHOLE-WHEAT BREAD

Crème Sénégalese with Apple

Turn into the top of a medium-sized double boiler with $1\frac{1}{2}$ inches water in the bottom, the contents of three 13-ounce cans Vichyssoise. Into $\frac{1}{3}$ cup apple juice stir 1 envelope dehydrated chicken broth, 1 heaping tablespoon curry powder, and one finely chopped, peeled, sharp-flavored apple. Add to soup and heat 15 minutes.

Crabmeat Salad Sandwiches

Butter 8 thin slices whole-wheat bread. Into any suitable receptacle, put contents of two 7¾-ounce cans crabmeat, drained. Pick over to remove any bits of shell and sinew. Add strained juice of 1 lemon, 1 teaspoon onion salt, 1 tablespoon each parsley flakes, chopped capers, and chopped green olives, and ¼ teaspoon garlic salt. Stir well; bind with mayonnaise. Spread on 8 slices unbuttered whole-wheat bread; cover with buttered slices. Cut in half if desired.

CREAM OF BROCCOLI SOUP

MEAT LOAF* OR LIVERWURST PÂTÉ SANDWICHES

ON WHITE BREAD

Cream of Broccoli Soup

Cook one package frozen chopped broccoli in the top of a medium-sized double boiler directly over a medium flame, in ½ inch chicken broth or the same amount of water with 1 envelope dehydrated chicken broth sprinkled over the vegetable at the time it is placed on the fire. Drain, saving the liquid in any convenient largish heatproof container. Add to it ⅔ cup undiluted evaporated milk and two 10½-ounce cans undiluted condensed cream of mushroom soup, ½ teaspoon celery salt, salt, white pepper, and a pinch of dry mustard. Add broccoli, stir well, and return to top of double boiler, this time over bottom part with 1 inch boiling water in it. Heat 15 minutes. Add strained juice of 1 lemon or 2 tablespoons bottled lemon juice before serving.

Meat Loaf* or Liverwurst Pâté Sandwiches

For meat loaf* sandwiches, spread 8 thin slices white bread generously with mayonnaise. Slice meat loaf* about ¼ inch thick and lay on 8 slices plain white bread. Season to taste. Cover with mayonnaise-coated slices. For liverwurst pâté, mash 10 thin slices liverwurst till smooth; season with 1 grated onion, salt, coarse-ground black pepper, and a little Worcestershire sauce. Bind with mayonnaise. Spread on plain white bread; cover with buttered white bread. Cut in half if desired.

BLACK BEAN SOUP

ROAST BEEF* SANDWICHES ON

SOUR RYE BREAD

Black Bean Soup

Place in the top of a medium-sized double boiler contents of two 10½-ounce cans undiluted condensed black bean soup, one 10½-ounce can undiluted condensed consommé, and ½ of a 13-ounce can undiluted evaporated milk. Stir thoroughly to dissolve all lumps. Add salt, coarse-ground black pepper, ½ teaspoon each onion salt, celery salt, and dry mustard, and 1 tablespoon sherry. Heat over 1½ inches of boiling water for 15 minutes.

CLEAR CUCUMBER SOUP

CHICKEN AND WATER CHESTNUT SANDWICHES ON

WHOLE-WHEAT BREAD

Clear Cucumber Soup

Peel, seed, and dice 2 large cucumbers. In the top of your largest double boiler, directly over a low fire, cook for 3 minutes in 2 tablespoons butter. Add salt, white pepper, and ½ teaspoon each ground ginger, onion salt, and celery salt. Stir well, and then add two 13¾-ounce cans undiluted condensed chicken broth. Fill one broth can with white wine, add, and stir again. Put 2 inches water into the bottom of the double boiler, assemble boiler, raise flame to medium, and cook soup for 15 minutes, covered.

Chicken and Water Chestnut Sandwiches

Spread 8 slices whole-wheat bread generously with mayonnaise. Salt and pepper all of them. Empty into any suitable receptacle one 5-ounce can boned cooked chicken; chop finely. Drain one 5-ounce can water chestnuts, chop finely, and mix with chicken. Squeeze over chicken mixture the juice of ½ lemon or sprinkle on about 1 tablespoon bottled lemon juice. Bind with mayonnaise; spread on 8 uncoated slices whole-wheat bread. Cover with coated slices. Cut in half if desired.

FIVE SALAD-AND-COLD-MEAT LUNCHES

CAESAR SALAD
BREAD (FRENCH, IF POSSIBLE) AND BUTTER
CANNED APRICOTS

Caesar Salad

Tear up 2 large heads romaine lettuce, first discarding all outside leaves that are wilted or darkened by exposure and also most of the tough stalky parts. Wash well and place in the largest bowl or suitable receptacle you have. Sprinkle with 1/2 teaspoon each dry mustard and coarse-ground black pepper, 1/4 teaspoon garlic salt, 1 teaspoon onion salt, and 1 rounded teaspoon salt. Grate enough Roquefort cheese to make 1/2 cup and add to salad. Pour on 7 tablespoons olive oil and strained juice of 2 lemons. Break 2 raw eggs over the salad and toss until no trace of egg is apparent. Just before serving, add 2 cups plain croutons, bought ready-made or made before starting the salad by frying 2 cups 1/2-inch cubes of white bread in olive oil over low fire. Keep oil handy because the bread soaks up more than you think it's going to, and shake or stir the cubes frequently, watching constantly for signs of burning. When toasty brown, remove and drain on paper. After adding croutons, toss salad again.

TUNA-FISH SALAD
RYE BREAD AND BUTTER
MELON OR CANNED BLACK CHERRIES

Tuna-fish Salad

Into a bowl or any suitable container break into big chunks the drained contents of three 7-ounce cans solid pack tuna fish. Add 2 green peppers, pith and seeds removed, and cut into shoe-string strips; 1 medium-sized red onion, peeled, the ends cut off, and sliced into thin rings; ¾ cup sliced black olives; 3 hard-boiled eggs, cut lengthwise into eights; 4 smallish tomatoes cut lengthwise into ¾-inch-wide wedges. Toss lightly. In an 8-ounce screw-top jar or bottle put 1 rounded teaspoon salt, ½ rounded teaspoon coarse-ground pepper, and a scant ¼ teaspoon each sugar, dry mustard, and garlic salt. Add 6 tablespoons olive oil and 2 tablespoons white or red wine vinegar. Close jar and shake well. Pour over salad and toss. Chill ½ hour or so if possible, though not essential.

Melon or Canned Black Cherries

If you choose melon, dress each serving with 1 tablespoon rum. If black cherries (one No. 2 (16-ounce) can is plenty), drain off half the juice before serving. Add 1 ounce kirsch over the entire amount of cherries, then serve in small bowls.

ROAST BEEF* SALAD MAISON I
BREAD OR ROLLS AND BUTTER
CANNED PINEAPPLE SLICES

Roast Beef* Salad Maison I

Cut into shoestring strips about 2 inches long, or into ½-inch cubes, enough cold cooked roast beef* to make 2 cups. Put into a large bowl or any vessel. Add 2 tablespoons each finely chopped white onion or scallion and chopped pickles (any kind except fruit) or garden relish. Add 1 cup sliced cooked potatoes* and ½ cup each cooked string beans cut into short pieces (not French-style) and sliced cooked baby beets. All or any of these three last ingredients can come from cans. Make a dressing as for Tuna-fish Salad (page 69), adding, just before shaking it up, 1 scant table-spoon chili sauce and a dash of Tabasco. Pour over salad. Toss lightly but thoroughly.

Canned Pineapple Slices

For four, use a 1-pound can, and not much of the juice.

ESCAROLE WITH PROSCIUTTO, PROVOLONE,
AND PIMIENTO
SLICED TOMATOES
TOASTED SPLIT SOFT ROLLS
CANNED PEACHES

Escarole with Prosciutto, Provolone, and Pimiento

Tear into fairly small pieces the green leafy parts of 1 head escarole, after first discarding the outside wilted or darkened leaves. Wash well, shake off excess water, and place in large bowl or suitable vessel. Add ½ cup each prosciutto ham and provolone cheese, cut into shoestring strips about 2 inches long; ⅓ cup sliced green olives; and ¼ cup pimiento, also cut into shoestring strips. Make a dressing as for Tuna-fish Salad (page 69), using half the amount of vinegar and making up the difference with red wine, and also decreasing the oil by 1 tablespoon. Pour over salad; toss well. Chill for ½ hour or so, if possible.

Toasted Split Soft Rolls

These are done most efficiently with two stainless steel frying pans, both over a low fire. Split any kind of soft roll you wish, butter the split sides, place split side down in the pan, and toast quickly, keeping a sharp watch for over-browning.

Canned Peaches

Use those labeled *Elberta Halves, Home Style*. Pour off half the juice before serving. Sprinkle generously with ground ginger as a flavor-booster.

POTATO SALAD MAISON I OR II
GREENS WITH TOMATOES
BREAD AND BUTTER
CANNED FIGS

Potato Salad Maison I—Red

Peel 4 or 5 medium potatoes and put in saucepan with one 10½-ounce can undiluted condensed consommé and enough additional water to cover, or sprinkle with 3 envelopes dehydrated beef broth, then add water to cover. Add 1 clove garlic or ⅛ teaspoon instant minced garlic. Cook, covered, till done but not mealy (about 15 minutes). Drain and remove garlic, if fresh whole clove was used. While still warm, slice potatoes into a bowl or any suitable receptacle, and cover with red wine. Let stand for 20 minutes or ½ hour. Meantime, in another bowl or vessel, put 4 small cooked beets (fresh or canned), sliced; a few shreds of cooked or canned ham; 1 tablespoon each parsley flakes or chopped fresh parsley, and chopped pickle (any kind except fruit); 2 tablespoons finely chopped white onion, and 4 table-spoons finely grated Parmesan or Romano cheese.

Separately, make a dressing of 4 tablespoons each olive oil and red wine vinegar, seasoning with ½ teaspoon salt, ¼ tea-spoon coarse-ground black pepper, and a scant ¼ teaspoon each sugar and dry mustard. Drain potato slices and place in a large receptacle. Add other solid ingredients. Shake or stir dressing vigorously, and pour over salad. Toss to mix well.

Potato Salad Maison II—White

Peel 4 or 5 medium potatoes and put in saucepan with one 13¾-ounce can undiluted condensed chicken broth, adding water to cover, or sprinkle with 3 envelopes dehydrated chicken broth, then add water to cover. Cook, covered, till done but not mealy. Drain and let cool till comfortable to handle. Slice thinly into a bowl or any suitable receptacle, and cover with dry white wine. Let stand till cold. Meantime, lift out and cut in half each heart contained in one 4½-ounce jar artichoke hearts, and place in a second bowl or suitable container. Add ⅓ cup each sliced green and black olives, ⅓ cup finely chopped white onion or scallion, and 1 tablespoon each parsley flakes or chopped fresh parsley and chopped capers.

Separately, make a dressing of 1 teaspoon salt, a scant ¼ teaspoon sugar, ¼ teaspoon white pepper, ½ teaspoon celery salt, 5 tablespoons olive oil and 2½ tablespoons white wine vinegar or tarragon vinegar. In a large salad bowl or receptacle, put the drained potatoes and other solid ingredients. Pour dressing over, after stirring it well or shaking it in a jar. Toss to mix completely.

Greens with Tomatoes

Tear up and wash well the leafy green parts of three from among these different kinds of greens: escarole, chicory, romaine, Boston lettuce, Bibb lettuce, watercress. After shaking off excess water, place in a salad bowl or similar vessel. Cut 4 smallish tomatoes into large dice and put on top of greens. Make dressing as for whichever potato salad (Red or White) you have decided to serve, pour over salad, and toss well.

Canned Figs

Prepare this between breakfast and lunch. Drain all juice from one No. 2 (16-ounce) can or two 8-ounce cans figs. In the top of a medium-sized double boiler, over 1½ inches boiling water, heat ½ cup red wine, 1 tablespoon sugar, and 1 teaspoon lemon juice, fresh or bottled. When hot, add figs. Cook 5 minutes. When cooled, place in container with snug cover and store in icebox.

SIXTEEN DINNERS

(All first courses are planned to serve with drinks
before the meal, and can be ignored if so desired.)

First Day

FRIDAY

ONION CREAM CHEESE SPREAD*

MY FAVORITE RAGOUT*

THIN NOODLES

WATERCRESS AND ENDIVE SALAD

SLICED FRESH PEACHES

Onion Cream Cheese Spread*

Soften two 3-ounce packages cream cheese till easily mashed. Add 2 scant tablespoons undiluted evaporated milk. Mash with fork till milk is completely blended in and there are no lumps. Add 1 grated white onion about the size of a golf ball, season well, then "green" with parsley flakes, and chill.

This spread may be made up to a week before using.

My Favorite Ragoût*
This is brought on board from home, where it was cooked. (See recipe, page 305.) Tonight it merely needs a thorough heating over two asbestos pads and a low fire. Allow a full 45 minutes for this.

Thin Noodles
The recipe is given on page 212, under Fettuccini Parmigiana, but omit cheese.

Watercress and Endive Salad
Wash and break into medium-sized pieces 1 large or 2 small bunches watercress. Add cut-up leaves of 2 Belgian endives. Toss with French dressing* brought aboard from home.

Second Day   SATURDAY

LIZ'S LIVERWURST* WITH PARTY RYE
COLD FRIED CHICKEN I*
POTATO SALAD III*
BEET AND ONION SALAD
SKILLET BISCUITS I
LOGANBERRIES AND ANGEL CAKE

Liz's Liverwurst*
This spread can be made at home and brought aboard, up to 10 days before using, or it can be made aboard at lunchtime on the day you want it, and chilled until dinnertime. (See recipe, page 303).

Cold Fried Chicken I*
This can be made aboard or brought aboard already cooked at home. In either case, the recipe is the same (see page 305).

Potato Salad III*

Like the chicken, this can be made at home and brought aboard, or made right after the lunch dishes are done, and put to chill in the icebox. (See recipe, page 309).

Beet and Onion Salad

Open and drain one 1-pound can whole baby beets. Slice into a bowl or any convenient receptacle, and add to them 1 medium-sized white onion, peeled and sliced into very thin rings. Put in 1 teaspoon salt, ½ teaspoon coarse-ground black pepper, ½ teaspoon dry mustard, 3 teaspoons olive oil and 1½ tablespoons non-wine vinegar. Stir to blend. Chill or not as desired.

Skillet Biscuits I

Recipe is given on page 55.

Third Day   SUNDAY

CUCUMBER WEDGES
COLD MEAT LOAF*, SLICED
CORN ON THE COB
SLICED TOMATOES AND RED ONIONS I
CAFÉ LIÉGOIS WITH CAKE

Cucumber Wedges

Peel 3 cucumbers; cut lengthwise into eighths, then in half crosswise. Wrap in aluminum foil and place next to the ice till ready to serve with saltines and salt.

Cold Meat Loaf*, Sliced

This is cooked at home and brought aboard ready to eat. (See recipe, p. 306.)

Corn on the Cob

Boil it any way that you personally prefer, but for no longer than 3 minutes, and save the water it cooked in for dishwashing.

Sliced Tomatoes and Red Onions I

On a large plate or platter arrange alternate slices of ripe tomatoes and peeled red onions sliced ¼ inch thick. Add a pinch each thyme and basil (whole, not powdered) to ⅓ cup French dressing* brought aboard from home; pour over the tomatoes and onions.

Café Liégois

Per person, mix ¾ cup double-strength hot or warm coffee with ½ cup fresh milk. Chill in a 1½-quart container. When ready to serve, add to each portion 2 tablespoons each heavy cream and soft ice cream (chocolate, maple, pecan, or walnut flavor). Serve in mugs after stirring well.

Fourth Day

MONDAY

PICKLED HERRING

PICKLY BEEF*

MASHED POTATOES I

RED CABBAGE VIN ROUGE

PINEAPPLE CHUNKS II, WITH LIME

Pickled Herring

There are several varieties of pickled herring available. My own preference is for Bismarck, with an occasional switch to Mätjes. Sometimes I add thin slices of fresh white onion and a dollop of sour cream to each portion of Bismarck. In any case, if not bought that way, the herring should be cut into bite-sized pieces, served with rye-flavored crackers or rye-flavored Melba toast.

Pickly Beef* (à la Fermière)

Slice thinly enough cold cooked roast beef* or pot roast* to have 3 slices per person. Set aside in a shallow vessel. In an 8-inch frying pan melt 3 tablespoons butter, and in it sauté 1 cup finely chopped white onion until golden. Stir in 2½ tablespoons flour till combined smoothly with butter. Add 1 cup undiluted condensed canned consommé, ½ cup pulp of canned tomatoes, ½ teaspoon salt, and ¼ teaspoon coarse-ground black pepper. Stir until sauce comes to a boil. Add ⅓ cup chopped dill pickle and ½ teaspoon each dry mustard, mild vinegar, and prepared horse-radish. Place the sliced beef in the pan, cover with sauce by spooning it over the meat, cover and heat through. Do not let it boil up again.

Mashed Potatoes I

Using the top of a medium-sized double boiler, prepare the dehydrated kind and follow directions on the box. For milk called for, use evaporated milk diluted half-and-half with water. Set aside over 1½ inches hot water in the double boiler bottom, placed on asbestos pads.

Red Cabbage Vin Rouge

Shred coarsely 1 large red cabbage or 2 small ones, and put with 6 tablespoons butter into the top of your largest double boiler with 2 inches water in the bottom, or in a saucepan nested into a larger one. Add 1 cup each red wine and undiluted condensed consommé. Cover and steam over moderate flame for 30 minutes. Season with salt and coarse-ground black pepper. Serve, using tongs or 2 forks.

Pineapple Chunks II, with Lime

Drain off ½ to ⅔ of the syrup from one No. 2 (16-ounce) can pineapple chunks. Lift fruit out into individual serving dishes. Into the remaining syrup mix the strained juice of 1 lime or 1 tablespoon bottled lime juice, stir and pour over fruit. Chill or not as you desire, and serve with cookies of any kind.

Fifth   T U E S D A Y
Day

SHRIMP SPREAD*

CHICKEŃ COMTESSE

SPAGHETTINI AL BURRO

CANNED ASPARAGUS SALAD

CANNED APRICOTS WITH CHOCOLATE COOKIES

Shrimp Spread*

This is made at home and brought aboard. (See recipe, page 303.)

Chicken Comtesse

Slice thinly enough peeled white onions to make ⅔ cup. Slice, after scrubbing and destemming, ½ pound mushrooms, or open and drain four 3-ounce cans sliced mushrooms. Remove from bones the equivalent of ½ cooked chicken*, or open three 5½-ounce cans chicken and discard the jellied broth in which it is packed. Cut meat into bite-sized pieces. Sauté the onions till golden in 3 tablespoons butter. Add mushrooms, and more butter if needed, and sauté till tan, if fresh, or heated through, if canned. Put in the chicken pieces, along with one 13-ounce can Vichyssoise, 1 teaspoon strained lemon juice, 1 tablespoon sherry, Madeira, or Marsala, and salt and black pepper to taste. Bring to a boil; simmer 5 minutes.

Spaghettini al Burro

Use about two-thirds of a 1-pound package of No. 9 spaghetti. Fill a large pot with water to within 1 inch of the top. Pour on the water about 1 tablespoon olive or vegetable oil. Cover and bring to a boil. Break the pasta in half with your hands and put it in the pot. Stir with a wooden spoon until the water reboils, replace the cover so as to cover only about two-thirds of the mouth of the pot, and cook for no more than 9 minutes. Drain, saving the water for dishwashing, and putting the spaghettini into a heat-proof bowl. Add 3 or 4 tablespoons butter cut into ½-inch pieces for quicker melting and 4 tablespoons grated Parmesan cheese. Toss as vigorously as a salad. Cover and keep warm by setting the bowl into a pan containing very hot water, and placing this arrangement near the stove on three or more asbestos pads.

Canned Asparagus Salad

Use two No. 303 cans asparagus spears, either green, white, or mixed. Chill from lunch to dinner. Open, drain carefully, and lay the spears neatly on a large, fairly shallow dish. Pour over them a French dressing made with strained lemon juice instead of vinegar.

Sixth   WEDNESDAY   *Go Ashore*
Day   *and*
                       SHRIMP TOAST   *Market*
                   ROAST BEEF* SALAD II   *Today*
              BAKED BEANS À LA RUSSE
              CUCUMBERS FINLANDIA
         FRESH CHERRIES WITH CAKE

Shrimp Toast

Cut 8 slices white bread, trimmed of their crusts, into four triangles each. Open and drain one 7-ounce can wet-pack shrimp; place in a bowl and mash with fork or small pestle. Add 4 finely chopped water chestnuts and 1 teaspoon each salt, sugar, and cornstarch. Mix well. Beat 1 egg lightly and add to shrimp mixture, stirring in completely. In a heavy frying pan, heat ½ inch oil. When smoking hot, gently place in it about eight triangles spread with the shrimp mixture, shrimp side down. After 1 minute turn over and fry a few more seconds. Drain on paper. Spread eight more triangles and repeat. Continue until all triangles are spread and cooked. Serve hot.

Roast Beef* Salad II

Cut cold roast beef* into 2-inch-long strips the thickness of a pencil to fill 2 cups, and place in a large bowl or vessel. Add ½ cup sliced radishes, ½ cup diced peeled cucumber, ½ white onion, finely chopped, and ⅓ cup sliced green olives. Pour over the beef mixture a dressing made by thinning ¼ cup mayonnaise with the strained juice of ½ lemon, then stirring in 1 tablespoon each garden relish or any chopped pickle (except fruit pickle), parsley flakes, and chili sauce. Toss well. Chill before serving, if feasible.

Baked Beans à la Russe

Drain well one No. 2 (16-ounce) can vegetarian baked beans, and place in a bowl. Mix about 2 tablespoons each mayonnaise and catsup, add salt and coarse-ground black pepper to taste, combine well, and pour over beans. Stir to blend.

Cucumbers Finlandia

Peel 2 large cucumbers, cut them in half lengthwise, scoop out seeds with paring knife and discard. Slice thin and spread in a large shallow dish. Sprinkle generously with salt, and cover with cold water. Refrigerate, if possible, for about an hour; if not possible, keep covered, wherever safest and coolest. When ready to serve, drain well and sprinkle with coarse-ground black pepper, parsley flakes, and 3 tablespoons white wine vinegar.

Seventh
Day

THURSDAY

SARDINES AND SALTINES
BEEF COLLOPS WITH RUSSIAN SAUCE
CARAWAY NOODLES
BIBB LETTUCE WITH CUCUMBERS
CANTALOUPE RINGS WITH BLUEBERRIES

Sardines and Saltines

Open and drain thoroughly two 3½-ounce cans of whichever sort of sardines you like best. Lay neatly side by side in individual serving dishes, then carefully pour about 1 tablespoon fresh or bottled lemon juice over each portion. Serve with salad forks and a bowl of saltines.

Beef Collops with Russian Sauce

Place 1 pound raw chopped beef in a bowl or any convenient receptacle, even a plastic bag. Add ½ cup fine bread crumbs, 1 teaspoon salt, and ¼ teaspoon coarse-ground black pepper. Mix well. Add ½ cup any kind of liquid milk and mix again. Roll into balls about 1 inch in diameter, setting each as it is formed into a shallow dish or on wax paper or aluminum foil. Melt 3 tablespoons butter or drippings in a large heavy frying pan and sauté the meat balls, crowding as many as you can into the pan. Shake frequently to keep varying surfaces exposed to heat and to prevent sticking. As meat balls become browned all over, remove with tongs to drain on paper towel, newspaper or a flattened brown paper bag, and continue cooking until all meat balls are browned, adding more butter from time to time if necessary, though this is not likely. After all meat balls are out of the frying pan, add to the butter remaining, 4 tablespoons flour, and combine well. Add 2 cups stock made by mixing ½ cup water with one 10½-ounce can undiluted condensed beef broth and ½ cup catsup. Stir sauce till it comes to a boil, then stir in 1 cup sour cream, return the meat to the sauce, turn flame low, and simmer 5 minutes.

Bibb Lettuce with Cucumbers

Into whatever container you plan to serve the salad, put the ingredients for a basic French dressing using lemon juice instead of vinegar, and combine well; or use 4 tablespoons French dressing* prepared at home and brought aboard. Peel ½ a cucumber and slice very thinly into the dressing. Break up, wash, and drain 3 or 4 heads Bibb lettuce, wrap in a towel, and put into icebox. When ready to serve, combine the two and toss thoroughly.

Cantaloupe Rings with Blueberries

Peel and seed 1 medium cantaloupe. Cut crosswise into 4 slices and place in individual bowls. Pour ½ teaspoon lime juice, fresh or bottled, over each portion. Wash and pick over 1 pint fresh blueberries and divide equally among the portions. Spoon ½ ounce (1 tablespoon) rum over each serving. It may, but need not be, chilled till ready to serve.

FRIDAY

GUACAMOLE <u>CHEZ MOI</u> ON MELBA TOAST
CRABMEAT FRANKLIN
POTATO BALLS
HOT SCALLIONS
RUSSIAN PLUMS

Guacamole Chez Moi

Mash 1 fairly large avocado in a bowl or any convenient receptacle, using a pestle or fork. Add 2 tablespoons lemon juice, fresh or bottled, 1 tablespoon finely grated white onion (about ½ a small onion), and stir well. Season with ½ teaspoon each salt and chili powder, ¼ teaspoon each coarse-ground black pepper and cayenne, and mix well again. Chill if possible, though this is not essential.

Crabmeat Franklin

Open and drain two 7¾-counce cans crabmeat and pick over to remove all bits of shell, bone, and sinew. Place into any bowl or suitable vessel, and add to it enough undiluted condensed cream of shrimp or cream of mushroom soup to make a thick paste. Sauté 8 slices boiled ham until the edges curl markedly. Put into the top of a medium-sized double boiler over 1½ inches very hot water and set aside on asbestos pads to keep hot. Over very low heat, in the pan the ham was cooked in, heat crabmeat paste till hot, stirring carefully occasionally. Place the ham "cups" on heated plates, two "cups" per person; spoon crabmeat mixture into the "cups" and serve.

Potato Balls

Peel 2 very large or 3 medium-large potatoes. With melon-ball cutter, scoop out as many potato balls as possible, dropping each ball into a vessel of cold water as it is scooped from the large potato. Keep enough water in the receptacle to cover the potatoes, so as to prevent discoloration. When all potato balls are made, drain and place in a deep saucepan, cover with fresh cold water, and bring to a boil slowly. When water begins to boil, drain, saving water for dishwashing later. Spread potato balls on newspapers or dish towel, roll up and rub until fairly dry. In a heavy large frying pan melt 6 tablespoons butter; add salt, coarse-ground black pepper and potato balls. Cover and shake well to coat with butter. Cook, covered, over low flame till turning color and soft but not mushy (about ½ hour to 40 minutes).

Hot Scallions

Prepare these exactly as you would fresh asparagus, allowing 1 bunch scallions per person. Cut off the roots and strip away the outer membranes of each stalk first; then chop off a part of the green tops, but leave at least 3 inches of the green. Tie with kitchen string into one big bunch and stand upright, root end down, in the bottom of a drip coffeepot or the main chamber of a non-electric percolator or other suitably tall fireproof vessel (a double boiler will do nicely, the scallions upright in the bottom, the top overturned and placed over the scallions). Add enough water to cover the white part of the scallions and boil gently for 5 minutes. Drain, untie and serve.

Russian Plums

Open and drain fully one No. 2 (16-ounce) can plums. Place in any convenient receptacle, cover with sour cream, and sprinkle generously with brown sugar. Serve unchilled.

Ninth Day

SATURDAY

"BABY" FRANKFURTERS
COLD CHICKEN* SAINT SEBASTIEN
TOMATOES WITH CHILI SAUCE
BEAN SPROUT SALAD
GINGERED PEARS

"Baby" Frankfurters

Cut apart into individual sausages 2 pounds cocktail frankfurters and peel if needed. Cook slowly, shaking pan often, in a large frying pan over a low flame, for 6 or 7 minutes. Meantime, set out one plate per person, spoon a dollop of prepared mustard into each egg cup from the egg poacher, or any similar small vessel and place one on each plate. With a spatula, slide an equal number of sausages onto each plate; serve.

Cold Chicken* Saint Sebastien

In a bowl or any suitable receptacle, toss together 1½ cups diced cold fried chicken* or diced canned chicken and ⅓ cup each thinly sliced celery and water chestnuts. Make ½ cup French dressing using 2 parts oil to 1 part combined white wine vinegar and lemon juice, fresh or bottled; or use the same amount of French dressing* prepared at home and brought aboard. Pour over chicken mixture and toss. Let stand ½ hour, then add 1¼ cups cold cooked rice*, 3 tablespoons slivered almonds, and ⅔ cup sour cream. Season with 1 teaspoon salt and ½ teaspoon coarse-ground black pepper. Stir lightly. Though the dish is best served chilled, this is not really necessary.

Tomatoes and Chili Sauce

Slice 4 medium-sized tomatoes into ¼-inch slices and place in any suitable bowl or vessel. In a small measuring cup, put 3 tablespoons chili sauce and stir into it the juice of 1 lemon or 2½ tablespoons bottled lemon juice. Season tomatoes with salt and course-ground black pepper, pour sauce over them, and set aside until serving. Refrigeration is not needed.

Bean Sprout Salad

Open and drain thoroughly two 1-pound cans bean sprouts, and put into a bowl or any convenient receptacle. Pour over them a dressing made in a screw-top jar, bottle or other container from these ingredients: ⅛ teaspoon garlic salt; ¼ teaspoon coarse-ground black pepper; a scant ¼ teaspoon sugar; 2 teaspoons each slivered green olives, parsley flakes, chopped pickles (any kind except fruit pickles) , and chopped capers; juice of ½ lemon or 1 tablespoon bottled lemon juice; 1 tablespoon malt or tarragon or white wine vinegar; and 4 tablespoons olive oil. Shake or stir vigorously. Toss salad thoroughly and chill in a tightly closed plastic bag as long as convenient. Drain off dressing just before serving.

Gingered Pears

Open and drain off ⅔ the juice from one No. 2 (16-ounce) can halved Bartlett pears. Place pears in the top of a medium-sized double boiler with remaining juice and 2 tablespoons finely chopped candied ginger. Set over double boiler bottom with 1½ inches water in it, and cook over low heat for 5 minutes. Let cool, then turn into an icebox container with tight lid, close and chill till ready to serve.

Tenth Day   SUNDAY

TUNA CANAPÉS ON ONION ROUNDS
ROAST BEEF* HASH
GREEN BEANS WITH HORSERADISH SAUCE
MINTED APPLESAUCE WITH RED CANDY BITS

Tuna Canapés

Mix together ¼ cup mayonnaise, 2 tablespoons sherry or a similar wine, and 1 tablespoon each Worcestershire sauce, prepared mustard, and paprika, then add a dash of Tabasco. Blend in drained and flaked contents of one 7-ounce can tuna fish. Spread on onion rounds, or serve onion rounds separately and pass the container of tuna fish, encouraging everybody to spread their own.

Roast Beef* Hash

In a stout plastic bag, put 2 cups each diced cooked roast beef* and diced cooked potatoes*, either or both of which may alternatively be canned and drained before dicing. Add 1 tablespoon fresh or ½ teaspoon dried minced onion, 1 teaspoon salt, ¼ teaspoon coarse-ground black pepper, 1 teaspoon Worcestershire sauce, and 1 tablespoon parsley flakes or chopped fresh parsley. Close bag tightly and gently squeeze and knead to mix thoroughly. Add 1 cup undiluted condensed beef bouillon, re-close bag, and mix again. Melt 2½ tablespoons butter in a heavy, large frying pan over a low flame; spoon or pour hash into it, spreading hash till flat and evenly distributed. Sprinkle with 3 tablespoons red wine, and set two asbestos pads under the skillet. Cook, un-covered, about 45 minutes, or until brown crust forms on the bottom. (Check this by gingerly lifting one corner of the hash with a small spatula to see how it's coming). To serve, turn out of pan, crust side up, onto a large round plate or piece of wax paper or foil, and cut into wedges. Or cut into wedges while still in the pan, and turn out each portion with spatula or pancake turner, crust side up.

Green Beans with Horseradish Sauce

In the top of your largest double boiler, with 2 inches water in the bottom, melt 2 tablespoons butter; add 2 tablespoons flour and blend till smooth. Add 1 cup undiluted evaporated milk, remove to direct high-medium flame and cook, stirring constantly, till thickened. Put back over hot water and add 1 tablespoon prepared horse radish, stirring in well. Open and drain two No. 2 (16-ounce) cans cut green beans and stir beans into sauce. Heat for 15 minutes, then remove double boiler to asbestos pads near the stove to keep warm, and to free burner.

Minted Applesauce with Red Candy Bits

Open one 1-pound can applesauce and place in any con-venient receptacle. Stir in any *one* of these: 2 tablespoons mint jelly, 3 or 4 drops peppermint extract, or 1½ tablespoons green crème de menthe. Chop finely, or crush with a heavy bottle, 2 tablespoons hard red cinnamon candies (or use an equal amount of cinnamon-flavored candy "pills" sold for cake decorating, and stir through the applesauce. Chill before serving if possible.

                    R A D I S H E S ,   S C A L L I O N S ,   A N D   *Market*
                              S A L T I N E S   *Today*
                        P A N - F R I E D   S T E A K   I
                    M O U N T A I N   G R E E N E R Y
                          G R E E N   S A L A D
                          W A T E R M E L O N

Radishes, Scallions and Saltines

You will need 2 bunches or packages of radishes, 3 bunches of scallions and enough saltines to fill a capacious receptacle. Scrub radishes well (first snipping from their leaves if in bunches), and cut off roots, tops and any imperfections. Lay cleaned radishes on two or three thicknesses of newspaper or paper towel, then wrap up and refrigerate. Cut off roots and strip away outside membrane of the scallions, also cut off all but about 4 inches of the tops. Lay on two thicknesses of newspaper or paper towel, wrap up and refrigerate. When ready to serve, divide the vegetables evenly among 4 plates, set on each plate a small dish of salt (plastic, foil, or a cup from the egg poacher) and hand around saltines.

Pan-Fried Steak I

Choose sirloin or porterhouse 1- to 1½-inch thick, weighing 3 to 3½ pounds. Cut out the large lump of fat that each type of steak possesses and trim fat around edge down to ¼ inch in thickness. Every 2 inches, slash the remaining fat diagonally clear through to the flesh. Rub steak all over, both sides, with oil. Heat your largest heavy frying pan to the sizzling point—which is when a few drops of water sprinkled on the surface dance a jig and immediately disappear. Put 1 tablespoon butter into the pan, then the steak. Expect much smoke, so have portholes and companionway open. Cook 2 minutes, turn with tongs and cook 2 minutes on the second side. Turn again. For blood-rare meat, cook 2 more minutes on each side; for medium rare, turn two more times, with 2 minutes cooking between each turning. Shut off fire, and serve as soon as possible.

Mountain Greenery

Open one 16-ounce can small whole boiled potatoes and one 8-ounce can peas. Drain, saving the combined liquids. Dice the potatoes coarsely. In the top of a medium-sized double boiler with 1½ inches water in the bottom, melt 2½ tablespoons butter; while it is melting, season well, add 2½ tablespoons flour, blend till smooth. Dilute 5 ounces evaporated milk (or one small can) with an equal amount of the combined vegetable liquids and discard balance of vegetable liquid. Add to butter-flour mixture. Remove top of double boiler to high direct flame on same burner, setting aside lower chamber on asbestos pads near stove for the moment. Stir constantly till sauce comes to a tentative boil and is thickened. Lower flame, replace bottom part of double boiler, and put upper chamber in it. Add potatoes and peas, stirring just to blend. Cover and keep hot.

Green Salad

The recipe is given on page 226.

Twelfth
Day

TUESDAY

CHEESE-AND-CHUTNEY WITH
PUMPERNICKEL
LAMB CHOPS, SAUTÉED
BROCCOLI PARMESAN
HOME-FRIED POTATOES I
COFFEE MARSHMALLOW CREAM

Cheese-and-Chutney

Make the day before you will serve it. Mash thoroughly two softened 3-ounce packages cream cheese. Chop finely enough chutney to make ⅓ cup; stir into the cheese with 2 tablespoons chutney syrup and 2 teaspoons curry powder. Pack into tight-lidded container and chill.

Lamb Chops, Sautéed

Trim off about half the fat around six loin or shoulder lamb chops. Heat over medium-high flame a heavy frying pan, and brown chops on both sides without additional fat or butter. Remove to shallow dish. Lower flame. Stir up browned bits in pan with a mixture of ½ cup white wine and ½ cup undiluted condensed consommé. Add 1 teaspoon salt, ½ teaspoon coarse-ground black pepper, ½ teaspoon dry mustard, and 1 tablespoon red or white wine vinegar. Stir to blend. Put chops back into the pan, cover, and simmer for 30 minutes. Serve with sauce.

Broccoli Parmesan

Separate 1 bunch fresh broccoli into easily manageable spears, cutting off half of the root end of each large stalk and slicing it lengthwise into pieces ½ inch in diameter. Place in saucepan with the stalks at bottom, the floweret pieces on top, and add water to the depth of ¾ inch. Bring to a fast boil over high heat. Lower flame considerably and cook 10 minutes. Drain and put broccoli in top of your largest double boiler with 2 inches water in the bottom, or use the pot the broccoli cooked in as a substitute, setting it into a pan suitable for nesting. Add 2 tablespoons butter and 3 tablespoons grated Parmesan cheese. Toss well, cover, and keep warm near the stove on asbestos pads.

Home-fried Potatoes I

Slice thinly 3 large cold cooked potatoes* or the drained contents of one No. 2 (16-ounce) can cooked potatoes. Be not startled at what will look like far too many for one meal; potatoes shrink in the frying. In an 8-inch frying pan melt 2½ tablespoons butter, add the potatoes, and shake to coat with butter. Sauté over low flame very slowly (you might need to slip an asbestos pad under the pan to slow down the cooking) until golden or a bit tan, shaking from time to time. Do not expect these potatoes to be crisp; they should be soft and buttery.

Coffee Marshmallow Cream

Prepare this dessert right after lunch.

Into a container with a tightly-closing top and a wide

mouth, cut ½ pound marshmallows in small pieces, preferably with scissors. Pour over them ½ cup hot triple-strength coffee. Cool. In a bowl or large measuring cup whip ½ pint heavy cream till stiff, fold into marshmallow-coffee mixture, cover, and chill 4 hours.

Thirteenth Day   WEDNESDAY

LIEDERKRANZ CHEESE

VEAL BONNE FEMME

DILLED GREEN BEANS

BROWN RICE

GREEN GRAPES

Liederkranz Cheese

Let the cheese stand unrefrigerated for at least an hour before serving, to soften to runny consistency inside. It is very good with almost any kind of cracker except cheese-flavored varieties.

Veal Bonne Femme

Heat 3 tablespoons butter in your largest heavy frying pan having a cover, and brown in it quickly 4 large shoulder veal chops from which fat has been cut off. Remove to a dish on the side. While veal is browning, or beforehand, put 16 small white onions in a saucepan, cover with cold water, and bring to a boil over low fire. When water boils, remove onions from fire, drain, reserving the water, and plunge onions into cold water. When cool, remove skins and a bit off each end of each onion. Set onions aside. Finely chop 2 cloves garlic or measure out ¼ teaspoon instant minced garlic. Wash and quarter 10 firm white mushrooms. Put the onions in the frying pan; brown well, shaking to prevent burning, and remove to dish holding meat. Put garlic and mushrooms into the frying pan and cook for 2 minutes. Remove to dish holding meat and onions.

Take pan from fire, put on three or four asbestos pads or on bread board, add 1 tablespoon butter, and, when melted, add 3 tablespoons flour, ¾ cup white wine, and ½ cup undiluted condensed consommé. Season with salt and coarse-ground black pepper. Return to fire; stir till smooth and boiling. Put chops, onions and mushrooms into pan with sauce. Add 1 bay leaf and 1 tablespoon dehydrated parsley flakes. Cook, covered, for 35 to 40 minutes. Remove bay leaf before serving.

Dilled Green Beans

Use either fresh or canned whole green beans. If fresh, snip off the ends of 1¼ pounds young beans. If canned, use two 16-ounce cans. Lay fresh or canned beans evenly in an 8-inch stainless steel frying pan. To cook fresh beans, add a scant ¼ inch cold water, salt, and coarse-ground black pepper; bring to fast boil over high heat, turn flame low, and cook only 8 minutes more. Drain, add 1 tablespoon dried dill weed and 1 tablespoon butter. After draining canned beans, add butter and dill weed, and heat over low fire. In either case when butter is melted, set pan over saucepan big enough for it to nest in, the latter with 1 inch water in it, bring water to boil, and set aside on asbestos pads to free the burner for cooking the brown rice.

Brown Rice

Cook according to directions on the box, adjusting proportions for four persons.

Fourteenth Day   T H U R S D A Y

C A P O N A T A

FIXED-UP CANNED BEEF STEW

M U S T A R D Y   L I M A   B E A N S

C O R N   E N S E Ñ A D A

CANNED PEACHES WITH GINGERSNAPS

Caponata (Eggplant Appetizer)

Two 4¾-ounce cans will suffice. Open and divide among individual small bowls. Season each serving with salt, coarse-ground black pepper, and a pinch each of oregano and basil. Serve with any crackers except those that are cheese flavored.

Fixed-up Canned Beef Stew

Open two 1-pound cans beef stew or one 2-pound can. Drain over bowl or any suitable vessel, setting gravy aside in 16-ounce, or larger, measuring cup. Pick out potatoes, cut into smaller pieces and put back in stew. Place stew in a large bowl. Drain two 8-ounce cans or one 16-ounce can each boiled small onions and baby carrots. If 16-ounce cans are used, add only two-thirds of contents to solid ingredients of stew; for small cans, use total contents. Add to gravy enough half-and-half red wine and undiluted condensed beef broth to make a total of 2 cups. Melt 2 tablespoons butter in large, heavy frying pan, add 2 tablespoons flour, and allow to tan after blending. Put in 1 teaspoon salt, a rounded ½ teaspoon coarse-ground black pepper, 1 tablespoon Escoffier Sauce Diable, ¼ cup sliced green olives, and one drained 3-ounce can sliced mushrooms. Simmer 3 minutes. Add solid ingredients and simmer 7 minutes more.

Mustardy Lima Beans

In the top of a medium-sized double boiler over 1½ inches of boiling water, melt 4 tablespoons butter. Add a dash of sugar, 1 teaspoon dry mustard, 2 teaspoons strained lemon juice, ½ teaspoon salt, ¼ teaspoon coarse-ground black pepper, and a dash of ground nutmeg. Drain 2 medium-sized (16-ounce) cans lima beans, either baby green limas or the bigger variety. Add to sauce. Stir. Heat for 10 minutes, then set aside on asbestos pads, to free the burner.

Corn Enseñada

To two 12-ounce cans whole-kernel corn, drained and placed in a frying pan over low flame, add ¼ cup each diced pimiento and green pepper or green olives, ½ teaspoon salt, ¼ teaspoon coarse-ground black pepper, and 2 tablespoons butter. Heat till butter melts, stirring occasionally. Make up a double-boiler arrangement using the frying pan as upper part, and keep hot over very low fire, using asbestos pads if necessary.

Canned Peaches with Gingersnaps

Crumble 12 gingersnaps into a small bowl or any suitable receptacle. Add 4 tablespoons rum or bourbon. Open one No. 2 (16-ounce) can halved *Elberta Peaches, Home-Style,* and drain off two-thirds of the juice. Distribute the fruit evenly into individual small bowls. Spoon a little of the gingersnap-and-liquor mixture into the hollow of each peach half. Pour over each portion about 1½ tablespoons juice from the can.

Fifteenth *Day*	FRIDAY	*Go Ashore* *for Final* *Marketing*

BLACK BEAN SPREAD
WITH SESAME CRACKERS
SALMON CAKES
CANNED PETITS POIS I
BOILED POTATOES
BLACK CHERRIES

Black Bean Spread

In any suitable container, with a fork mash two 3-ounce packages softened cream cheese. Add ½ can undiluted condensed black bean soup, ½ teaspoon each ground thyme and chili powder, 1 teaspoon onion salt, 1½ teaspoon salt, 1 tablespoon Worcestershire sauce, and 1 teaspoon lemon juice, fresh or bottled. Combine well and chill.

Salmon Cakes

Open, and drain two 16-ounce cans best-quality canned salmon. After picking over to pull out and discard all bones and skin, place in a stout plastic bag. Flake coarsely with fingers. Add juice of 1 lemon or 2½ tablespoons bottled lemon juice, ¼ teaspoon each ground thyme, mace, and curry powder, and 1½ teaspoons celery salt, 1 tablespoon parsley flakes and 1 small onion, grated, or 2 teaspoons onion salt. Separately, beat 3 eggs slightly, add to salmon and seasonings, close bag tightly and squeeze and knead to mix well. Open bag and with fingers blend in bread crumbs until the mixture reaches a consistency that can be formed into cakes. These should be about 3 inches across and ¾ inch thick. Fry slowly in plenty of butter in a heavy large frying pan till well browned on both sides, adding dabs of butter as the pan seems to dry out. While cooking, set up a double-boiler arrangement of suitable capacity, heat till water in bottom boils, and set aside on asbestos pads. As cakes cook, remove to this edifice to keep warm.

Canned Petits Pois I

Into the top of a medium-sized double boiler, drain the liquid from two 16-ounce cans *petits pois,* leaving peas in the cans. Put over direct high flame, and boil, uncovered, until reduced by half. Add peas, 1 tablespoon butter, and seasoning to your taste. Put 1½ inches water in the doble boiler bottom, put top over it, cover, lower flame, and heat 10 to 15 minutes.

Sixteenth   SATURDAY
Day

ARTICHOKE HEARTS

SPANISH CHICKEN PIE

BOILED RICE

FIXED-UP CANNED SPINACH

CHOCOLATE PUDDING WITH COOKIES

Artichoke Hearts

After breakfast, or early in the day, put to chill two 4½-ounce jars marinated artichoke hearts. When ready to serve, open jars and lift out each heart with fork or knife, and cut lengthwise in half. Divide contents evenly among 4 individual dishes. Serve with crackers or Melba toast. Discard excess oil, or keep for future salad dressing.

Spanish Chicken Pie

Canned or cold cooked fresh chicken may be used. You need about 3 cups meat, cut into fairly large pieces. Chop coarsely 1 large yellow onion, put a large heavy frying pan over a moderate flame, put 2 tablespoons any kind of fat or oil in it and, when melted or heated, add onion and sauté. While onion is cooking, remove pith and seeds from 2 green peppers and cut into strips lengthwise. When onion turns golden, add pepper strips. When peppers start changing color a little, add 2 cups canned tomatoes, measured from pulp in a 16-ounce can, adding juice only if there is not enough pulp to make 2 cups. Stir well. While mixture is heating, slice enough pitted black olives to make 1 cup, and add, along with 1/4 teaspoon instant minced garlic, 1 teaspoon salt, 1/2 teaspoon coarse-ground black pepper and 1/4 teaspoon cayenne. Stir to mix. Add chicken pieces, bring to a simmer, and cook, uncovered, for 10 minutes; then cover and keep at a very slow simmer for 20 minutes more.

Boiled Rice
See Robinson Rice recipe, page 63.

Fixed-Up Canned Spinach
In the top of your largest double boiler with 2 inches water in the bottom, place contents of two drained 1-pound cans chopped or unchopped spinach and stir in 1 1/2 tablespoons butter and 2 tablespoons grated Parmesan or Romano cheese (fresh is preferable but commercial is admissible). Heat for 15 minutes. When hot, set aside on asbestos pads to keep warm and free burner. Before serving, season with salt and coarse-ground black pepper.

Chocolate Pudding
Early in the day, if there's enough ice, chill 4 individual-serving cans prepared chocolate pudding, or 1 large can. Or, serve it right out of the can in small bowls. Or make up a powdered instant chocolate pudding, between lunch and dinner and chill, if possible. Serve either of them with cream, if there's enough on board.

Three Weekends~ Three Weathers

These menus and recipes use the same basic ingredients for each meal from Friday night dinner through Sunday lunch whether the weather is fair and warm, rainy but not cold, or windy and almost cold, but not wet. The shifts of menu, and therefore of stores, caused by the shift in weather are fairly slight. The wise cook who knows the weather changes possible in the waters she'll be sailing will make her preboarding marketing list include what she may need, be the elements fair or foul.

~

WEEKEND I

FRIDAY NIGHT DINNER

Fair and Warm

LOBSTER SPREAD I
STROGANOFF SALAD
SALADE LAFAYETTE
SKILLET BISCUITS II
PEPPERMINT CHOCOLATE ICE CREAM*

Lobster Spread I

Drain well one 7-ounce can lobster meat, put into any suitable receptacle, sprinkle over 1 tablespoon lemon juice, salt, pepper, 1 teaspoon onion salt, 1 teaspoon dried tarragon, ½ teaspoon chervil, 1 tablespoon chili sauce. Stir well, bind with mayonnaise.

Stroganoff Salad

Into a salad bowl, cut enough cold roast beef* for four persons into strips about 2 inches long and ½ inch wide. Season well with salt and pepper. Drain well one 3-ounce can sliced mushrooms. Add to meat strips. Squeeze 2 tablespoons lemon juice over both. Cut 16 pitted large ripe olives into quarters lengthwise, peel and slice thinly 1 bunch scallions, peel and quarter 1 red onion, slice each quarter into thin rings, and add all to meat and mushrooms. Mix 1 pint sour cream with 1 tablespoon lemon juice, 2 dashes Tabasco, 1 teaspoon Worcestershire sauce, and 1 teaspoon prepared horseradish. Combine with other ingredients. Pile salad to center of bowl and ring with large fresh leaves of romaine.

Salade Lafayette

Peel and slice fairly thickly 3 or 4 ripe tomatoes, depending on size. Overlap the slices in a shallow bowl. Sprinkle with ¼ cup grated Parmesan cheese and season well with salt and pepper. Mix ⅓ cup dry white wine and 3 tablespoons olive oil in a screwtop jar. Shake well and pour over tomatoes.

Skillet Biscuits II

With fork, mix 2 cups prepared biscuit mix with ⅔ cup water, diluted evaporated milk, or fresh milk. If dough seems too stiff, add 1 to 2 tablespoons more liquid. Grease a skillet 10 inches or larger. Line with oiled or buttered foil, being sure not to have the foil snug against the rim of the pan, as this would prevent the cover from fitting tightly. Heat over low flame. While pan is heating, knead dough once or twice, on wax paper. Spread out to ½-inch thickness, by patting it with your hand or rolling it out, using a filled quart bottle as a rolling pin. Cut dough into 2-inch rounds with the open end of an empty can or cut it into squares roughly the same size. Place the biscuits in the heated skillet. Cover. Cook 3 minutes to brown on one side, turn over, and cook 3 more minutes to brown the other side. Insert a flame-tamer between skillet and flame, turn fire to medium low, and cook 10 minutes.

Peppermint Chocolate Ice Cream*

This is made at home and brought on board. (See recipe, page 309.)

Rainy, Not Really Cold

LOBSTER SPREAD I
ROAST BEEF* SLICES WITH SAUERBRATEN SAUCE
MASHED POTATOES II
RED, GREEN OR WHITE CABBAGE
PEPPERMINT-CHOCOLATE ICE-CREAM*

Lobster Spread I

Prepare as in *Fair and Warm* Friday dinner menu.

Roast Beef* Slices with Sauerbraten Sauce

In a saucepan or skillet or deepish frying pan, mix into 2 cups cold water, ½ cup malt vinegar, 10 whole cloves, 3 bay leaves, 8 broken-up gingersnaps, 1 tablespoon sugar, a few drops bottled gravy sauce. Season, bring to a boil, turn flame low, cover and simmer 10 minutes. Then add 3 slices cold roast beef per person and heat.

Mashed Potatoes II

While sauce for meat is heating, in top of a double boiler cook instant mashed potatoes according to directions on package, and set aside. Heat water in lower container of double boiler, put potatoes on it, cover, and lower flame to keep hot.

Red, Green or White Cabbage

For four servings, 6–7 cups shredded cabbage should do; green cabbage, especially, has a way of shrinking in volume. In the top of your largest double boiler put enough water to cover the bottom. Remove double boiler with mashed potatoes and asbestos pads to counter top. Bring cabbage to quick boil; put 3 tablespoons butter on top of cabbage. Lower flame to simmer, and re-cover. Green or white cabbage needs no more than 8 or 9 minutes to be done; red cabbage needs more than twice as long— about 25 minutes. Place cabbage, when done, over the lower chamber of the double boiler, and keep hot.

Windy, Cold, but Not Wet

LOBSTER SPREAD I

STOVETOP EMPANADA

SKILLET BISCUITS II

APPLE SLICES HEATED IN HONEY

Lobster Spread I
Prepare as in *Fair and Warm* Friday dinner menu.

Stovetop Empanada
This pseudo-empanada has been a favorite way to use any leftover meat or mixture of meats for many years.

Begin by preparing the dry ingredients. These are: 1 white or yellow medium-sized onion, 1 medium-sized green pepper, 1 dozen seedless raisins (optional), 6 or 7 medium-sized fresh mushrooms or one 3-ounce can drained sliced mushrooms, ½ cup black or green olives of any kind, 1 or 2 hard-boiled eggs, and 2 cups cubed cooked beef.*

Into one bowl, chop coarsely the onion and green pepper, pith and seeds removed; slice the mushrooms, if fresh. Into second bowl, slice or cut olives crosswise into sizeable pieces, cut the egg lengthwise into eighths, and add the raisins and the cubed meat.

In a frying pan, 8 inches or bigger, heat 2½ tablespoons butter, oil, leftover meat fat, bacon fat, shortening, or a combination of all; add onion, green pepper, and mushrooms. Sauté till brown. Add all other dry ingredients, stir well, and set aside.

About 2 cups brown gravy is needed, made either from scratch as a thickened brown sauce, or by emptying a can of undiluted brown, beef, or mushroom gravy into the top of a biggish double boiler and then heating over hot water. To make gravy from scratch: melt 2½ tablespoons butter, beef or bacon fat, or shortening in top of double boiler over hot water; stir in 2½ tablespoons all-purpose flour. Season with salt and coarse-ground black pepper. When blended, add one 10½-ounce can un-diluted condensed beef broth. Remove top of double boiler to direct heat. Stir till gravy comes to a boil and thickens. Put gravy—canned or "scratch"—back over lower chamber of double boiler, and add dry ingredients. Stir gently just to mix and keep warm. Serve in bowls on split biscuits, cooked when convenient and kept warm off the fire on a hot flame-tamer plus two asbestos pads.

Skillet Biscuits II
Prepare as in *Fair and Warm* Friday dinner menu.

Apple Slices Heated in Honey
Drain two 16-ounce cans pie apples, saving the liquid. In the top of a medium-sized double boiler, arrange slices carefully in layers, dusting each layer with cinnamon and nutmeg and over it dribbling a moderate amount of honey. Add just enough of the reserved liquid barely to cover the bottom, put them over the lower part of the double boiler with 1 inch water in it, cover, insert two asbestos pads under, and heat over low flame no more than 15 minutes, or until ready to serve.

SATURDAY
BREAKFAST

Fair and Warm

JUICE
FRIED SLICED COLD COOKED HOMINY GRITS
WITH COUNTRY SAUSAGE PATTIES
SKILLET MUFFINS
BLACKBERRY OR APRICOT PRESERVES

Skillet Muffins
Over a high flame, preheat for 10 minutes a heavy 12-inch dome-lidded skillet, covered and with a rack in it. While skillet is heating, line an 8-by-8-inch cake pan with foil and butter the foil. Prepare any variety of muffin mix you desire according to

the directions on the package, using fresh, diluted evaporated, or reconstituted dry milk and fresh or powdered egg. Pour batter into pan, put pan on rack in skillet, lower flame somewhat, cover skillet tightly, and bake for 30 minutes. Cut muffins into squares and serve with jam and butter.

Fried Sliced Cold Cooked Hominy Grits with Country Sausage Patties

Friday night, after dinner, cook enough hominy grits for four servings. This takes about 20–25 minutes. Pour the hot grits into an oblong pan or dish and set aside to cool overnight.

For Saturday breakfast, while the muffins are baking on one burner and the sausage patties are frying on the other, slice the grits ½ to ¾ inch thick. As each patty is ready, remove to a plate and replace with a slice of grits, pouring off any excess fat. Fry on each side until a little darker than brown wrapping paper. When done, put a slice of grits on a patty, and, when all are done, lower flame, slide the grits and patties back into the skillet, cover, insert flame-tamer under skillet, set flame very low, and serve when muffins are ready.

Rainy, Not Really Cold

JUICE
COOKED COUNTRY SAUSAGE CRUMBLED INTO
HOT HOMINY GRITS
SKILLET MUFFINS
BLACKBERRY OR APRICOT JAM

Skillet Muffins

Prepare as in *Fair and Warm* Saturday breakfast menu.

Cooked Country Sausage Crumbled into Hot Hominy Grits

Over a high flame, heat the bottom of a double boiler with 1 inch water in it until water boils vigorously. Cover and remove to an asbestos pad.

Directly over the same flame, cook instant hominy grits for

four servings as directed on the package and set aside over bottom part of boiler, but do not turn off flame.

Over same flame, heat a large skillet. When hot, add 1 pound sausage meat, stirring with wooden spoon to break up and fry evenly, then stir from time to time to keep frying evenly. When moderately brown throughout (about 20 minutes), add grits and stir well together. Serve each portion in a deep bowl.

Windy, Cold, but Not Wet
(Use same menu as for Rainy, Not Really Cold.)

LUNCH

Fair and Warm

CORNED BEEF SANDWICHES
POTATO SALAD IV
SLICED TOMATOES
COLD CANNED RUMMY PEACHES

Corned Beef Sandwiches

Any corned beef may be used—canned, home-cooked, or store-bought. For canned corned beef, if you are not able to chill it well, crumble rather coarsely with fingers. Otherwise, slice it.

Allow four sandwiches per person. For each sandwich, spread beef on 1 slice of rye bread cut in half lengthwise; season well with salt and course-ground black pepper, cover with mayonnaise, then cover thinly with horseradish. Spread other half of sandwich thinly with mayonnaise if you wish.

When using crumbled corned beef, mix with mayonnaise and horseradish, combined to spreadable consistency.

Potato Salad IV

Slice 4 cooked peeled potatoes into $1/4$-inch slices and place in a salad bowl. Drain well one 8-ounce can sliced beets, chop finely 1 small white onion, and add to potatoes with 1 tablespoon dehydrated or freshly chopped parsley and 1 tablespoon chopped sweet gherkins, sweet garden relish, or piccalilli. Stir well. Pour over this mixture 2 tablespoons white wine vinegar, 1 tablespoon lemon juice (fresh or bottled), and 4 tablespoons olive oil (or half-and-half olive oil and vegetable oil, or all vegetable oil). Season well with salt and coarse-ground black pepper, toss to mix, and chill or not as you prefer.

Sliced Tomatoes

Slice 1 medium-sized tomato per person and arrange in a bowl or in individual dishes. We recommend any one of three different dressings for them:

(1) simple oil and vinegar, salt and coarse-ground black pepper;

(2) sugar sprinkled over the tomatoes;

(3) 1 teaspoon fresh or bottled lemon juice and 1 table-spoon chili sauce mixed well before spooning over the tomatoes.

Cold Canned Rummy Peaches

Drain 1 large can Elberta peach halves, saving the syrup. Over low flame, heat syrup in a saucepan until it boils and simmer 5 minutes. Add ¼ cup dark or light rum, pour over peaches, and let cool.

Rainy, Not Really Cold

JANE'S POTATO-TOMATO SOUP

DEVILED CORNED BEEF ON HOT-DOG ROLLS

COLD CANNED RUMMY PEACHES

Jane's Potato-Tomato Soup

Allow 1 precooked potato and 1 medium-sized fresh or canned tomato per person.

Dices potatoes, put into a cooking pot, and mash coarsely. Add one 10½-ounce can condensed beef bouillon diluted with ½ soup can water, and 1 large or 2 medium cloves garlic, finely chopped. Put on medium flame; cut tomatoes lengthwise into eighths and add. Cover, lower flame, and simmer for about 20 minutes.

Add salt, coarse-ground black pepper, about 2 tablespoons

butter, and ¼ cup undiluted evaporated milk or light cream. When hot, remove to a flame-tamer heated on the other burner, then remove both pot and tamer, and set aside.

Deviled Corned Beef on Hot-Dog Rolls

For four servings, allow 10 hot-dog rolls, 1¼ cups canned corned beef, or other cooked corned beef, and 1 cup processed American or cheddar cheese.

Split rolls, remove soft centers, and discard them. Heat a large, heavy skillet and butter the bottom lightly, protecting your hands by putting the butter on a wadded-up paper towel or piece of newspaper before greasing skillet. Spread rolls, split side down, on skillet bottom, and put a flame-tamer, with pie pan or shallow saucepan on it, on the other burner to heat over a medium flame. When rolls are browned, remove to pan on flame-tamer to keep warm, then remove flame-tamer and pan to free burner for sandwich filling.

Meanwhile, grate cheese, mix with crumbled or shredded corned beef, and add ⅓ cup catsup, 2 tablespoons chopped onions, 1 tablespoon Worcestershire sauce, a dash of Tabasco, and enough mayonnaise to bind.

Fill hot rolls with beef-cheese mixture, wrap each roll in waxed paper, and twist ends. Line the hot skillet with buttered foil, put filled rolls in it, cover, lower flame, and cook 20 minutes.

Cold Canned Rummy Peaches

Prepare as in *Fair and Warm* Saturday lunch menu.

Windy, Cold, but Not Wet

CORNED BEEF INTO HASH

TOASTED HOT-DOG ROLLS

STEWED TOMATOES I

HOT CANNED PEACHES WITH APRICOT JAM

Corned Beef into Hash

Over high flame, heat for 12 minutes a 12-inch, heavy skillet with rack in it, covered. Meanwhile, into a large bowl crumble one 12-ounce can corned beef or 1½ cups other cooked corned beef brought aboard. Dice finely fairly large white or yellow onions, and add. Peel 3 fairly large cooked potatoes, dice into ¼-inch squares, and add to onions and meat; then add ½ cup undiluted condensed beef bouillon. With fingers, mix all together.

Butter an 8-inch square cakepan, spread mixture in it, place on rack in skillet, cover, and lower flame to medium. Bake 15 minutes, lower flame to low, insert flame-tamer, and bake 20 minutes more.

Toasted Hot-Dog Rolls

Allow 3 rolls per person. On burner not occupied by hash, heat a medium-sized double boiler till water in lower part is boiling; set aside on two asbestos pads to keep warm. In large skillet over low flame, put 1 tablespoon butter to melt. Meanwhile, split each roll in half lengthwise, then put, cut side down, in skillet to toast. As done, remove to top of heated double boiler.

Stewed Tomatoes I

Fresh or canned tomatoes may be used. For fresh, peel 4 fairly large tomatoes, slice thickly, and place in saucepan with 3 tablespoons butter, ½ teaspoon basil, salt, and coarse-ground black pepper. Cook over low flame no longer than 7 minutes.

For canned whole tomatoes, drain one 29-ounce can and cook as for fresh, but only long enough to heat thoroughly.

Hot Canned Peaches with Apricot Jam

Drain one 29-ounce can Elberta peach halves, saving the liquid. Boil ¾ cup peach liquid with 3 tablespoons each raspberry and apricot jam for 5 minutes, add 2 tablespoon kirsch, pour hot syrup over peaches, and serve when ready.

DINNER

Fair and Warm

HOT DEVILED WALNUTS
CHICKEN* AND CORN SALAD
ARTICHOKE HEART AND GREEN OLIVE SALAD
BANANAS MAISON

Hot Deviled Walnuts

Over low flame, in an 8-inch heavy frying pan, melt 4 table-spoons butter, stir in 2 tablespoons bottled Sauce Robert and 4 cups walnut meats, sprinkle with salt and 3 dashes cayenne, and stir well to coat nut meats. Cover, put three asbestos pads under pan, cook for 10 minutes, and remove to keep warm.

Chicken* and Corn Salad

In a large bowl combine 2 cups diced cooked* or canned chicken; one 12-ounce can corn kernels, well drained; 5 fresh tomatoes, cubed; and 2 coarsely diced green peppers, pith and seeds removed. Stir in 1 cup mayonnaise, salt, and coarse-ground black pepper; then add 2 hard-boiled eggs, cut lengthwise into eighths, and 1 small white onion, finely chopped.

Pile salad in center of bowl, line bowl with lettuce leaves, and spread salad to fill bowl. Dust with paprika and serve.

Artichoke Heart and Green Olive Salad

Line a salad bowl with the leaves of any sort of salad green you have on hand, drain two 4½-ounce jars of marinated artichoke hearts into a separate bowl, and put the hearts themselves into the salad bowl. Slice into thirds crosswise enough pimiento-stuffed green olives to make ⅔ cup and add to artichoke hearts.

Into the marinade saved from the jars of artichoke hearts, strain enough fresh lemon juice to make it somewhat tart, tasting as you add. Season highly with salt and coarse-ground black pepper, and stir briskly. Spoon enough dressing over salad bowl to moisten well, reserving leftover dressing for another occasion.

Garnish salad with 2 heaping soupspoons of mayonnaise and sprinkle parsley flakes over all. Toss well before serving.

Bananas Maison

Allowing ½ banana per person, peel and slice, not too thinly, into individual serving bowls, sprinkle with lemon juice to keep from turning brown, spoon about 1 teaspoon fine-ground sugar over each serving, and dust with ground cinnamon and ground ginger. Brown sugar may be used instead of white, and sour cream may be added.

Rainy, Not Really Cold

HOT CHILI PEANUTS
CHICKEN*-WALNUT-CORN SKILLET CASSEROLE
HOT ARTICHOKE HEARTS AND GREEN OLIVES
BANANAS IN THE FIST

Hot Chili Peanuts

In a skillet melt 2 tablespoons butter over a low flame, add 1 pound unsalted peanuts, and toast until golden, shaking the pan once in a while, as you would when making croutons, for even toasting. Mix 1 tablespoon chili powder (or more, if you like a truly hot flavor) with 1 tablespoon salt, turn off flame, stir the chili-powder–salt mixture into the hot peanuts, and serve hot or cooled. Cashews or Brazil nuts are also good prepared in this manner.

Chicken*-Walnut-Corn Skillet Casserole

In a bowl, mix well 2 cups diced or lengthwise-cut strips of cooked chicken* with ¾ cup corn kernels (fresh or canned), ¾ cup coarsely chopped walnuts, 1 tablespoon finely chopped onion, 3 tablespoons lemon juice (fresh or bottled), 1 cup mayonnaise, salt, and coarse-ground black pepper.

Over a high flame, heat a well-buttered skillet, add the chicken-mayonnaise mixture, cover, turn heat to medium low, and cook for 15 to 20 minutes. Just before serving sprinkle thickly with grated Parmesan cheese.

Hot Artichoke Hearts and Green Olives

Drain two 4½-ounce jars marinated artichoke hearts, reserving 1 tablespoon marinade for this dish and saving the balance for use in salad dressing on another occasion. Slice crosswise into thirds enough pimiento-stuffed olives to make ¾ cup, dice enough fresh or drained canned celery to make ¾ cup, and mince finely 1 large or 2 medium sized cloves garlic.

Into the top of a double boiler, over direct medium heat, pour the reserved artichoke marinade. Lower flame, heat, add garlic, and steep for 5 minutes, then add all other ingredients and stir well. Put over bottom of double boiler with 1 inch water in it, cover, and cook 15 minutes.

Windy, Cold, but Not Wet

CHILLED ARTICHOKE HEARTS

SKILLET CHICKEN AND GREEN OLIVES WITH

CREAM SAUCE AND COOKED RICE

CANNED PETITS POIS II

CORN ON THE COB

BOURBON BANANAS, HOT

Chilled Artichoke Hearts

Open two 4¾-ounce jars marinated artichoke hearts. Drain, saving the marinade for use some other time. Cut each heart in half lengthwise and divide evenly into four individual dishes or bowls. Season well with salt and pepper. Squeeze 1 teaspoon lemon juice over each portion. Serve with sesame-flavored crackers, French bread, or rye wafers.

Skillet Chicken and Green Olives with
Cream Sauce and Cooked Rice

Butter a large heavy aluminum or iron skillet and line with buttered foil and into a bowl, dice 2 cups cooked fresh* or canned chicken. Chop coarsely 1 green pepper, pith and seeds removed, and 1 medium-sized white onion; slice into thirds enough pimiento-stuffed green olives to make ¾ cup. Add one 10½-ounce can undiluted condensed cream of chicken soup and half of a

10½-ounce can undiluted condensed cream of mushroom soup. Mix all ingredients well together.

Line the buttered foil in the skillet with 2 cups cooked rice. Carefully pour chicken mixture into the center, spread top with shredded cheddar cheese, cover, and heat over high flame 7 minutes. Lower flame, insert flame-tamer or three or four asbestos pads, and cook 30 minutes more, or until cheese is melted.

Canned Petits Pois II

Open three 8-ounce cans tiny peas. Drain, place liquid into top of double boiler directly over high flame, and add ½ teaspoon each celery salt, onion salt, and lemon juice. Season well with salt and pepper; bring to a boil, then lower flame to low and simmer till reduced by half. Add peas, place over lower chamber of double boiler, add ¼ teaspoon sage and ½ tablespoon butter, and stir well. Heat for 10–15 minutes. Set aside, to free burner for corn.

Corn on the Cob

See recipe on page 75.

Bourbon Bananas, Hot

Into a saucepan or skillet, slice peeled bananas, allowing ½ banana per person. Sprinkle with lemon juice to prevent discoloration. Sprinkle with brown sugar and dust generously with nutmeg. Over a very low flame and two asbestos pads, heat banana slices, then pour over them 2 teaspoons bourbon per each banana half. Turn off flame and put pan over hot water to keep hot.

SUNDAY BREAKFAST

~~~~~~~~~~~~~~~~~~~~~~~~~

Fair and Warm

RAW APPLE OR APPLE JUICE
CHOPPED SCRAPPLE AND SCRAMBLED EGGS
CINNAMON-RAISIN BREAD TOAST

Chopped Scrapple and Scrambled Eggs

Dice enough canned scrapple to make 1⅓ cups. Break 8 eggs into a bowl and add ½ cup undiluted evaporated milk. Beat with fork, manual eggbeater, or whisk till blended.

Over medium-high flame, heat a skillet, add scrapple, and sauté till done. If not enough fat has extruded from scrapple, add butter to the skillet. Turn flame high, add eggs and stir constantly as they cook. On the other burner, prepare the toast.

Cinnamon-Raisin Bread Toast

Place your largest skillet over a low flame. Put in 1½ tablespoons butter and, when butter melts, add as many pieces of cinnamon-raisin bread as skillet will hold. With spatula, and watching toast closely, turn as browned and cook other side. Keep hot in top of double boiler over hot water.

Rainy, Not Really Cold

APPLESAUCE WITH APRICOT JAM
SAUTÉED SCRAPPLE SLICES
HOME-FRIED POTATOES II
HOT MAPLE BISCUITS

Applesauce with Apricot Jam

For four, empty into a bowl 1 large or 2 medium-sized cans applesauce and stir in 4 tablespoons apricot jam. Serve in individual bowls or mugs.

Home-Fried Potatoes II

Allow 50 minutes to cook this dish, using precooked fresh potatoes or the canned variety, and figuring on the equivalent of half of a large raw potato or half a 1-pound can, drained, per portion.

Cut potatoes into slices ¼-inch thick. Over a fairly high flame, in a good-sized heavy skillet, melt 4 tablespoons butter. Add potatoes, turn flame low, and put two asbestos pads under the skillet, adding a third pad if needed. The cooking must be slow or the potatoes will not brown well. Serve in bowls, with scrapple slices on top.

Hot Maple Biscuits

Prepare as for Skillet Biscuits II (page 97), but before putting dough into skillet, spread over it any one of these: ⅔ cup sugar mixed with ⅓ cup maple syrup; 1 cup maple sugar; or ¾ cup white or brown sugar mixed with 1 tablespoon maple extract. When cooked, set aside to free burner for scrapple.

Sautéed Scrapple Slices

Slice 1 pound chilled scrapple into slices ½ inch thick. Over high flame, heat a large skillet and when hot, melt 1½ tablespoons butter in it, lower flame, and add scrapple slices. Cook slowly for about 15 minutes, turning once or twice.

Windy, Cold, but Not Wet

HOT APPLESAUCE WITH APRICOT JAM
SCRAMBLED EGGS, CHOPPED SCRAPPLE ADDED
CINNAMON-RAISIN BREAD WITH
BLACK CURRANT JAM

Hot Applesauce with Apricot Jam

Over high flame, put to heat the bottom part of a medium-sized double boiler with 1 inch water in it. Empty one 1-pound can applesauce into the top of the double boiler, stir in thoroughly ⅔ cup apricot jam or preserves, cover, heat over hot water for 10 minutes, and set aside.

Scrambled Eggs, Chopped Scrapple Added

Prepare as in *Fair and Warm* Sunday breakfast menu.

LUNCH

~~~~~~

Fair and Warm

RED BEAN AND ITALIAN SAUSAGE SALAD
COLESLAW I
BROWNIES

Red Bean and Italian Sausage Salad

Drain, rinse, and drain again one 29-ounce can red kidney beans and put into a salad bowl. Mince finely 2 large or 3 medium-sized cloves garlic and put into a large-mouthed screw-top jar or deep bowl.

Slice 6 anchovies in half lengthwise, then cut crosswise into pieces slightly less than ½ inch long and add to garlic, with ¼ teaspoon crushed dried hot red pepper, ½ teaspoon dried marjoram leaves, 1 teaspoon salt, ⅓ cup mixed peanut oil and olive oil in any proportion you like. Shake or beat, pour over beans, and set aside to marinate.

Just before serving, slice thinly 1 fairly small peeled red onion, separate into rings, and stir into salad with 2 tablespoons chopped fresh parsley or dried parsley flakes.

Poke into the edges of the salad bowl any kind of salad green leaves as lining. Arrange half-slices of Italian sausage (such as salami, cervelat, mortadella, or galantina) around edge of salad, neatly overlapping.

Coleslaw I

Into a bowl, shred finely enough green or white cabbage to make 3 cups. Cut from stems 1 bunch radishes, snip off roots, scrub well, slice thinly, and stir into cabbage.

In another bowl or large-mouthed jar, thin ¾ cup mayonnaise with 3 tablespoons white wine or lemon juice (fresh or bottled), season with salt and coarse-ground black pepper, then add 1 teaspoon each chopped capers, bottled chopped chives, chopped sweet or sour gherkin, onion salt, and chopped fresh or dried parsley. Stir thoroughly, pour over cabbage and radishes, and toss well.

Brownies

Over high flame, preheat for 10 minutes a 12-inch heavy dome-lidded skillet with a rack in it. While skillet is heating, prepare ½ package brownie mix according to the directions on package, cutting ingredients in half. Put balance of mix into an airtight container and enclose the directions torn off the package.

Butter an 8-by-8-inch cake pan and line with buttered foil or wax paper, taking care that the foil is not snug against the sides of the skillet. Spread batter evenly over the bottom, place on rack in skillet, cover, lower flame to medium, and bake, without lifting the lid, for 30 to 35 minutes.

Rainy, Not Really Cold

RED BEAN AND ITALIAN SAUSAGE
STOVETOP CASSEROLE
COLESLAW I
CHOCOLATE-NUT PUDDING

Red Bean and Italian Sausage Stovetop Casserole

Over medium heat, in a generous-sized heavy skillet or saucepan, heat 2 tablespoons oil or melt 2 tablespoons butter. Chop coarsely 1 medium-sized onion (white or yellow), mince 2 large or 3 medium cloves garlic, and put in pan to sauté. Meanwhile, cut ½ pound any kind of Italian sausage into shoestring strips, add to skillet, and continue sautéing till all are lightly browned.

Drain, rinse, and drain again one 29-ounce can red kidney beans. Add to them ¼ teaspoon crushed dried hot red pepper, ½ teaspoon dried marjoram leaves, and 1 teaspoon salt. Turn into skillet, stir well, and then stir in half of a 10½-ounce can undiluted condensed black bean soup and ¼ cup red wine. Cover and simmer for 10 to 15 minutes.

Coleslaw I

Follow recipe given in *Fair and Warm* Sunday lunch menu.

Chocolate-Nut Pudding

Use prepared packaged frozen chocolate pudding or canned or powdered chocolate pudding. For frozen, thaw till soft; for canned, empty into a bowl; for powdered, prepare as directed on package, using undiluted evaporated, or reconstituted dry, milk, and set aside to cool.

Stir into pudding 3 tablespoons rum, bourbon, or crème de cacao and ½ cup coarsely chopped walnuts or hazelnuts or Brazil nuts, or a mixture of the three.

Windy, Cold, but Not Wet

RED BEANS WITH RED WINE AND MOLASSES
HOT SAUTÉED ITALIAN SAUSAGE SLICES
COLESLAW II, HOT
BROWNIES

Red Beans with Red Wine and Molasses

Over a high flame, in a good-sized heavy skillet, heat 4 tablespoons bacon fat, meat fryings, butter, or oil. Meanwhile, chop coarsely 1 medium-sized onion, white or yellow; when fat is hot, add onion and sauté till lightly browned, then pour in ½ cup red wine, bring to a boil, and boil 3 minutes. Put in 2 tablespoons brown sugar, molasses, or any kind of syrup (more, if you like more sweetness) and ¼ cup catsup; stir well and simmer for 10 minutes.

Drain well one 29-ounce can kidney beans, add to skillet, and cook 20 minutes more. Just before serving, stir in 1 coarsely chopped green pepper, pith and seeds removed, and 1 tablespoon minced fresh or dehydrated parsley.

Coleslaw II, Hot

Shred finely enough green cabbage to make 3 cups, rinse and drain, place in top of double boiler, add ¼ cup water, and cook over direct medium flame for 5 minutes.

Meanwhile, thin ¾ cup mayonnaise with 3 tablespoons undiluted evaporated milk. Stir in 2 tablespoons hot prepared mustard, salt and coarse-ground black pepper, 1 tablespoon caraway seeds, and ½ teaspoon or more dried tarragon leaves.

Reduce flame under cabbage, stir in seasoned mayonnaise and 1 tablespoon butter, and cook over very low flame no more than 5 minutes. Set aside over hot water to free burner for sausage slices.

Hot Sautéed Italian Sausage Slices

Over medium heat, in skillet or saucepan or top of large double boiler, heat 2 tablespoons oil, add ½ pound sliced Italian sausages of any kind, and lower flame. Cook for 10 to 15 minutes, turning occasionally, and serve at once.

Brownies

Follow recipe in *Fair and Warm* Sunday lunch menu.

WEEKEND II

FRIDAY NIGHT DINNER

Fair and Warm

CAMEMBERT MARINÉE*
ON HEATED FRENCH BREAD SLICES
SALAD OF SHRIMPS AND ARTICHOKE HEARTS
GREEN SALAD
SLICED TOMATOES
LEMON CHIFFON TARTS

Camembert Marinée*

This appetizer is prepared at home and brought aboard. (See recipe, page 303.)

Salad of Shrimps and Artichoke Hearts

Bring on board along with other provisions, in a tightly closed heavy plastic bag, 1 package cooked, cooled frozen artichoke hearts and 20 cooked, shelled, cooled medium-sized shrimps and place in icebox.

When ready to prepare, into a large salad bowl, put 1 egg yolk, ½ cup combined olive and peanut oil (or olive oil only, as you choose) , ¼ cup white wine vinegar (with or without tarragon or shallots) , 1½ tablespoons Dijon-style mustard, 1 tablespoon parsley flakes, 2 teaspoons onion salt, and 2 tablespoons frozen chopped chives. Beat well. Remove the plastic bag containing the shrimps and artichokes from the icebox, pour the dressing into the bag, shake well to blend, close bag, and replace in icebox. Reserve the used salad bowl.

When ready to serve, line the same salad bowl in which dressing was made with just a few leaves of the greens you plan to use for the tossed salad, take the bag of shrimp salad out of the icebox, shake once more, and pour into bowl.

Green Salad
One recipe for this can be found on page 226. No doubt you have your own pet combination of greens for when you make this basic salad.

Sliced Tomatoes
Some like them skinned, some prefer tomatoes unpeeled; some like big ones, some think smaller tomatoes are sweeter. Personally, I like all kinds and suggest you slice your tomatoes your own way.

Lemon Chiffon Tarts
Bakery-bought and brought aboard.

Rainy, Not Really Cold

HOT HERBED RAVIOLI

STOVETOP SHRIMP CASSEROLE

BOWKNOT OR SHELL MACARONI

SLICED TOMATOES

LEMON CHIFFON TARTS

Hot Herbed Ravioli
Over medium flame put a 1½-quart double boiler with 1 inch water in the bottom. Empty two 15-ounce cans beef ravioli into top of double boiler, stir to mix sauce through, and add salt,

pepper, 3 tablespoons grated Parmesan cheese, 1 pinch each oregano, basil, thyme, and marjoram leaves and stir again, cover, and heat 15 minutes.

Bowknot or Shell Macaroni

Put a saucepan of 2½- or 3-quart capacity, three-quarters full of water, over a high flame on second burner, cover and bring to a vigorous boil, then put in one 1-pound package bow-knot or shell macaroni, dribble about 1 tablespoon oil over water, and boil, uncovered, for 9 minutes. Drain macaroni into colander and place colander into the cooking pan; cover, insert flame-tamer or three asbestos pads, and turn flame very low. It will stay hot until serving time.

Stovetop Shrimp Casserole

Bring on board along with other provisions a heavy plastic bag, tightly closed, containing one package cooked, cooled frozen artichoke hearts and 20–24 medium-sized cooked, cooled, shelled shrimp, with shrimp on top of artichokes. Open one 3-ounce can sliced broiled-in-butter mushrooms and one 10½-ounce can condensed golden mushroom soup. Chop finely 2 shallots and one large or two medium-sized cloves of garlic and mix on chopping board. Empty undiluted soup into bowl, add mushroom liquid and juice of ½ lemon to soup, and stir.

In a skillet or saucepan, over medium flame, heat ¼ cup oil of any kind. While heating, remove shrimp from plastic bag, add to hot oil, stirring constantly, and sauté no more than 3–5 minutes. Then stir in shallots and garlic, cook 2 minutes, and add artichokes, mushrooms, ¼ teaspoon thyme leaves, 1 tablespoon parsley flakes, salt, and black pepper. Cook till just heated through (about 4–5 minutes). Add diluted soup, blend well with other ingredients, lower flame, and cook only till sauce starts to bubble a little.

Windy, Cold, but Not Wet

HOT HERBED RAVIOLI
SHRIMP CREOLE IN HEAVY CREAM
SKILLET BISCUITS I
GREEN SALAD WITH ARTICHOKE HEARTS
HOT LEMON CHIFFON TARTS

Hot Herbed Ravioli
Prepare as in *Rainy, Not Really Cold* Friday dinner menu.

Shrimp Creole in Heavy Cream
Bring on board along with your provisions a heavy plastic bag, tightly closed, containing at the bottom one package cooked, cooled, frozen artichoke hearts, and on top of them 20–24 medium-sized shrimp, cooked, cooled, and shelled.

Skin, seed, and chop coarsely 2 medium-sized tomatoes and set aside, then drain two 3-ounce cans broiled-in-butter sliced mushrooms. Over a medium flame, melt 2 tablespoons butter in a large skillet, add tomatoes, and cook over slightly higher flame till well dissolved (about 10 to 15 minutes). Stir in 3 tablespoons flour and cook, stirring, till mixture thickens. Add mushrooms.

Remove shrimp from plastic bag and replace bag in icebox. Add shrimp to skillet containing tomatoes, stir well, lower flame, cook 3 minutes, and then add 2 tablespoons sherry, bourbon, or brandy, salt and coarse-ground black pepper, 1/4 teaspoon ground nutmeg, and 1/2 teaspoon ground ginger. Stir well. Blend in 1 cup heavy cream, fresh or canned; cover, turn flame very low, and heat until mixture starts to bubble a little. Serve in bowls over split hot biscuits spread lightly with prepared hot mustard.

Green Salad with Artichoke Hearts
Drain one 6-ounce jar marinated artichoke hearts over a bowl. Cut artichokes lengthwise into halves and put in a salad bowl. Wash well any salad greens on hand, tear or cut into bite-sized pieces, add to artichokes, and toss well.

To the artichoke marinade, add 1 teaspoon salt, 1/2 teaspoon coarse-ground black pepper, ⅛ teaspoon sugar, ½ teaspoon onion salt, a good dash Worcestershire sauce, and 2 tablespoons white wine vinegar. Beat well, pour over salad, toss, and serve.

Skillet Biscuits I

Prepare as for recipe on page 55. When biscuits are done, remove from stove, but do not turn off flame, as you will need it for the dessert.

Hot Lemon Chiffon Tarts

Remove biscuit pan from skillet and put skillet, covered, on stove over medium flame. In a lightweight 8-inch aluminum pie plate, or in heavy-duty foil bent to make a "pan", put 4 bakery-bought lemon chiffon tarts. Cover, turn flame to low, and heat no more than 20 minutes. Serve in individual bowls with spoons.

SATURDAY BREAKFAST

Fair and Warm

SLICED PEACHES AND CREAM
CHEESE MUFFINS
SCRAMBLED EGGS
HOT KIPPERS

Sliced Peaches and Cream

Peel, pit, and slice 1½ fresh peaches per person, and place in serving bowl, retaining all the juice possible. Pour over fruit 1 tablespoon lemon juice, fresh or bottled, to prevent discoloration. Serve with fresh or canned heavy cream.

Cheese Muffins

Over high flame, place to preheat for 10 minutes a 12-inch heavy dome-lidded skillet with a rack in it. While it is heating, put 2 cups prepared biscuit mix into a heavy plastic bag of suitable size and add ½ teaspoon hot prepared mustard, 1 teaspoon paprika, 2 tablespoons sugar, and ½ cup dry grated American, Parmesan, or Romano cheese. Close bag tightly, squeeze contents to blend thoroughly, open bag, and pour in ¾ cup fresh (or diluted evaporated, or reconstituted dry) milk, 2 tablespoons vegetable oil, and 1 raw egg. Close bag and squeeze again to mix all ingredients well (batter should be lumpy, not smooth) .

Grease an 8-by-8-inch cake pan and pour in batter, spreading evenly. Sprinkle more cheese on top. Put pan in skillet, cover, and cook over high flame 20 to 30 minutes, lifting lid only after 20 minutes to check doneness. When done, cut into squares and serve.

Scrambled Eggs

Over high flame, on burner not occupied by muffins, cover and set to heat the lower part of your largest double boiler with 2 inches water in it. Meanwhile, break 8 eggs into a bowl, add ½ cup fresh or undiluted evaporated milk, and with fork, whisk, or egg beater, beat to blend.

Remove lower part of double boiler from stove, place over two asbestos pads to keep hot, put top of double boiler directly on same flame, and in it melt 4 tablespoons butter. When sizzling, pour in eggs; stir vigorously and constantly to prevent eggs from sticking and to cook evenly. When eggs are about half done, stir in ⅓ cup seasoned bread crumbs. When eggs are almost done, remove from fire and place over hot water in lower part of double boiler to free the burner for the kippers. The eggs will cook a bit more while they wait.

Hot Kippers

Lower considerably the flame on which the eggs have been cooked and place a large skillet on it, add 3 to 4 tablespoons butter to melt. While butter is melting, open one 14-ounce can or four 3¼-ounce cans kipper fillets, drain on newspaper or paper towels, and remove bones.

Pour off the melted butter into a heatproof measuring cup, mug, or pitcher, fill the bottom of the skillet with kipper fillets laid side by side in one layer, and cook only till tan. If skillet is not of a size to hold all fillets in one layer, put first batch on a plate or shallow dish that fits between the cover and top of the double boiler containing the eggs, to stay hot while you cook the rest. One more layer should certainly do it.

When all kippers are cooked, return to skillet, dribble melted butter over them, sprinkle with coarse-ground black pepper, and squeeze lemon juice generously on top. Cover skillet, heat for 5 minutes, and turn off flame.

Rainy, Not Really Cold

SLICED RUMMY PEACHES

KIPPERS WITH SCRAMBLED EGGS

RY KRISPS AND CHEESE

Sliced Rummy Peaches

Following recipe for Peaches and Cream in *Fair and Warm* Sunday breakfast menu, omitting cream and adding 3 tablespoons rum to peaches 15 minutes before serving.

Kippers with Scrambled Eggs

Before starting to prepare the eggs, set over a high flame the lower part of your largest double boiler, covered, with 2 inches water in it, and on the other burner, put a large heavy skillet to preheat for 5 minutes over a medium flame. Drain one 14-ounce or four 3¼-ounce cans kipper fillets and lay side by side on newspaper or paper towels to drain further. Remove bones and skin, and set fillets aside. While kippers are draining, put 4 tablespoons (½ stick) butter in top of double boiler and place directly over a low flame.

Break 8 eggs into a bowl, add ½ cup fresh or undiluted evaporated milk, and beat with fork, whisk, or eggbeater just until well blended. When butter is sizzling, pour in eggs, turn flame high, and cook eggs, stirring frequently so they will not stick and will cook evenly. Between stirrings break up the kippers into ½-inch bits. When eggs are about half done (still moist but firming up), stir in the kipper bits and finish cooking.

Put top of double boiler on lower part, cover, and turn flame as low as possible to keep hot until served.

Ry Krisps with Cheese

Since the weather is wet, one must give a thought to the cockpit occupants, rapidly getting soaked. Ry Krisps, water biscuits, hardtack, Swedish dry rye bread, etc., are what is needed as a starch for this breakfast.

Mix 4 tablespoons (½ stick) butter with 2½ tablespoons grated cheese such as American cheddar, swiss, Parmesan, or Romano. Spread mixture on pieces of hard bread and put an unspread piece on top of each.

Melt 2 tablespoons butter in heated skillet, lay "sandwiches" in one layer on bottom, cover, turn flame low, and cook for 10 minutes. Hand out to cockpit personnel with bowls of kippers and eggs.

Windy, Cold, but Not Wet

HOT SLICED RUMMY FRESH PEACHES
KIPPERS WITH SCRAMBLED EGGS
HOT CHEESE MUFFINS

Hot Sliced Rummy Fresh Peaches

In a saucepan or skillet over a high-medium flame, melt 1½ tablespoons butter. Peel and slice 1½ fresh peaches per person, and put in skillet. Turn flame to low. Pour over peaches 3 tablespoons light or dark rum, cover, and cook till heated through (about 5–7 minutes).

You should have no burner problems if you reserve one burner for the muffins, starting them first. Heat the peaches on the other burner and set aside to keep warm over two asbestos pads, then use that burner for the Kippers with Scrambled Eggs.

Kippers with Scrambled Eggs

Prepare as in *Rainy, Not Really Cold* Saturday breakfast menu.

Hot Cheese Muffins

Prepare as in *Fair and Warm* Saturday breakfast menu.

LUNCH

Fair and Warm

HAM, SPINACH AND RAW MUSHROOM SALAD
BUTTERED SWEDISH KRISPBRÖT
FRESH APRICOTS OR PLUMS

Buttered Swedish Krispbröt

These very thin, rye-flavored wafers are available in cardboard packages in most stores with gourmet pretensions, as well as in the delicacy departments of department stores. Stow them with all your crackers, but only after removing them from the box. Before serving, spread thinly with softened butter.

Ham, Spinach and Raw Mushroom Salad

Bring on board and place in icebox one heavy plastic bag filled with one package fresh raw spinach, carefully picked over, washed, and drained, and another plastic bag containing 1¼ cups diced boiled or baked ham.

Dressing does not need to be refrigerated. In a large-mouthed screw-top jar, or bowl, put 2 tablespoons lemon juice, fresh or bottled, 4 tablespoons olive oil, 1 teaspoon salt, a good dash of coarse-ground black pepper, ¼ teaspoon dry mustard, ½ teaspoon sugar, and 1 teaspoon celery seed. Mince finely 1 clove garlic and add, together with the yolk of 1 egg, but do not blend.

Scrub 6 or 7 medium-sized raw mushrooms, slice, and set aside. Into a large salad bowl, empty the spinach and ham, and strew the mushrooms on top. Shake or beat the dressing to mix thoroughly. Pour over salad, toss well, and serve.

Fresh Apricots or Plums

Some people eat fruit as is, unpeeled, in the first; others are happier when the fruit is peeled. To accommodate the latter, peel, pit, and halve 1 dozen fresh apricots or plums, or some of each, and serve in bowls with forks.

Rainy, Not Really Cold

HAM AND CHEESE SKILLET CASSEROLE
SAUTÉED SPINACH
HOT BUTTERED SWEDISH KRISP-BRÖT
FRESH APRICOTS OR PLUMS

Ham and Cheese Skillet Casserole

Bring on board, layered in a tightly closed heavy plastic bag, 1½ cups diced uncooked ham steak (about ½ pound) and 4 hard-boiled eggs, cut into eighths. In another tightly closed plastic bag, bring aboard 1 pound fresh spinach, washed and dried on a towel, the towel discarded before placing the spinach in the bag. Place both in icebox.

Over a high flame, put the lower chamber of your smallest double boiler with ¾ inch water in it, then put the top part over it with 1¼ cup fresh or undiluted evaporated milk, the contents of 2 envelopes dehydrated chicken broth, 1 teaspoon salt, ½ teaspoon dry mustard, 1 teaspoon celery seed, and 1 teaspoon onion salt. Cover and lower flame to medium.

On the other burner, in a capacious skillet, over a low flame, melt 2 tablespoons butter. While it is melting, measure out 2 tablespoons flour, wash and scrub well ¼ pound mushrooms and slice or open and drain one 3-ounce can broiled-in-butter sliced mushrooms. When butter is melted, add flour, stir till blended, and add the seasoned heated milk, stirring to make sure there are no lumps. Lower flame as much as you can, then insert two or three asbestos pads or a flame-tamer under skillet. When sauce comes just to a bubble, add ham, hard-boiled eggs, and mushrooms, and stir to blend. Add ¼ cup dry grated American, Parmesan, or Romano cheese; stir once more and cover. Serve in bowls over spinach and Krisp-Bröt.

Sautéed Spinach

On burner freed by removing double boiler, over medium flame, place a largish skillet. Put in 2 tablespoons olive oil. Remove from icebox plastic bag containing spinach. When oil is hot (but not steaming or smoking), empty spinach into skillet, add salt and pepper, toss well, set flame very low, and cook no more than 3 minutes. Remove from burner to any heatproof surface, but do not turn off the flame.

Hot Swedish Krisp-Bröt

Over the same low flame, put a saucepan with 1½ tablespoons butter. When butter is melted, add contents of 1 package Krisp-Bröt (or Ry Krisp or similar crisp rye bread or cracker), stir slices to coat with butter, and cook till heated through.

Windy, Cold, but Not Wet

HOT CLAMATO
CREAMED HAM WITH BROWN RICE
SAUTÉED SPINACH
HOT FRESH APRICOTS OR PLUMS
IN RUM, PORT, OR BOURBON

Hot Clamato

This unfortunately named mixture is very good hot, when the wind is piping and the crew shivers. It need not be carried on board as is—one 16-ounce can tomato juice and two 6-ounce bottles or cans clam juice mixed together are just as restoring. The trick is in the seasonings.

Light a high flame on one burner, put 1 inch water in lower part of a medium-sized double boiler, cover, and put to heat. Into the top part, empty one 29-ounce can "Clamato" or mixture of clam juice and tomato juice. Add juice of 2 lemons or 4 tablespoons bottled lemon juice, 1 teaspoon salt, ½ teaspoon coarse-ground black pepper, 3 teaspoons each celery salt, onion salt, and Worcestershire sauce, 1 teaspoon dry mustard, and 6 good dashes Tabasco. Stir and put over bottom of double boiler, turn flame to low, and heat 10 minutes. Serve in mugs.

Creamed Ham with Brown Rice

Bring aboard Friday, in a tightly closed heavy plastic bag or other airtight container, 3 cups cooked brown rice. In another, bring 1½ cups diced cooked ham—boiled, baked, or steak. Place both in icebox.

When ready to prepare, remove rice and ham from icebox, drain into a bowl two 3-ounce cans broiled-in-butter sliced mushrooms, and open one 10½-ounce can condensed cheddar cheese soup.

Over medium flame, in a large skillet, melt 2 tablespoons butter or drippings or fat of any kind. When melted, add ham and sauté 6 or 7 minutes or until ham is brown on all sides. Stir in 1 tablespoon flour, ¼ teaspoon coarse-ground black pepper, 1 teaspoon celery seed, 1 tablespoon paprika, and 2 teaspoons Worcestershire sauce, and turn flame as low as possible.

Add undiluted soup and mushroom liquid to skillet, blend well, turn up flame slightly, and cook until sauce bubbles a little. Stir in rice, cover, and cook until ready to serve in bowls over sautéed spinach.

Sautéed Spinach
Prepare as in *Rainy, Not Really Cold* Saturday lunch menu.

Hot Fresh Apricots or Plums in Rum, Port, or Bourbon
Peel, halve, and pit 12 fresh apricots or plums, or a mixture of the two. In a saucepan, over a low flame, put 1 tablespoon butter; let melt. Stir in fruit, pour over it 3 tablespoons rum, port, brandy, or bourbon, cover, and heat no more than 10 minutes. Serve in bowls or mugs.

DINNER

Fair and Warm

SAVORY SPREAD ON MELBA TOAST
COLD FRIED CHICKEN II
COLESLAW III (MENAGÈRE)
HEATED BAKERY ROLLS
POUND CAKE WITH LIQUEUR RASPBERRIES

Savory Spread
Bring on board one heavy plastic bag, tightly closed, containing two chopped hard-boiled eggs, 2 tablespoons minced pimiento, 2 tablespoons dry grated Parmesan cheese, ½ teaspoon

salt, and 1 tablespoon parsley flakes. Place in icebox. When ready to prepare, into a medium bowl put ¼ cup mayonnaise, ½ teaspoon Worcestershire sauce, 3 tablespoons catsup, juice of 1 lemon, salt, and coarse-ground black pepper to taste, and blend well. Add to bag containing egg mixture, reclose bag tightly, and knead to blend all ingredients well. Turn back into bowl in which dressing was mixed. Serve with Melba toast slices.

Cold Fried Chicken II

Prepare this dish after the breakfast dishes are done.

Remove from icebox 1 quartered uncooked frying chicken. Discard giblets and cut away any extraneous fat. Place chicken, skin side up, in any skillet, saucepan, shallow dish, or 8-by-8-inch baking pan. In a bowl, or capacious screw-top jar, put juice of 1 lime, or 2 tablespoons bottled lime juice, ¾ cup dry white wine, 1 clove garlic minced, salt, black pepper, and imported paprika to taste, and ½ cup olive oil. Stir gently, pour over chicken, and set aside to marinate for 2 hours. Then set a large skillet over a high flame and put 2 tablespoons chicken marinade and 2 tablespoons olive oil in skillet. When hot, pick chicken out of marinade and sauté, skin side down, turning flame to low after 10 minutes. Turn meat to other side and, when chicken is almost done (about 10 more minutes), pour over it the rest of the marinade; cover and cook 10 minutes longer. Let cool in skillet, then empty into a heavy plastic bag and put in icebox.

Coleslaw III (Menagère)

Bring on board in a tightly closed plastic bag 2 cups finely shredded cabbage. In another bag bring 4 slices Muënster cheese, cut into strips or diced, 16 quartered pitted black olives, and 16 coarsely chopped radishes. Place both bags in icebox. In a salad bowl, put ½ cup mayonnaise, 2 tablespoons malt vinegar, 1 teaspoon sugar, salt, black pepper, and a good shake of garlic salt. Stir to blend. Mix into cabbage, toss well, strew over salad the contents of second plastic bag, and serve.

Heated Bakery Rolls

Bring on board Friday night 1 dozen fresh-baked soft rolls—
Parker House, dinner, or any other kind you fancy. Set the lower
chamber of your largest double boiler, with 1½ inches water in it,
over a high flame. When water is boiling, put top of double boiler
with rolls in it over lower chamber, cover, turn flame low, and
heat for 15 minutes.

Liqueur Raspberries

Bring aboard Friday night 2 packages frozen raspberries and
put in icebox. By Saturday evening they should be thawed. Parcel
out into four shallow bowls. Over each bowl, pour 1 tablespoon
Cointreau or Curaçao and serve.

Rainy, Not Really Cold

HOT SAVORY SPREAD

CHICKEN MORNAY—WHITE RISOTTO

SLICED TOMATOES AND RED ONIONS II

TOASTED ANGEL FOOD WITH

HOT RASPBERRY SAUCE

Hot Savory Spread

Prepare mixture as in *Fair and Warm* Saturday dinner
menu, but heat over hot water in your smallest double boiler for
10 minutes. At the same time, on the other burner, in a larger
double boiler, heat over hot water as many crackers as the
double boiler top will hold. Use any kind of crackers you prefer,
or substitute Melba toast (rye, white, or whole wheat). Remove
both vessels to heat-proof surface until ready to serve.

Chicken Mornay

Early in the day, or the day before, prepare 1 quartered
chicken, following recipe for Special Cold Fried Chicken in *Fair
and Warm* Saturday dinner menu, but undercook by 20 minutes.

When ready to prepare for this dinner, remove chicken from
icebox, skin, remove meat from bones, and cut into sizeable
pieces. In a large skillet, heat one 10½-ounce can undiluted con-

densed clear chicken broth, add chicken and all marinade, turn flame low, cook for 15 minutes, remove chicken, set aside in skillet to cool.

Meanwhile, prepare Sauce Mornay. Put water to the depth of 1 inch in the lower chamber of your medium-sized double boiler, add the upper part, and put both over high-medium flame. In the top of the double boiler, put 3 tablespoons butter, salt, white pepper, and 1 teaspoon dry mustard. While butter is melting, measure out $2\frac{1}{2}$ tablespoons flour and $1\frac{1}{4}$ cups diluted evaporated milk, open 2 envelopes powdered chicken broth, and grate coarsely enough Swiss cheese to make $\frac{1}{4}$ cup. Set flame low and add flour; stir till smooth and blend in milk and powdered chicken broth. When the sauce has thickened (stir it occasionally to make sure there are no lumps), add the grated cheese and stir until it melts into the sauce. When done, remove double boiler to two asbestos pads on counter.

Now chop 2 medium-large white onions and 2 large stalks celery, leaves removed. Open and drain, reserving the liquid, one 5-ounce can whole water chestnuts. Slice eight of them and put the remaining water chestnuts into the icebox, with enough of their own liquid to cover, in an airtight container.

On same burner put a smaller heavy skillet, with 2 tablespoons butter in it, and sauté onions till golden. Remove onions, sauté celery and water chestnuts in the same skillet until tan but not soft, and remove skillet from flame. Pour broth-marinade from chicken into an airtight container and put into icebox, leaving chicken meat in the large skillet. Place skillet over medium flame and sauté chicken meat (with a little more butter if needed) until tinted. Put onions, celery, and water chestnuts over chicken meat. Pour Sauce Mornay over all, cover, insert flame-tamer or two or three asbestos pads, turn flame as low as possible, and keep hot until ready to serve.

White Risotto

On burner freed from double boiler, over a low flame, put to melt 4 tablespoons ($\frac{1}{2}$ stick) butter in a deep saucepan. While it is melting, chop finely two small white onions or enough to make $\frac{1}{2}$ to $\frac{2}{3}$ cup and sauté till transparent. Add $1\frac{1}{4}$ cups noninstant raw rice, 2 teaspoons salt, and ½ teaspoon white pepper to onion-butter blend and stir until rice turns opaque, but do not let it brown. Add one 10½-ounce can undiluted condensed clear chicken broth, cover pan, and cook gently until broth has been entirely absorbed by the rice. If at that time the rice does not test done, add ¼ cup water and cook a little longer. Just before serving, stir in ¼ cup grated Parmesan or Romano cheese. Serve in individual bowls with the Chicken Mornay over it.

Sliced Tomatoes and Red Onions II

Slice medium-thin 2 or 3 tomatoes. Peel and slice thinly enough red onion to equal in bulk half the tomatoes. Arrange onions and tomatoes in overlapping slices in one layer on platter or shallow dish; sprinkle with 2 tablespoons olive oil and 1 tablespoon white wine vinegar; dust with salt, a very small amount of sugar, coarse-ground black pepper, about 1 teaspoon celery seed, and 1 tablespoon chopped fresh dill or 1½ teaspoons dried dill weed.

Toasted Angel Food with Hot Raspberry Sauce

Cut enough angel food into ½-inch slices to have 1½ slices per person. Empty one box thawed frozen raspberries into a small saucepan, put over high-medium flame, and cook till juice is reduced by half. While fruit is cooking, on the other burner place a large heavy skillet over a low flame. In it melt 1 tablespoon butter, tilting skillet to spread the butter evenly. Fill the bottom of the skillet with one layer of angel food slices. Heat until tan on one side; turn over and tint the other side.

Place 1½ slices toasted cake in each of four individual bowls, pour hot raspberries over cake, and douse with rum, bourbon, sherry, or brandy.

Windy, Cold, but Not Wet

HOT SAVORY SPREAD

DEVILED DRUMSTICKS WITH BROWN RISOTTO

COLESLAW IV (HOT)

TOASTED ANGEL FOOD WITH

HOT RASPBERRY-APRICOT SAUCE

Hot Savory Spread

Prepare as in *Rainy, Not Really Cold* Saturday dinner menu.

Deviled Drumsticks with Brown Risotto

Bone (or not, if you prefer) four cold fried chicken drumsticks. Chop 2 medium-large yellow onions. Light both burners and turn flames to medium. On one burner place a 9-inch heavy skillet and on the other a deep, heavy saucepan. In each, melt 4 tablespoons butter. When butter is melted, divide onion evenly between the two pans and sauté until a good dark brown.

While the onions are sautéing, measure out 1¼ cups non-instant raw rice and open one can condensed beef broth. Lower flame under the skillet and to the browned onions add 2 tablespoons parsley flakes, 2 teaspoons Dijon-style prepared mustard, 2 teaspoons Worcestershire sauce, and 2 tablespoons tarragon or red wine vinegar. Stir sauce well to blend. Simmer 3 minutes and turn off flame if not yet ready to cook drumsticks.

To the browned onions in the other pan, add the rice, stir well, and keep stirring frequently until rice turns quite brown.

To the skillet with the sauce in it, then add the drumsticks and light a medium flame. Cook no more than 15 minutes. When done, cover and keep warm over low flame, with flame-tamer or three asbestos pads under the skillet, until ready to heat coleslaw.

To the browned onions in the other pan, add the rice, stir well and keep stirring frequently until rice turns quite brown, then add entire can of condensed beef broth, lower flame to lowest possible, cover, and cook until all broth has been absorbed by the rice. If at that time the rice does not test done, add ¼ cup water, re-cover, and cook 10 minutes longer. Just before serving, stir in ¼ cup grated Parmesan or Romano cheese. Pass rice and drumsticks separately.

Coleslaw IV (Hot)

Over one burner place lower chamber of your largest double boiler, with 1½ inches water in it, and turn flame high. Off the fire, place in the top of the double boiler one pint cole slaw, homemade or store-bought and brought aboard. Add 15 pitted black olives cut in quarters, 12 scrubbed radishes cut into eighths, and 1 minced small white onion. Cover, place over lower chamber of double boiler, and lower flame. While heating, grate coarsely enough Muënster cheese to make ¼ cup. Add to cole slaw, blend thoroughly, insert flame-tamer or three asbestos pads under pot, and keep warm until ready.

Toasted Angel Food with Hot Raspberry-Apricot Sauce

Prepare angel food as in *Rainy, Not Really Cold* Saturday dinner menu, but make sauce as follows: Drain one box thawed frozen raspberries and put in a small saucepan. Set over lowest possible flame, add 2 heaping tablespoons apricot preserves or jam, stir well, and heat till bubbling.

SUNDAY BREAKFAST

Fair and Warm

AMBROSIA WITH WHITE WINE

LAMB HASH

OATMEAL-RAISIN-CINNAMON SKILLET BREAD

Ambrosia with White Wine

Drain one 1-pound can pineapple slices, cut the slices into eight wedges each, and place in any suitable receptacle. Peel 3 oranges (preferably seedless), cut them in half crosswise, then into sections, and add to the pineapple. Sprinkle 1 cup shredded coconut over the fruit and mix well. Pour ½ cup chilled white wine over all.

Lamb Hash

Bring on board Friday night, along with your other provisions, a stout plastic bag containing 3 cups finely diced cold cooked roast lamb. Put in icebox.

When ready to prepare, remove lamb from icebox. Over a medium flame, place a heavy skillet, with cover set aside, with 4 tablespoons butter in it. While butter is melting, chop finely 2 golf-ball–sized white onions, stir into butter, and sauté until transparent and just beginning to brown.

While onions are cooking, drain into a bowl one 3-ounce can broiled-in-butter sliced mushrooms, leaving mushrooms in the can; open one 10½-ounce can brown gravy, and measure out 2 tablespoons flour. When onions are ready, stir in flour, blending well. Add liquid from can of mushrooms, stir till smooth, add brown gravy, stir till smooth, and season with salt, coarse-ground black pepper, and 2 teaspoons Worcestershire sauce. Mix in lamb, sprinkle generously with parsley flakes, cover, and heat 10 minutes.

Oatmeal-Raisin-Cinnamon Skillet Bread

Into a heavy plastic bag put ¾ cup all-purpose flour, 1¼ cups noninstant rolled oats, 2 slightly rounded teaspoons baking powder, 2 teaspoons cinnamon, ½ teaspoon salt, 4 tablespoons sugar (preferably brown), and ½ cup raisins. Close bag tightly, squeeze and knead until all ingredients are well mixed. If some other container is unavoidable, stir ingredients well to mix thoroughly.

Into the bag with dry ingredients put 3 tablespoons oil or melted shortening of any kind and ½ cup hot water or milk. Reclose bag, squeeze and knead till a stiff dough is formed. Squeeze dough onto a floured board that has been generously sprinkled with oats, and put a large, heavy skillet or griddle to heat over high-medium flame while you shape the dough into four rounds about ½ inch thick, then cut the rounds into wedges. Brush skillet or griddle with oil or butter, and put one full layer of wedges into it.

Brown on each side about 2 minutes, reduce flame to medium low, cover, and bake 5 minutes more. Split and insert dab of butter. Keep hot while next batch is cooking; brush skillet or griddle with more butter between batches.

Rainy, Not Really Cold

HOT AMBROSIA WITH RUM

LAMB HASH

OATMEAL-RAISIN-CINNAMON SKILLET BREAD

Hot Ambrosia with Rum

Put lower part of a medium-sized double boiler, with 1 inch water in it, over a medium flame. Prepare Ambrosia as in *Fair and Warm* Sunday breakfast menu, omitting wine. Put in double boiler top, stir 3 tablespoons rum into fruit and juices, put over lower part, cover, and heat for at least 15 minutes.

Lamb Hash

Prepare as in *Fair and Warm* Sunday breakfast menu.

Oatmeal-Raisin-Cinnamon Skillet Bread

Prepare as in *Fair and Warm* Sunday breakfast menu.

Windy, Cold, but Not Wet

HOT AMBROSIA WITH RUM

PENNY'S BAKED BEANS

PLAIN OATMEAL SKILLET BREAD

Hot Ambrosia with Rum

Prepare as in *Rainy, Not Really Cold* Sunday breakfast menu.

Penny's Baked Beans

Set a large, heavy skillet over high-medium flame to preheat for 5 minutes. Meanwhile, chop finely 1 small white onion and open two 16-ounce cans baked beans of any kind. Put 1 tablespoon butter or oil in skillet to melt and, when melted, add onions, sauté till golden, add beans, then stir in 2 tablespoons chili sauce, 2 tablespoons brown sugar, 2 tablespoons molasses, and salt. Reduce flame to low and cook for 30–45 minutes.

Plain Oatmeal Skillet Bread

Prepare according to recipe for Oatmeal-Raisin-Cinnamon Skillet Bread in *Fair and Warm* Sunday breakfast menu, omitting cinnamon and raisins.

LUNCH

~~~~~~

Fair and Warm

HORS D'OEUVRES VARIÉS
ON ANY BREAD, BISCUITS, OR CRACKERS LEFT OVER
MELON WEDGES, IF ANY, OR
CANNED BLACK CHERRIES

After the breakfast dishes are done, go through the icebox and pull out any meat or vegetables left over from previous meals during the weekend.

For four persons, a selection of no more than 6 to 8 hors d'oeuvres is ample to provide the main course for lunch. Variety of texture and flavor is the secret of the well-put-together hors d'oeuvres tray. Ideally there should be one egg dish, one of fish, one of meat, two of vegetables, and one of legumes. Whatever you lack to round out your selection, obtain from cans in the locker. The twelve recipes that follow call for ingredients previously mentioned in the recipes for this weekend, plus some from cans.

I. HORS D'OEUVRES FROM LEFTOVERS OF THE WEEKEND'S DISHES

Tomato and Red Onions III

If there is enough to serve four, put in a bowl, add a bit of French dressing, and toss gently. If not enough, add leftover raw green pepper and a few black olives.

Chicken and Almonds

Into a bowl, cut into julienne strips enough cold cooked chicken to make 1¼ cups. Stir in ¼ cup slivered almonds, 1 teaspoon parsley flakes, ½ cup diced celery, 1 teaspoon onion salt, salt, and black pepper. Add enough French dressing to moisten and toss again. Just before serving, dress with 2 table-spoons sour cream, or fresh heavy cream, or cream that has started to go sour.

Baked Bean Salad

Put in a bowl ½ cup drained leftover baked beans, or drain one 8-ounce can baked beans of any kind. In a separate container, put 2 tablespoons mayonnaise, 1 tablespoon chili sauce, and (optional) 2 tablespoons garden relish or chopped pickle of any kind. Blend well, then stir in the beans.

Coleslaw

Into 1 cup any leftover Coleslaw III, partially drained, stir 1 tablespoon each celery seed and caraway seed.

Mustard Celery

Slice thinly, on a pronounced diagonal, enough celery to make ¼ cup; put in a bowl. In another container, put 2 table-spoons mayonnaise, 1 tablespoon lemon juice, 1 tablespoon hot prepared mustard and blend in well. Pour over celery and toss.

Hard-boiled Eggs with Shrimp and Louis Dressing

Use any shrimp left over from Friday night's dinner in this recipe. Peel and slice 4 hard-boiled eggs and arrange in over-lapping slices on flat dish or plate. Over eggs, strew leftover shrimp salad, or drained leftover shrimp-with-artichokes, or shrimp creole over eggs.

Louis Dressing

Mix 4 tablespoons mayonnaise and 2 teaspoons chili sauce, then add 1 tablespoon lemon juice, 4 chopped green or black olives, 2 teaspoons capers, and 1 finely chopped gherkin; stir into mayonnaise mixture. Pour over eggs-and-shrimp mixture; garnish with any leftover Savory Spread from Saturday night.

II. HORS D'OEUVRES FROM OTHER SOURCES

Hard-boiled Eggs à la Russe

Shell and slice thinly 4 hard-boiled eggs. Arrange on shallow dish. Thin ¼ cup mayonnaise with 1 tablespoon lemon juice or pickle juice. Stir in 1½ tablespoons tomato catsup and spread over eggs.

Pseudo-Pâté

Empty into a bowl one 4¾-ounce can or two smaller cans liver pâté spread. Stir in 2 tablespoons imitation bacon bits and 1 finely chopped small white onion, then blend in 1 tablespoon brandy, or bourbon, or rum, or sherry. Add 1 teaspoon onion salt, ¼ teaspoon garlic salt, 1 teaspoon celery salt, and 1 teaspoon prepared horseradish. Keep cold until served.

Beet Salad

Drain one 8-ounce can sliced or small whole beets. If the latter, slice thinly. Slice thinly 1 small white onion and intermingle onion slices with the beets. Sprinkle with salt and coarse-ground black pepper. Pour 1½ tablespoons tart French dressing over the salad and toss well.

Sauerkraut Slaw I

Drain thoroughly one 1-pound can sauerkraut. Place in saucepan over low flame with 1 whole peeled small onion. Sprinkle over sauerkraut the contents of ½ envelope dehydrated chicken broth. Add ½ cup water. Simmer 20 minutes. (This can also be done in the top of a double boiler while the lower chamber, if it is deep enough, is occupied by 4 eggs in the process of being hard-boiled.) Cool sauerkraut. Remove onion and chop it finely, mix into sauerkraut, and toss with bland French dressing.

Sardine Hors d'Oeuvre

Drain 2 cans brisling sardines without removing fish from cans. With fork or broad-bladed knife, remove sardines carefully to shallow bowl. Season with salt, coarse-ground black pepper and 2 tablespoons lemon juice. Garnish with mayonnaise if desired.

Green Bean Salad I

Drain one 8-ounce can cut green or wax beans, place in a bowl, stir in 10 to 12 scrubbed radishes, sliced or cut into eighths, and toss with French dressing.

Pickled Mushrooms I

Put in a bowl one 3-ounce can or bottle well-drained whole mushrooms. Over low flame, heat ½ cup white vinegar. Pour over mushrooms and let cool. Just before serving, stir in 2 tablespoons olive oil and ½ teaspoon coarse-ground black pepper.

Rainy, Not Really Cold

DANISH VEGETABLE DINNER
ON CUT-UP TOAST
LEFTOVER FRESH FRUIT OR
CANNED PINEAPPLE SLICES

Danish Vegetable Dinner on Cut-Up Toast

Assemble in a bowl any leftover vegetables you have in the icebox (this may include celery, radishes, mushrooms, artichokes, even olives), and mix well. If not enough to make 3 cups, add drained string beans, carrots, peas, etc., from small cans to make 3 cups, but not spinach or any leafy vegetable.

Light both burners of the stove. Place a large double boiler, with water to the depth of 2 inches in the bottom, over a high flame.

In the top of double boiler put 3 tablespoons butter to melt. While butter is melting, measure out 3 tablespoons flour, ¼ cup milk (fresh, reconstituted dry, or undiluted evaporated), and 1¼ cups mayonnaise. Add flour to butter, blend, add milk, and stir to make sure there are no lumps. Remove double boiler and put top over direct flame; stir mixture until thickened. Season with salt, pepper, celery seed, and 1 teaspoon onion salt. Reassemble double boiler and put back over lowest possible flame and stir in 1 cup mayonnaise. Blend well, then stir in vegetables. Cover and cook 15 minutes.

On the other burner, fry over low flame 16 slices bacon. As

done, drain on paper towel, brown paper bag, or newspaper. When all bacon is done, set aside on plate. Bacon does not have to be warm for this dish.

Drain off bacon fat, and in the hot pan melt 1 tablespoon butter. Toast 4 slices bread of any kind in skillet.

Set up four capacious individual bowls. Into each, place one slice of toast, cut into bite-sized pieces, and on this put bacon and ½ of a tomato herring, split, boned, and drained. Pour vegetable mixture over this, and serve with spoons.

Windy, Cold, but Not Wet

CHICKEN AND TOMATO JUICE SOUP
CURRIED VEGETABLES ON
LEFTOVER RISOTTO
HOT CANNED PINEAPPLE WITH BOOZE

Chicken and Tomato Juice Soup

Over a high flame, put the lower part of a large double boiler, with 2 inches water in it. In the top of the double boiler, off the stove, blend together one 10½-ounce can undiluted condensed cream of chicken soup and one 8-ounce can tomato juice. Season with salt, pepper, 1 teaspoon each dried basil, onion salt, and celery seed and set over double boiler bottom. Cover, and lower flame to medium. When heated, empty soup into a quart-sized large-mouthed thermos, close tightly, and set aside.

Curried Vegetables on Leftover Risotto

Put in the top of your largest double boiler 2½ cups leftover risotto, combined with fresh-cooked rice if needed. Place over bottom part containing 1½ inches water, cover, and heat for 15 minutes over a medium flame.

Drain the sauce from any leftover vegetables in cream or other sauce into a bowl or dish. Drain well any other leftover vegetables you have in the icebox, discarding the liquid. Peel and chop coarsely enough raw fresh fruit (melon, orange, apple, pear, etc.) to make ½ to ¾ cup. Cut into sizeable dice any raw vegetables that are on hand (such as celery, green peppers, and radishes).

A total of 3 cups of fruits and vegetables is needed. Spread drained and raw vegetables and fruit on a large piece of wax paper and sprinkle generously with flour. Scoop up sides and ends of wax paper to make a sort of bowl, and roll fruit and vegetables around to coat with flour.

Over medium flame heat a large heavy skillet, put in 4 tablespoons leftover meat-or-bacon-fat or butter or oil, and when hot, add floured fruits and vegetables. Sauté till golden, stirring frequently. Meanwhile, measure into a container 3 tablespoons curry powder, 1/8 teaspoon cayenne, 2 teaspoons ground ginger, and 1/2 teaspoon each ground cinnamon, cloves, and nutmeg. Then add 2 teaspoons onion salt and 1/2 teaspoon garlic salt. With small spoon, stir until all spices are well mixed, sprinkle over fruits and vegetables, and blend well.

When fruits and vegetables are done, add all sauce reserved from sauced leftover vegetables with one 10½-ounce can condensed beef broth and stir till well blended. If amount of liquid does not equal amount of solid material, add any fruit juice on hand to make it so, stir again, reduce flame very low, cover, and cook 10 to 20 minutes or until curry sauce is thickened to your taste.

WEEKEND III
FRIDAY NIGHT DINNER

Fair and Warm

BRIE ON FRENCH BREAD
PAN-BROILED STEAK
POTATOES HASHED IN CREAM*
GREEN BEANS À LA FAÇON DE CHEZ MOI*
STRAWBERRIES AND CREAM
ANGEL FOOD CAKE

Brie on French Bread

For four persons, ½ pound Brie is ample. Leave Brie unrefrigerated long enough to become runny (2–3 hours). Slice sourdough French bread thinly and pile into a bowl.

Pan-Broiled Steak

Allow a 3- to 4-pound porterhouse or sirloin steak at least 1 inch thick for four people. If frozen, thaw before bringing aboard. Trim off all but ½ inch of fat and gash remaining fat on a slant at 2-inch intervals all around, then set steak aside to warm to galley temperature.

Over the hottest flame you can produce, heat a very heavy 11-inch (or larger) frying pan until drops of water shaken onto it disappear immediately. Brown meat quickly on both sides. Reduce flame to high-medium and cook till desired degree of doneness but do not turn again.

There is no such thing as a rule of thumb on timing the pan-broiling of a steak because too many imponderables exist: how cool the meat is when cooked, how thick it is, how lean or fat, and how rare, medium, or well-done you and your guests prefer it.

Potatoes Hashed in Cream*

Remove precooked hashed potatoes, brought aboard with your provisions (see recipe, page 307), from icebox; bring to galley temperature. Over a direct low flame in the top of your largest double boiler, melt 1½ tablespoons butter. When melted, add potatoes, stir well, insert flame-tamer or two or three asbestos pads under pan, and heat for 10 minutes. Remove from stove, with flame-tamer or pads, but do not turn off flame.

Green Beans à la Façon de Chez Moi*

Remove precooked green beans, brought aboard with your provisions (see recipe, page 308), from icebox; bring to galley temperature.

On the burner freed by removing potatoes, over the same flame, put the bottom of your largest double boiler, with 2 tablespoons butter in it. When butter has melted, add green beans, stir well, then add 3 tablespoons white wine. Take flame-tamer or asbestos pads from under the double boiler top, insert under boiler bottom, put top over bottom, cover, and heat until ready to serve, but no more than 15 minutes.

Rainy, Not Really Cold

BRIE ON FRENCH BREAD

BEEFSTEAK BITS SAUTÉED

SPECIAL STEAK SAUCE

POTATOES HASHED IN CREAM*

GREEN BEANS À LA FAÇON DE CHEZ MOI*

STRAWBERRIES AND CREAM

ANGEL FOOD CAKE

Brie on French Bread

Prepare as in *Fair and Warm* Friday dinner menu.

Beefsteak Bits Sautéed

This may be prepared at home and brought aboard, if desired.

To prepare: cut all fat from a 3-pound porterhouse or sirloin steak at least 1 inch thick and remove bone. (If frozen, thaw at home before bringing on board.)

Cut meat vertically into ¼-inch-thick slices, then cut each slice crosswise into 2- to 3-inch lengths and pile in a bowl. In a large frying pan, over a high flame, heat 3 tablespoons butter or oil, or a combination of the two. When sizzling, place one good full layer meat bits in the pan, turn flame to high-medium and sauté quickly on each side. Remove to bowl or dish fitted onto top of double boiler in which potatoes and green beans are heating.

Repeat, adding butter as needed, until all beefsteak bits are cooked and removed. Turn flame very low, heat Special Steak Sauce to slow simmer, and pour over steak bits.

In individual bowls, place a layer of potatoes, then one of green beans, with meat and sauce over all. This is a spoon meal.

Special Steak Sauce

On burner freed by removing steak bits, over a low flame place a saucepan with the contents of two 10½-ounce cans mushroom gravy in it. Stir in 1 teaspoon celery salt, ¼ teaspoon powdered thyme, the content of 4 envelopes dehydrated beef broth, and 1 bay leaf. Simmer, uncovered, until reduced by one-third. Now add 2 tablespoons tomato sauce and 1 tablespoon black currant jelly. Stir until jelly has melted, and add 4 table-spoons (¼ cup) red wine, preferably claret. Bring to a simmer, turn off flame, and remove from stove.

On the burner thus freed, place a medium-sized skillet containing 3 tablespoons butter. Add 2 finely chopped shallots and sauté until golden; then add ½ cup dry white wine, bring to a simmer, and cook uncovered for 20 minutes.

Meanwhile, chop 1 large dill pickle, measure out ⅓ teaspoon dried tarragon leaves and ½ teaspoon dried parsley flakes, and add to reduced red wine and gravy. Bring again to a simmer, add shallot-and-white-wine mixture, bring once more to a simmer, cover, and remove from stove. Pour over steak bits and serve as directed in recipe for Beefsteak Bits Sautéed above.

Potatoes Hashed in Cream*
Prepare as in *Fair and Warm* Friday dinner menu.

Green Beans à la Façon de Chez Moi*
Prepare as in *Fair and Warm* Friday dinner menu.

Windy, Cold, but Not Wet

HOT HERBED POTATO CHIPS
SMOTHERED STEAK SLICES À LA SMITANE
HASHED BROWN POTATOES* I
GREEN BEANS À LA FAÇON DE CHEZ MOI*
HOT STRAWBERRIES WITH BOOZE
ANGEL FOOD CAKE

Hot Herbed Potato Chips
Empty potato chips into heavy plastic bag, or two lighter bags, one inside the other. Melt 3 tablespoons butter over low flame. Spoon 1 teaspoon each thyme and basil leaves into bag with potato chips. Close mouth of bag and shake vigorously. Pour melted butter into bag and shake again once or twice, with bag upside down and your hand at all times holding the mouth closed. Empty into a bowl and keep warm.

Smothered Steak Slices à la Smitane

With a very sharp knife, cut all fat from a 3-pound sirloin or porterhouse steak; then remove meat from bone and slice it as best you can into ½-inch pieces. Put a heavy 12-inch dome-lidded skillet, uncovered, over highest possible flame to preheat for 10 minutes. Meanwhile, cut 2 medium-sized green peppers, pith and seeds removed, into ¼-inch strips and place in covered container. Peel and slice into ¼-inch rings 2 tennis-ball-sized yellow onions and put on top of peppers.

Without fat of any kind, sear a layer of meat slices in heated skillet once on each side and remove. Repeat until all steak slices are seared and removed. Put onion rings in pan, stir in 2 table-spoons oil, lower flame, and sauté till onions are golden. Then add pepper strips and continue sautéeing until peppers are tinged with color.

Put in seared beef slices, stir just to mix, and add 1 cup red wine, salt, coarse-ground black pepper, garlic salt, and celery salt to taste. Cover and simmer 15 minutes.

Meanwhile, open a 10½-ounce can beef gravy and one 8-ounce container sour cream. When steak is done, stir in gravy and then sour cream. Put asbestos pads or flame-tamer under skillet, cook 5 minutes more, and serve over potatoes and beans in shallow soup plates or fairly large bowls.

Hashed Brown Potatoes I*

Melt 3 tablespoons butter in top of large double boiler and add Potatoes Hashed in Cream (brought on board; see recipe, page 307). Put, uncovered, directly over low flame to cook for 20 minutes. Turn from time to time, to make sure potatoes are browning and cream in which they were originally cooked is being absorbed. When approaching a good shade of dark tan, remove from heat and cover.

Green Beans à la Façon de Chez Moi

Prepare as in *Fair and Warm* Friday dinner menu.

Hot Strawberries with Booze

Over a low flame, place a medium-sized double boiler with 1 inch water in the bottom. In the top, put 2 pints washed and hulled fresh strawberries. Add 3 tablespoons superfine sugar and 3 tablespoons any fruit liqueur you wish, or rum, or bourbon. Stir well, cover, and heat no more than 8 minutes. Serve over ¾-inch-thick angel food wedges in individual bowls.

SATURDAY BREAKFAST

Fair and Warm

GREEN GRAPES IN WHITE WINE
CHICKEN LIVERS SAUTÉED WITH
TOMATOES AND WINE
CINNAMON-RAISIN WHOLE WHEAT BREAD, SAUTÉED

Green Grapes in White Wine

After washing well a 1-pound bunch of seedless green grapes, detach fruit from stem and divide into four individual dishes. Pour 3 to 4 tablespoons chilled dry white wine over each dish of grapes, stir lightly, and serve.

Chicken Livers Sautéed with Tomatoes and Wine

Drain one 1-pound can whole tomatoes, reserving juice for another use. Place tomatoes in large heavy skillet with 1 tablespoon butter over a medium flame, and cook, uncovered, till most of juice still in tomatoes has evaporated. Remove from skillet and set aside. Add to skillet, over same flame, ½ stick (4 tablespoons) butter and heat till butter is sizzling.

While butter is heating, cut 1 pound chicken livers into halves, removing and discarding any fat. When butter is hot, add livers and sauté over high heat for 4 to 5 minutes, shaking occasionally so they won't stick. Remove livers onto tomatoes and add ⅓ cup red wine to butter remaining in skillet. Scrape and stir up into the wine all the brown bits at the bottom, lower flame to medium, and cook, uncovered, until slightly reduced (about 6 or 7 minutes).

Lower flame, return chicken livers and tomatoes to skillet, cover, and heat till bubbling.

Cinnamon-Raisin Whole Wheat Bread, Sautéed

Set up a double boiler with 1 inch water in lower section, cover, and over high heat bring water to a rolling boil. Without turning off fire, remove double boiler and put it on two or three asbestos pads to keep warm.

Lower flame, and in a large skillet melt 1 tablespoon butter, tipping pan from side to side to coat bottom with butter. Put in as many slices of whole wheat cinnamon-raisin bread as skillet will accommodate and sauté till brown on both sides, removing to top of double boiler as done. Repeat, adding more butter as needed, until enough bread has been cooked for four persons.

Serve with apple butter as a spread.

Rainy, Not Really Cold

GREEN GRAPES IN WHITE WINE
CHICKEN LIVERS SAUTÉED. WITH
SHERRY AND WINE
SAUTÉED ENGLISH MUFFINS

Green Grapes in White Wine

Prepare as in *Fair and Warm* Saturday breakfast menu.

Chicken Livers Sautéed with Sherry and Wine

In a large, heavy skillet melt $2\frac{1}{2}$ tablespoons butter over high heat. While butter is melting, cut 1 pound chicken livers into halves, removing and discarding all fat. Fry chicken livers quickly, shaking occasionally to turn. When well browned, remove livers from skillet, lower flame somewhat, and stir in 3 tablespoons dry sherry to bring from the skillet bottom all brown bits; then add 1 cup dry white wine and cook until reduced by half. Return chicken livers to skillet, cover, turn off fire, and let sit in hot pan till served.

Sautéed English Muffins

Set up your largest double boiler, with 2 inches water in lower section, cover, and over high heat bring water to a rolling boil. Without turning off flame, remove double boiler from stove and put it on two or three asbestos pads to keep warm.

Lower flame, and in a large heavy skillet melt 2 tablespoons butter, tipping pan from side to side occasionally to coat bottom with butter. While butter is melting, with fork split 6 to 8 English muffins three quarters through. Spread in skillet as many split muffins as will fit into one layer, split side down. Sauté till brown or golden, according to taste; fold each muffin together again, as done, and then remove to top of double boiler. Repeat, adding more butter as needed, until all muffins are cooked.

Make sandwiches by inserting a few hot chicken livers into each muffin, and hand to wet skipper in the cockpit and to crew, whether below or topside.

Windy, Cold, but Not Wet

HOT SPICED CRANBERRY JUICE
CHICKEN LIVERS IN RED WINE
ON SAUTÉED ENGLISH MUFFIN HALVES

Hot Spiced Cranberry Juice

Pour a 1-quart can or bottle of cranberry juice into a large deep saucepan over a medium-low flame. Add juice of 2 lemons or 4 tablespoons bottled lemon juice, 4 sticks cinnamon, 1 teaspoon ground cloves, and ½ teaspoon ground nutmeg. Cover, heat, and serve in mugs, putting 1 stick of cinnamon into each.

Chicken Livers in Red Wine

Drain two 3-ounce cans whole or sliced mushrooms, leaving mushrooms in cans, and fill each can with halved green olives, stuffed or not. In a large skillet, over medium flame, melt 1½ tablespoons butter, add olives and mushrooms, and sauté for 3 minutes. Meanwhile, cut 1 pound chicken livers into halves, removing and discarding any fat. Without changing the flame, with slotted spoon remove olives and mushrooms, melt 4 tablespoons (½ stick) more butter in the skillet, turn flame high, add chicken livers, and fry quickly until well browned, stirring to prevent sticking. Return the mushrooms and olives to skillet, stir well, add ¼ cup red wine, season to taste, cover, and simmer 10 minutes. Serve in bowls on sautéed English muffin halves.

Sautéed English Muffin Halves

Prepare as in *Rainy, not Really Cold* Saturday breakfast menu, but split the muffins clear through instead of only three-quarters of the way.

LUNCH

~~~~~

Fair and Warm

COLD SQUASH SOUP
SARDINE PÂTÉ SANDWICHES ON RYE
MÉLANGE OF CANNED FRUITS IN WHITE WINE

Cold Squash Soup

Prepare at least 3 hours before serving.

In a deep saucepan, over heat recommended on the package, cook 1 package frozen mashed yellow squash, using, instead of the water called for in the directions, an equivalent amount of broth from one 10½-ounce can undiluted condensed chicken broth. While squash is cooking, cut into large cubes 3 peeled medium-sized raw potatoes, 3 stalks celery, 3 carrots, and 2 tennis-ball–sized yellow onions; add to squash with balance of can of chicken broth, plus a second 10½-ounce can broth and 2 envelopes dehydrated beef broth.

Cook over low-medium flame until vegetables are soft. Turn off flame and let cool. Mash vegetables thoroughly through soup and stir in ¾ cup heavy cream or undiluted evaporated milk together with salt, coarse-ground black pepper, and a generous grating of nutmeg (about ½ teaspoon, if ground nutmeg is used).

Put soup in covered airtight container. Refrigerate, if icebox has space, though this is not necessary.

Sardine Pâté Sandwiches on Rye

Begin with 4 hard-boiled eggs, either brought on board from home or cooked right after breakfast dishes are done, using the same water that the dishes were washed in—which will not affect the eggs.

Drain into a bowl three 3¾-ounce cans Norwegian brisling sardines and their oil and mash. Chop finely the hard-boiled eggs and 2 small white onions, and add to sardines with 2 teaspoons anchovy paste, 1 tablespoon parsley flakes, and 1 teaspoon brandy. Add enough mayonnaise to make pâté spreadable; season with salt, coarse-ground black pepper, and 1 tablespoon lemon juice, fresh or bottled. Stir thoroughly and serve with rye bread cut into quarter-slices.

Mélange of Canned Fruits in White Wine

Drain into a saucepan the juices of one 8-ounce can each sweet white cherries, apricot halves, and crushed pineapple. Mix fruit in a serving bowl. Over low flame bring juices, uncovered, to a simmer, add ⅓ cup white wine, cook until reduced by half, and cool. Pour over fruit and serve.

Rainy, Not Really Cold

HOT SQUASH SOUP

SARDINE PÂTÉ SANDWICHES

ON RYE TOAST

PEPPERMINT PATTIES

Hot Squash Soup

Prepare as in *Fair and Warm* Saturday lunch menu, but reheat for 15 minutes in double-boiler arrangement before serving.

Sardine Pâté Sandwiches on Rye Toast

Prepare sardine mixture as for *Fair and Warm* Saturday lunch menu. Set up a large double boiler with 2 inches water in lower section. Over high flame, bring water to a rolling boil, and set aside on two or three asbestos pads to keep warm.

In a large skillet, over a low flame, melt 1 tablespoon butter, tipping from side to side to coat bottom evenly with butter. Add as many slices rye bread with caraway seeds as skillet will accommodate in one layer and cook on both sides to preferred shade of tan or brown, removing as done to top of double boiler. Repeat, adding more butter as needed, until 16 slices have been toasted. Make sandwiches of sardine mixture and toast, and serve.

Windy, Cold, but Not Wet

HOT SQUASH SOUP

HOT SARDINE SANDWICHES, SAUTÉED

HOT MIXED CANNED FRUITS

Hot Squash Soup

Prepare as in *Rainy, Not Really Cold* Saturday lunch menu; remove double boiler to asbestos pads to keep warm and to free burner.

Hot Sardine Sandwiches, Sautéed

One-half hour before preparing, remove 4 tablespoons (½ stick) butter from icebox to soften.

Over a high flame, put a large double boiler with 2 inches water in the bottom, bring water to a boil, remove double boiler from stove, and put on two or three asbestos pads to keep warm.

Over a low flame, melt 2 tablespoons butter in a small skillet, turn off flame, and add 1½ tablespoons Worcestershire sauce, 2 teaspoons anchovy paste, 1 teaspoon dry mustard, season well with salt and coarse-ground black pepper, and blend sauce well.

Drain four 3¾-ounce cans Norwegian brisling sardines, discarding oil. On the other burner, over a low flame, put a large skillet with 2 tablespoons butter in it. While butter is melting, dip sardines, one at a time, in sauce, lay 3 or 4 side by side on a half-slice of rye bread with caraway seeds, cover with another half-slice, and spread top with softened butter. Put sandwiches into skillet, buttered side up, as soon as put together, until skillet bottom is full. Sauté till brown on one side, turn, and brown buttered side. Meanwhile, continue making sandwiches until all sardines are used.

As sandwiches are done, place in empty double-boiler top, cover. Repeat, adding butter as needed, until all sandwiches are cooked.

Hot Mixed Canned Fruits

While sandwiches are cooking prepare the dessert, as in *Fair and Warm* Saturday lunch menu, but make this change:

When juices and wine have reduced, add fruit immediately while syrup is hot, cover, and turn off flame. The dessert will stay hot enough until ready to serve, with or without cream of any kind.

DINNER

Fair and Warm

SPICED CREAM CHEESE AND CAPERS
ON PUMPERNICKEL
COLD SLICED TONGUE
CELERY SALAD WITH MUSTARD DRESSING
RYE ROLLS
GOOSEBERRY FOOL WITH MAPLE WAFERS*

Spiced Cream Cheese and Capers

After lunch, set out two plates, on one put 1 stick butter and on the other two 3-ounce packages cream cheese. After 2 hours or more, in a fairly large bowl, using a slotted spoon, cream the two together, then beat until light and fluffy. Add 1 teaspoon each prepared hot mustard, caraway seeds, and paprika. Grate one very small white onion over all, and mix in 2 teaspoons each dehydrated parsley flakes (or fresh chopped parsley) and chopped capers. Chill, if feasible, and serve with thinly sliced dark pumpernickel.

Cold Sliced Tongue

This can be cooked at home, brought aboard, and kept chilled in the ice chest, or 1 chilled can whole cooked tongue can be opened and sliced.

Celery Salad with Mustard Dressing

Scrub thoroughly, after removing and discarding all leaves, the stalks of 1 large or 2 medium-sized bunches chilled celery. Cut stalks at a slant crosswise into ½-inch pieces and put into a large salad bowl.

In a separate receptacle, combine ⅓ cup mayonnaise, 3 tablespoons lemon juice (fresh or bottled), salt and coarse-ground pepper to taste, and 2 teaspoons prepared hot mustard. Add to celery; toss thoroughly.

Gooseberry Fool

Use 1 pint heavy cream, whipped, or 1 pint soft vanilla ice cream, or 1 pint prepared canned whipped cream. Put cream in a bowl, mix thoroughly with one 8-ounce jar gooseberry jam or preserves, and stir in 2 tablespoons brandy. Chill.

Maple Wafers*

The recipe for these is on page 309.

Rainy, Not Really Cold

SPICED CREAM CHEESE AND CAPERS
ON PUMPERNICKEL
HOT DEVILED TONGUE SLICES
CABBAGE SAUTÉED WITH BACON
CELERY SALAD WITH MUSTARD DRESSING
RYE ROLLS AND BUTTER
GOOSEBERRY TRIFLE

Spiced Cream Cheese and Capers

Prepare as in *Fair and Warm* Saturday dinner menu.

Hot Deviled Tongue Slices

Mix in a small bowl 2 tablespoons Worcestershire sauce, 1 teaspoon dry mustard, a pinch cayenne, ¼ cup canned tomato sauce, and 2 tablespoons chopped gherkins.

Put lower section of your largest double boiler, with 2 inches water in it, over a high flame. Bring water to a rolling boil and, without turning off fire, set aside on two or three asbestos pads. Meanwhile, slice cold cooked tongue, or canned whole tongue, into 14 thin slices, and sprinkle on both sides with flour, salt, and coarse-ground black pepper. On same burner, directly over a low flame, melt 3 tablespoons butter in top of the same double boiler, and in it sauté tongue slices, one layer at a time, till lightly browned on both sides. As done, remove to a plate or dish fitted into lower section of double boiler, and repeat until all tongue is done.

To the juices remaining in top of double boiler, add 1 tablespoon butter, melt, and stir in flavorings in small bowl. When sauce is hot, stir the tongue slices in gently, cover, and put over lower section to keep warm.

Cabbage Sautéed with Bacon

While tongue is sautéing, remove and discard outer leaves of 1 medium-sized head green cabbage; shred cabbage coarsely.

Over the same flame on which the tongue was cooked, put a deep saucepan with 4 slices bacon in it. Fry bacon until crisp, turning often; remove and drain on paper towels, newspaper, or brown paper bag. Add cabbage to saucepan, and toss frequently with fork and spoon (as you would a salad), as it cooks (about 12 to 15 minutes). While it is cooking, crumble bacon. When cabbage is done, season with salt and coarse-ground black pepper to taste. Stir in crumbled bacon and ½ cup sour cream, or undiluted evaporated milk, or heavy sweet cream, and stir all together well. Serve in bowls over tongue slices.

Celery Salad with Mustard Dressing

Prepare as in *Fair and Warm* Saturday dinner menu.

Gooseberry Trifle

Slice one 1-pound pound cake into eight ½-inch slices; then cut slices in half crosswise.

Melt 2 tablespoons butter in a large skillet over a low flame and toast cake on both sides until lightly browned. Spread with gooseberry jam, turn flame as low as possible, cover, and keep warm. Serve in shallow bowls topped with any kind of whipped cream.

Windy, Cold, but Not Wet

HOT BUTTERED RY KRISP WITH CARAWAY SEEDS
STOVETOP TONGUE AND CABBAGE CASSEROLE
MASHED CANNED SWEET POTATOES
HOT CELERY AND CHEDDAR CHEESE
HOT GINGERBREAD I WITH CREAM

Hot Buttered Ry Krisp with Caraway Seeds

Over high flame, preheat for 10 minutes a covered 12-inch dome-lidded heavy skillet with an 8-by-8-inch cake pan on a rack inside. Spread 18 slices Ry Krisp, or other hard bread, with soft butter, sprinkle each slice with caraway seeds and put into cake pan. Cover, lower flame to high-medium, and cook no more than 5 minutes. It should keep warm until ready to serve.

Stovetop Tongue and Cabbage Casserole

When you start preheating the 12-inch skillet, on the other burner, over a medium flame, put to heat the lower section of your largest double boiler with 2 inches water in it. Meanwhile, shred coarsely 1 medium-sized head green cabbage, unusable outer leaves removed, and cut 14 thin slices cold cooked tongue or canned whole tongue.

When water in lower section of double boiler is boiling, re-move this pot, and put it on two or three asbestos pads to keep warm. Lower flame to medium, and in top of double boiler over direct flame put to melt 2 tablespoons butter. While butter is melting, sprinkle in $\frac{1}{4}$ teaspoon thyme leaves, $\frac{1}{4}$ teaspoon dry mustard, salt, and coarse-ground black pepper. Stir well, then add cabbage and mix butter through it. Lower flame and cook no more than 10 minutes. Put tongue slices on cabbage and cook only until heated through. Set on bottom of double boiler to keep warm.

Mashed Canned Sweet Potatoes

While cabbage is cooking, on the free burner, over a medium flame, heat the covered bottom section of a medium-sized double boiler with $1\frac{1}{4}$ inches water in it, until water is at a rolling boil, then set flame as low as possible, to keep water at a simmer.

Meanwhile, drain one 29-ounce can, or two 1-pound cans, whole sweet potatoes without syrup and, off the stove, empty the potatoes into the top of the double boiler. Put over lower part, raise flame to medium, heat for 15 minutes, and remove from burner, leaving lower section on the fire. Lower flame again to keep water in lower section at a simmer.

With a slotted spoon or fork, mash potatoes coarsely. Season with salt, coarse-ground black pepper, and 1/4 teaspoon each ground cinnamon, cloves, ginger, and nutmeg. Then stir in 4 tablespoons dry sherry and 2 tablespoons butter. Return to double boiler bottom and cook for 15 minutes, then remove entire double boiler from stove to free burner. Potatoes will stay warm.

Hot Celery and Cheddar Cheese

Remove and discard unusable outer stalks from 1 large, or 2 medium, bunches celery. Scrub well each remaining stalk, and cut off all leaves. Cut celery into 1-inch slices and put into deep saucepan. Add 1½ cups water and 4 envelopes dehydrated chicken broth, bring to a boil, lower flame considerably, and cook 5 minutes.

While celery is cooking, open one 10½-ounce can condensed cream of celery soup, grate coarsely enough cheddar cheese to make 1 cup, and measure out ½ cup slivered blanched almonds.

When celery is done, leaving low flame on, remove from stove and drain. In the same saucepan, over the same low flame, put one layer celery, one scant layer almonds, one layer soup, and one layer cheese; continue, alternating layers, till all ingredients are used. Insert flame-tamer under pan, cover, and cook 20 minutes.

Hot Gingerbread I with Cream

Remove Ry Krisps from cake pan in skillet to shallow dish fitted as third tier over either double boiler you have keeping warm, and put skillet, covered, with rack in it over high flame to preheat for 10 minutes, leaving empty cake pan on work counter.

Using a stout plastic bag, prepare one package gingerbread mix, following directions on package. Butter and flour cake pan and squeeze batter into it, spreading evenly. Place in preheated skillet, cover, turn flame to medium and bake 30–35 minutes.

When done, shut off flame, remove gingerbread, turn over onto another rack, and let cool. Serve with plain or whipped cream.

SUNDAY BREAKFAST

Fair and Warm

PRUNES WITH LIME, HONEY, AND CREAM
BACON
SKILLET CORN BREAD
ONION FRITTATA

Prunes with Lime, Honey, and Cream

After the dishes are done Saturday night, put 1 pound dried pitted prunes to soak in a skillet, with water to cover. In the morning, add to prunes 1 stick cinnamon and 1 lime cut crosswise into six pieces. Light flame, turn to low, and simmer 20 minutes, while water for coffee is heating on the other burner.

When prunes are done, remove lime slices, drain, and stir in ¾ cup honey. Place in cockpit or other cool place, to chill enough for breakfast. Serve with cream, if possible.

Bacon

While prunes are cooking, on the other burner set your largest double boiler, with 2 inches water in the bottom, and, over a high flame, bring water to a boil. Remove from stove as soon as water boils, to free burner for cooking the bacon, but leave flame on and turn it low. In a large skillet, over this flame, fry 16 slices bacon, turning frequently, and removing as done to drain on paper towels, newspaper, or brown paper bag. When all bacon has drained, put into top of double boiler, pour all but about 2 tablespoons fat into another skillet about 9 inches wide, and place without heat, on burner freed by removing the prunes.

Skillet Corn Bread

Bring aboard Friday night, along with your other provisions, a tightly closed heavy plastic bag in which you have put 1¼ cups flour, 2 tablespoons sugar, 3 teaspoons baking powder, 1 teaspoon salt, and 1 cup cornmeal, yellow or white.

While bacon is frying, add to dry ingredients in plastic bag ⅓ cup oil, 1 egg, and ½ cup diluted evaporated, fresh, or reconstituted dry milk. Reclose bag and squeeze to a well-blended batter. Pour over the 2 tablespoons bacon fat in large hot skillet over low flame, spread smoothly, cover tightly, and cook until it tests done (15 to 20 minutes should do it). Lift onto a plate and cut in squares, or cut it in the pan if you wish.

Onion Frittata

While corn bread is cooking, chop coarsely 2 large onions and drain 1 medium-sized can whole tomatoes. Light high flame under the second skillet with bacon fat in it and, when hot, lower flame and sauté onions till golden. Next add tomatoes and ¼ teaspoon each garlic salt, thyme leaves, and basil. Cook for no more than 10 minutes. Turn off flame and remove skillet to cool the vegetables.

Into a bowl, break 8 eggs and beat lightly; season with salt and pepper. Relight flame, turn to low, place pan with onions and tomatoes over flame, and mix eggs in thoroughly. Cover snugly, and cook till firm, turning once. Cut into wedges, and serve with bacon and corn bread.

Rainy, Not Really Cold

PRUNES WITH LIME, HONEY, AND CREAM

CRUMBLED BACON IN SKILLET CORN BREAD

ONION FRITTATA

Prunes with Lime, Honey, and Cream
Prepare as in *Fair and Warm* Sunday breakfast menu.

Crumbled Bacon in Skillet Corn Bread
Since plain sliced bacon will be a little unappealing once it's been rained on, for the comfort of the cockpit personnel crumble the drained cooked bacon (it need not be hot) into bag with corn bread batter (see *Fair and Warm* Sunday breakfast menu) and

squeeze to mix bacon well throughout. Cook as for plain corn bread.

Onion Frittata

Prepare as in *Fair and Warm* Sunday breakfast menu.

Windy, Cold, but Not Wet

HOT COOKED PRUNES IN PORT WINE
CRUMBLED BACON IN SKILLET CORN BREAD
EGGS WITH FRENCH-FRIED ONION RINGS

Hot Cooked Prunes in Port Wine

After the dishes are done Saturday night, put 1 pound dried pitted prunes in the top of a double boiler of suitable size and cover with cold water. In the morning, add 1 stick of cinnamon to prunes, put over direct low flame, and simmer prunes 20 minutes. When prunes are done, drain and put back on fire, remove cinnamon stick, and add 1 cup port wine. Cook no more than 5 minutes. Meanwhile, heat 1 inch water in the lower part of a double boiler. When prunes are done, place over bottom of double boiler, cover, and set aside on two or three asbestos pads, freeing the burner for the corn bread and bacon.

Crumbled Bacon in Skillet Corn Bread

Prepare as in *Rainy, Not Really Cold* Sunday breakfast menu.

Eggs with French-Fried Onion Rings

Into a bowl, break 8 eggs and add 4 tablespoons of any of these liquids: cold water, any kind of milk or cream, bouillon, tomato juice, or V-8 juice. Beat eggs lightly. Open a medium-sized can of French-fried onion rings and break rings into thirds or halves. Put a 9-inch heavy skillet over high-medium flame to heat. When hot, add 3 tablespoons butter, tilting pan back and forth to spread melting butter evenly. Pour eggs into melted butter, add onion rings, and, with wooden spoon, stir through eggs. Turn flame high and cook quickly, stirring constantly, till eggs are well set.

LUNCH

<center>~~~~~~</center>

Fair and Warm

COLD CREAM OF SPINACH SOUP
SALAD OF TUNA FISH AND PINTO BEANS
ANY LEFTOVER FRUIT

Cold Cream of Spinach Soup

When the breakfast dishes are done, bring a package of frozen chopped spinach out of the icebox, and replace it with two 10½-ounce cans condensed cream of chicken soup and one 13-ounce can undiluted evaporated milk. (If you have as much as a cup of heavy cream on hand, use it instead of milk, even though it might be on the turn toward souring.)

If spinach has been in the icebox since Friday night, it has undoubtedly thawed. Put it in a deep saucepan, sprinkle 2 packets dehydrated chicken broth over it, and stir through; then add ½ cup water, bring to a boil, turn flame low, and simmer no more than 3 minutes. Drain well, saving the liquid, and cool. Then put both spinach and liquid into icebox.

Just before serving, empty into a bowl both cans of cream of chicken soup. Into one emptied can, pour the reserved spinach liquid and fill can with fresh or evaporated milk or heavy cream, and stir well into soup. Blend soup mixture into spinach and season with salt, white pepper, and a scant ½ teaspoon freshly grated nutmeg or ¼ teaspoon ground nutmeg.

Salad of Tuna Fish and Pinto Beans

Drain a 29-ounce can speckled pinto beans, and place beans in a salad bowl. Stir in ½ cup red wine vinegar, ½ teaspoon marjoram leaves, 1 teaspoon basil leaves, 3 finely sliced scallions, 1 tablespoon parsley flakes, salt, and pepper. Mince finely 2 cloves garlic and cut into strips 1 green pepper, pith and seeds removed, and add to beans. Drain one 7-ounce can tuna fish, breaking it into fairly large chunks as you remove it from can. Stir through bean combination. Stir together ½ cup olive oil and juice of ½ lemon or 1 tablespoon bottled lemon juice, pour over salad, and toss well.

Just before serving, garnish with any salad greens you still have on hand.

Rainy, Not Really Cold

HOT SPINACH GUMBO SOUP

STOVETOP TUNA CASSEROLE

FRIJOLES REFRITOS I

ANY FRESH FRUIT ON HAND WITH

ANY CAKE OR COOKIES ON HAND

Hot Spinach Gumbo Soup

When breakfast dishes are done, remove from icebox one package frozen chopped spinach. (If it has been there since Friday night, it undoubtedly has thawed.) Put it in a deep saucepan with ½ cup water, over a high medium flame, bring to a boil, lower flame, simmer no more than 3 minutes and then add 2 cans undiluted condensed chicken gumbo soup, and stir well. Next, add ½ cup water and ¼ cup red wine, stir again, bring soup to a boil, and turn off flame. Pour into one quart-sized and one pint-sized large-mouthed thermos bottle.

Stovetop Tuna Casserole

Butter generously the top of a double boiler of at least 1½-quart capacity. Put the lower part, with 2 inches water in it, over a medium flame and cover. While water is heating, open two 7-ounce cans tuna fish, one 10½-ounce can condensed cream of mushroom soup, and one 29-ounce can speckled pinto beans (for use in Frijoles Refritos, below).

Cut into strips 1 large green pepper, pith and seeds removed, slice thinly 1 medium-sized red onion, and grate enough cheddar, Parmesan, or swiss cheese to make ¾ cup. Drain fish, and put a layer of large tuna flakes into top of double boiler, strew a sparse layer of green pepper strips over it, add a rather more generous layer of red onion rings, and over all sprinkle 1 teaspoon parsley flakes. Repeat layers until all ingredients are used.

Empty the can of undiluted soup into a bowl, half fill the emptied can with fresh or undiluted evaporated milk or light cream, and stir into soup. Pour over ingredients in top of double boiler and sprinkle with the cheese. Put over lower chamber of double boiler, cover, turn flame down somewhat, and heat 20 minutes.

Frijoles Refritos I

Place a frying pan of suitable size over low flame. Dice 6 slices bacon and put into pan to cook. While bacon cooks, chop coarsely 1 large or 2 medium yellow onions and mince 1 clove garlic. Add to bacon, stir well, and continue cooking until onions are light brown. Meanwhile, drain and mash the 29-ounce can pinto beans. Stir in and fry till fat is absorbed (about 10 minutes). Serve in bowls, with tuna mixture spooned over the beans.

Windy, Cold, but Not Wet

GUMBO IN A MUG WITH WINE

STOVETOP TUNA, BEANS, AND

CHEESE CASSEROLE

STEWED TOMATO DRINK

HOT FRUIT ON HAND

Gumbo in a Mug with Wine

When the breakfast dishes are done, through a strainer drain into a deep saucepan 2 cans undiluted condensed chicken gumbo soup, and set strainer with solid matter aside. Add to saucepan one 13½-ounce can undiluted condensed clear chicken broth, cover, and put over a medium-low flame to heat. Empty strainer into a bowl, stir in one 8-ounce can drained *petits pois,* and mash well with a slotted spoon. Add to soup and stir thoroughly. When soup is near boiling, add 4 tablespoons (¼ cup) red wine. When soup has come to a boil, pour into one quart-sized and one pint-sized large-mouthed thermos.

Stovetop Tuna, Beans, and Cheese Casserole

Set up a double boiler of at least 1½-quart capacity with 1½ inches water in bottom, and place over a low flame to heat.

Open one 10½-ounce can each condensed cream of mushroom soup and condensed cream of potato soup, one 29-ounce can of pinto beans, and one 7-ounce can of tuna fish. Grate cheddar, swiss, or Parmesan cheese to make ¾ cup, dice 1 large green pepper, pith and seeds removed, and chop coarsely 1 small red onion.

Put soups and cheese into top of double boiler, and stir well. Cook until cheese is thoroughly blended in. Drain beans and stir in, then add green pepper, onion, and drained tuna in large flakes. Season well with salt, pepper, and at least 1 teaspoon paprika. Lastly, stir in 2 tablespoons parsley flakes. Cover and heat 20 minutes.

Stewed Tomato Drink

Without peeling, slice thickly all the fresh tomatoes you still have on hand. If not enough for four persons, open a medium-sized (16-ounce) can of whole tomatoes, but do not drain.

Set a deep saucepan with cover over medium-low flame and in it melt 2 to 3 tablespoons butter till sizzling and starting to turn brown. Sauté fresh tomatoes in it till somewhat brown. If canned tomatoes are needed, add when fresh are cooked. Season with salt, pepper, 1 teaspon sugar, and 1 teaspoon basil leaves. With slotted spoon, crush tomatoes to thick pulp. When beginning to simmer, pour into mugs or bowls and serve.

Hot Fruit on Hand

I can't think of any fresh fruit that cannot be heated with rum, bourbon or brandy, and served in either mugs or bowls. If melons are on hand, cut from rind, dice coarsely, and put in saucepan over low flame to heat, with 1 tablespoon rum, brandy, or bourbon added per cup of fruit. If you have green grapes, remove from stalks, cut a number in half, place in saucepan, and season the same way. Most other fruits should be peeled before heating. They need not be diced, but should have seeds and cores removed. Fruit slices, halves, or any combination of several fruits all may be treated in this manner. Serve in deep bowls with generous spoons to make sure the cockpit contingent gets its full share, despite the whipping wind and the movement of the boat.

Six Summer Dinners
at Quiet Anchor

Among cruising's most pleasurable hours are those spent in the early evening after the boat has been brought into a calm, snug, quiet harbor (hopefully pretty much unpopulated by other cruising groups), the hook is tossed over and holds nicely, and everybody on board settles into the cockpit with a contented sigh and his favorite predinner drink in hand to discuss the day's sail and ponder tomorrow's. Then is when what some sailors call a "holy calm" descends, and the cook is prompted to put forth extra effort to make dinner, from appetizer to dessert, a special meal.

The menus and recipes in this chapter are all planned with that kind of occasion in mind.

~

CRAB SPREAD

BLANQUETTE DE VEAU

COLD CURRIED RICE

GREEN BEAN SALAD II OR III

FRENCH BREAD

CHOCOLATE SUNSHINE

Chocolate Sunshine

Make this dessert just before starting to assemble the rest of the dinner. It needs only an hour in the icebox to "set."

Put 1 teaspoon plain gelatin in ¼ cup cold water to soak.

Put a small double boiler with ¾ inch water in the bottom over a medium flame. In the top chamber, put to melt 2 squares bitter chocolate. Meanwhile, separate 3 eggs, and beat ½ cup sugar into the yolks. Blend yolk mixture with the chocolate, and with wooden spoon beat hard until mixture thickens (about 4–6 minutes). Add ¼ teaspoon peppermint· extract, 3 tablespoons rum or bourbon, ½ teaspoon powdered cinnamon, and ½ teaspoon salt; stir.

Take top of double boiler off flame, stir in the soaked gelatin, and set aside to cool for 10 minutes. Beat egg whites until stiff, and gradually fold into the cooled chocolate mixture, a half cup at a time, stirring gently and lightly, never beating. Chill well.

Crab Spread

Drain two 7¾-ounce cans crabmeat and place in any suitable container. Pick over carefully to remove bones and sinew. With fingers, flake quite fine. Peel and dice small 1 large cucumber and stir into crabmeat. Stir in enough mayonnaise to make spreadable but not soupy. Season with salt, coarse-ground black pepper, and ½ teaspoon Worcestershire sauce. Hand the bowl into the cockpit with a dish of Melba rounds, plain or any flavor you fancy, and a spoon or broad-blade knife.

Blanquette de Veau

Remove bone, all fat, and connecting tissue from 2 pounds fresh or thawed frozen veal cutlet, cut into 1½-inch cubes or pieces, and place in heavy saucepan or skillet. Peel and slice 3 golf-ball-sized white onions and put on top of meat. Pour one 10½-ounce can undiluted condensed cream of chicken soup over meat and onions, then half fill the emptied can with white wine and pour over all. Cover, place on stove over low flame, and simmer 45 minutes to 1 hour, or until meat is tender. Make *beurre manié* by kneading together three tablespoons soft butter and 1½ tablespoons flour. Just before serving, add well-drained contents of one 6-ounce or two 3-ounce cans sliced or whole broiled-in-butter mushrooms, stir in *beurre manié,* and cook till sauce thickens somewhat.

Cold Curried Rice

Early in the day, cook 1 cup noninstant rice, drain, steam slowly for 20 minutes, and set aside to cool.

When ready to prepare, place cooled rice into a bowl, add ¾ cup sliced pitted black olives and 2 tablespoons curry powder, and stir till well blended. Toss gently with ½ cup French dressing to which has been added 2 tablespoons parsley flakes.

Green Bean Salad II

Drain two 1-pound cans cut green beans and place in bowl. Cut up coarsely 1 green pepper, pith and seeds removed, and 4 medium-sized tomatoes. Add to beans, stir in 2 tablespoons capers and 1 tablespoon dried basil, then toss with just enough French dressing to moisten.

Green Bean Salad III

Drain two 1-pound cans cut green beans and place in a bowl. Toss with just enough French dressing to moisten. On a plate, platter, or capacious shallow dish, place overlapping slices of tomatoes and green pepper rings and strew green beans over them.

CAVIAR CREAM CHEESE

HAM STEAK MENAGÈRE

CELERY CHEZ MOI

POTATOES NOISETTE WITH CARAWAY

CRÊPES ANTWERP

Caviar Cream Cheese

Right after breakfast, remove from icebox and place in a bowl one 8-ounce package cream cheese to soften.

When cream cheese is soft, mash well and thin with 4 tablespoons sour cream, or undiluted evaporated milk, or fresh heavy cream. Grate into it 1 peeled small white onion. Stir in 3 tablespoons red or black caviar and cool in icebox. Serve in the cockpit with tray of any sort of biscuits, Melba toast, or crackers, or combination thereof.

Ham Steak Menagère

Use a ham steak weighing a little less than 2 pounds and about 1½ to 2 inches thick. Cut off all but ¼ inch of the fat, reserving the fat cut off; gash remaining fat at 1½-inch intervals. Place over a high flame a heavy skillet big enough to accommodate the ham easily but do not put in the ham. While it is heating, dice the fat cut from the ham, turn flame to medium, and put fat in the skillet to "try out." Peel and slice thinly 2 medium carrots and 2 fairly large white onions. When the cubes of fat are well tried out, there should be enough melted fat to sauté the onions and carrots. Lower flame to medium low, spread carrot and onion slices in the skillet and sauté until golden. While vegetables are sautéing, open a 10½-ounce can beef gravy and measure out ⅓ cup Madeira or sherry. With slotted spoon, remove the vegetables and set aside. Raise flame high and sauté the ham for about 3 minutes on each side. Lower flame, spread vegetables over the ham, pour beef gravy over all, and stir in the Madeira or sherry. Cover and cook 15 minutes or a little more.

Celery Chez Moi

Fresh or canned celery may be used. In each case, some broth is needed for the sauce, and there should be enough celery, in 1½-inch slices, to make 4 cups. Put fresh celery in shallow saucepan or skillet, and add enough water to come two-thirds of the way to the top of the celery. Sprinkle with the contents of 2 envelopes dehydrated chicken broth, cover, put over high flame, and bring to a boil. The moment it boils, turn flame low, simmer 6 minutes, drain, reserving liquid, and set aside.

With canned celery, before slicing, drain into a saucepan, add 2 envelopes dehydrated chicken broth, cover, bring to a boil, turn flame low, simmer 6 minutes, and set aside. While liquid is simmering, slice the celery.

Put a medium or large double boiler, with 2 inches water in the bottom, over a high flame and bring to a boil. When boiling, turn flame to low. Empty one 10½-ounce can undiluted condensed cheddar cheese soup into top of double boiler, reserving the emptied can. Half fill can with liquid from canned celery or from cooking fresh celery. Stir in 2 more envelopes dehydrated chicken broth. Add cooked or canned celery, cover, and heat 15 minutes. Set aside on three asbestos pads to keep hot, and to free burner for ham or potatoes.

Potatoes Noisette with Caraway

Fresh or canned potatoes may be used. For four persons, use 16 small potatoes, or two 1-pound cans. Peel fresh potatoes, boil for 15 minutes, drain, and set aside. Canned potatoes need only be drained.

In the top of a large double boiler, melt ½ stick (4 tablespoons) butter directly over a low flame. Stir in the potatoes, and shake gently to make sure all are coated with melted butter. Put 2 inches water in bottom of double boiler, put top part on it, cover, and bring water in bottom to a boil. Stir in 3 tablespoons caraway seeds. Simmer 5 minutes. Remove double boiler to keep hot.

Crêpes Antwerp

Stir into ½ cup of any kind of preserves or jam 2 tablespoons rum, brandy, bourbon, or any liqueur. Break 2 eggs into a mixing bowl, add 4 tablespoons fresh, undiluted evaporated, or reconstituted dry milk, and mix. Add 4 tablespoons flour, ¼ teaspoon powdered cloves, ⅛ teaspoon lemon extract, 2 tablespoons sugar, and ½ teaspoon salt. Beat until smooth, then add enough more milk to batter to reduce to the consistency of thin cream. Set aside for ½ hour.

When ready to cook crêpes, fit a shallow dish into the top of one of the double boilers to heat. On free burner, heat a 5- or 6-inch heavy skillet over high-medium flame and grease with a little butter or vegetable oil. Using a large spoon, cover the bottom of the skillet with a thin coating of batter and brown carefully to a toasty tan on one side, lowering the flame if the batter seems to brown too fast. Turn, and brown the other side. Remove to dish in top of double boiler and cook all batter the same way.

When all crêpes are cooked, put 1 tablespoon jam-liqueur mixture in center of each, roll neatly, and sprinkle generously with confectioner's sugar. When all crêpes are rolled, place dish to keep hot in any manner convenient.

PICKLED MUSHROOMS II
COLD POACHED SALMON STEAKS
SPINACH FRITTATA
LIMA BEANS À LA SMITANE
APRICOT TRIFLE

Pickled Mushrooms II

These come in jars ready to serve, but are more tasteful when made on board. Canned mushrooms may be used. For four persons, you will need ½ pound scrubbed fresh mushrooms (sliced if large, whole if small) or 1½ cups drained canned button or sliced mushrooms.

Heat to boiling point 1 cup good white wine vinegar, and pour over mushrooms. Marinate for anywhere from 20 minutes to 2 hours, then add ¼ cup olive oil, 1 tablespoon parsley flakes, salt and coarse-ground black pepper, and stir well. Serve with crackers, bread, or biscuits.

Cold Poached Salmon Steaks

Allow one ½-inch-thick steak per person. After the breakfast dishes are done, place steaks side by side in the bottom of a large skillet, with enough water to cover. Pour off water into a measuring cup to ascertain how much bouillon you are going to need in which to cook them. Set aside the salmon. In the same skillet, put half-and-half white wine and water to equal the amount of water drained off the salmon. Add 1 sliced medium-sized onion, 1 sliced carrot, 1 teaspoon celery seed, 1 teaspoon onion salt, 1 bay leaf, salt, coarse-ground black pepper, 1 teaspoon parsley flakes, and ½ teaspoon thyme leaves. Cover, bring to a boil over high heat, then set flame low and simmer 15–20 minutes, but do not turn off flame. Strain, return broth to skillet over same low flame, and add salmon steaks. Re-cover, and simmer 7 minutes— no more. Lift salmon steaks to a shallow dish and allow to cool unrefrigerated.

Spinach Frittata

Use 1 package frozen, or one 1-pound can, leaf spinach. For frozen spinach, cook as directed on package, drain, and cool. For canned spinach, drain thoroughly and then squeeze with slotted spoon, or your hands, to remove still more moisture.

Break 8 eggs into a bowl, beat slightly with fork, and mix in 1 teaspoon salt, ½ teaspoon black pepper, ¼ teaspoon each ground nutmeg and thyme, and ⅓ cup grated Parmesan cheese. Stir in spinach, tearing into shreds as you add it. Over a low flame, melt 2½ tablespoons butter in a skillet or saucepan of suitable size. Turn flame high and pour in egg-spinach mixture. Cook until well set on one side, slide onto a plate, melt a dab more butter in pan, turn frittata back into it, and then cook till well set on the second side. Cut in wedges to serve.

Lima Beans à la Smitane

Two packages frozen, or two 1-pound cans, baby green lima beans may be used. For frozen, cook as directed on the package and drain. For canned, simply drain. Put the drained beans in the top of a double boiler, off the fire. Put the bottom of double boiler, with 1 inch water in it, over high flame to heat. Mix ½ pint (1 cup) sour cream with 2 tablespoons finely chopped shallot, white onion, or scallion, 1 tablespoon Dijon-style prepared mustard, and salt and coarse-ground black pepper to taste. Spoon over lima beans. Sprinkle with paprika, cover, put over bottom of double boiler, and heat 20 minutes.

Apricot Trifle

Stale or fresh ladyfingers, sponge cake, pound cake or angel food may be used. Drain into a saucepan the juice from one 29-ounce can apricot halves. Put fruit into a bowl, pour 4–5 tablespoons Cointreau, curaçao, or any fruit liqueur over fruit, and set aside to marinate. Over high heat, bring the fruit syrup to a boil and cook rapidly until reduced by half; pour over apricots.

Put slices of cake, spread thinly with currant jelly, in individual bowls. Spoon fruit and syrup over cake and serve.

FROMAGE BOURBONNAIS
BASS FILLETS RIMINESE
CORN CREOLE
EGGPLANT DORCHESTER
ORANGES ESTELLA

Fromage Bourbonnais

Several hours ahead, remove from icebox two 3-ounce packages cream cheese and one 4-ounce package Liederkranz cheese. When ready to prepare, mix the two cheeses together in a bowl and add 5 tablespoons sour cream or fresh heavy cream, 1 teaspoon celery seed, ½ teaspoon garlic salt, and salt and coarse-ground black pepper to taste. Beat or stir until mixture has a smooth, creamy texture. Stir in ¼ cup Madeira, Marsala, or sherry. Chill till ready to serve.

Bass Fillets Riminese

Depending on size, allow 1 or ½ fillet per person. Drain a 1-pound can sliced potatoes and two 3-ounce cans sliced mushrooms. Melt 4 tablespoons (½ stick) butter in a large skillet over medium flame; sauté fillets till brown on both sides and remove from skillet. Arrange sliced potatoes in bottom of skillet, strew mushrooms over potatoes, and lay fish on top. Pour over the fish the contents of 1 can condensed cream of mushroom soup diluted with ½ cup dry white wine, top off with 1 thinly sliced lemon, sprinkle with rosemary leaves, cover, and cook only till sauce begins to bubble.

Corn Creole

In a saucepan or skillet, heat 2½ ounces olive oil over low flame. Slice 8 scallions, including tops, and dice coarsely 1 green pepper, pith and seeds removed. When oil is hot, sauté them.

Into any suitable receptacle strain all the sauce from two 1-pound cans cream-style corn and set aside the corn itself. Stir into the corn sauce half of a 6-ounce can of tomato paste, 2 tablespoons imitation bacon bits, ¼ teaspoon dried rosemary leaves, 2 tablespoons minced parsley, fresh or dried, salt and coarse-ground black pepper to taste.

Stir drained corn into scallion–green pepper mixture, and sauté until corn merely starts to take on a tan. Then stir in corn liquid and tomato paste, blend, set flame as low as possible, and cook until thoroughly heated through. Remove and keep hot over two asbestos pads, to free the burner.

Eggplant Dorchester

Peel one eggplant about 8 inches long and cut crosswise into inch-thick slices. From the center of each slice cut out a 2-inch circle, and set aside into a bowl. Put a large skillet over high flame to heat, and pour 2 tablespoons olive oil into it. While oil is heating, with a fork mash the eggplant in the bowl till pulpy. Add to it ½ teaspoon garlic salt, 4 tablespoons chopped black olives, 1 finely chopped small white onion, salt and pepper, and mix well. When oil is hot, put eggplant rings in skillet and sauté on one side till brown. Turn, reduce flame to very low, and with spoon fill the center of the eggplant rings with the mixture in the bowl. Sauté till second side is brown. Sprinkle with grated Parmesan cheese, cover, and cook 5 minutes longer, then remove skillet, put over two heated asbestos pads to keep warm and free the burner for the dessert.

Oranges Estella

With a very sharp knife, peel the skins of 4 oranges, taking care not to include any of the bitter white outer coating of the flesh. If by chance any does come off, remove from peel with knife. Cut peel into julienne strips. Put the strips in a saucepan, cover with rum, bourbon, or brandy, and set aside.

Strip off and discard the white pith from the oranges. Slice them and arrange in a large skillet, then dot the slices with 2 tablespoons butter and 2 tablespoons sugar. Set skillet over low heat, cover, and cook for 10 minutes. On the other burner, over low flame, place the saucepan with peel and spirits, then add ½ cup maple syrup or any other syrup on hand, or a mixture of ⅓ cup water and 3 tablespoons sugar. Bring to a boil and cook till syrup is reduced slightly. Pour over orange slices and serve hot, with or without cream.

GUACAMOLE CHEZ MOI
CURRIED LOBSTER SALAD
ASPARAGUS VINAIGRETTE
GREEN PEPPERS AND CELERY À LA GRECQUE
HOT GARLIC-SESAME BISCUITS
WALNUT SPICE CAKE

Guacamole Chez Moi

The recipe for this appetizer is given on page 82.

Curried Lobster Salad

Use the meat from either 2 boiled lobsters, about 1½ to 2 pounds each, or from 2 packages frozen lobster tails, cooked according to directions on the package and cooled, or from three 5-ounce cans lobster meat, picked over carefully. Dice lobster coarsely and put into a heavy plastic bag. Add 1 cup sliced canned water chestnuts, drained and rinsed well in cold water, ⅓ cup minced scallions, tops included, ½ diced peeled cucumber with seeds and center removed, and ¼ cup toasted slivered almonds. Close bag tightly and shake well to mix.

Stir together 5 tablespoons each mayonnaise and sour cream and stir in 2 teaspoons or more curry powder (as you prefer), 1 tablespoon soy sauce, the juice of ½ lime or 1 tablespoon bottled unsweetened lime juice, and salt and white pepper to taste. Add to lobster mixture and shake well.

Line a salad bowl with leaves of any mild-flavored salad greens, add dressed lobster mixture, and sprinkle with paprika.

Asparagus Vinaigrette

Use 25 stalks precooked fresh asparagus, 2 packages cooked and cooled frozen asparagus spears, or 2 drained 1-pound cans green asparagus spears.

Over medium flame, heat asparagus, laid neatly side by side, in top of your largest double boiler with 1½ inches water in lower section. While asparagus is heating, make vinaigrette sauce.

Put into a large-mouthed screw-top jar, or a bowl, ½ teaspoon salt, ¼ teaspoon each coarse-ground black pepper, dry mustard, and celery salt, and a very scant ¼ teaspoon sugar. Add 2½ tablespoons olive or vegetable oil, or any combination of the two, and 1 tablespoon white wine vinegar. Shake or beat well, then add 1 teaspoon dehydrated or minced fresh parsley, ¼ teaspoon each dried tarragon leaves, chervil leaves, and frozen or dried chives, and ½ teaspoon chopped capers. Shake or beat again, pour over hot asparagus, and set aside to cool (it need not not be refrigerated).

Green Peppers and Celery à la Grecque

Cut crosswise, into broad diagonal slices, 4 stalks celery and 2 medium-sized green peppers, pith and seeds removed.

Off the stove, in a saucepan or skillet, combine 4 tablespoons olive or vegetable oil, or any combination of the two, the juice of 1 lemon or 2 tablespoons bottled lemon juice, 1 split clove of garlic or ⅛ teaspoon dried minced garlic, ½ teaspoon salt, 6 peppercorns, 1 bay leaf, and ¼ teaspoon dried tarragon leaves. Add the vegetables and enough hot water barely to cover. Stir well. Cook over low heat no more than 7 minutes but do not turn off the flame. With a slotted spoon, remove vegetables, set aside and continue to cook the liquid until it is reduced by half. Pour the hot liquid over the vegetables and let cool. This may be refrigerated when cooled, though it is not necessary.

Walnut Spice Cake

Sift into a bowl the contents of 1 box single-layer plain white cake mix, together with 3 tablespoons dry powdered cocoa, 2 teaspoons dry instant coffee, 1 teaspoon baking soda, 1 teaspoon ground ginger, ½ teaspoon allspice, 1½ teaspoons cinnamon, 1 teaspoon salt, and ½ cup brown sugar. Beat in the amount of liquid called for on box, using water, fresh milk, or diluted evaporated milk. Add 1 tablespoon oil and 1 egg. Beat until smooth, stir in ¾ cup walnut meats, and pour batter into 8-by-8-inch buttered cake pan.

Over a high flame, preheat for 10 minutes a heavy 12-inch dome-lidded skillet with a rack placed in it. Put cake pan on rack in skillet, turn flame low, cover, and cook 30 minutes without lifting cover. Then lift cover and touch top of cake with a finger tip. If it springs back into position, cake is done. If not, re-cover and continue cooking 5–10 minutes longer.

When done, turn off flame, remove cake pan but leave hot skillet on stove. Slide a knife or narrow spatula all around the inside of the pan to loosen cake, turn onto a plate, let cool, and serve in squares or slices.

Hot Garlic-Sesame Biscuits

An adaptation of Skillet Biscuits II (page 97), with these changes: before adding liquid to the mix, blend in ½ teaspoon garlic powder (not garlic salt), ½ teaspoon salt and ¼ cup minced parsley, fresh or dried. After dough is in skillet, strew generously with sesame seeds, then cook and serve hot.

KIPPERS WITH VINEGAR

CASSOULET FROM CANS

SAUERKRAUT SLAW II

BLACKBERRY COBBLERETTES

Kippers with Vinegar

Put into a bowl two 7-ounce cans kipper fillets and with fingers flake coarsely. Sprinkle 1 tablespoon red wine vinegar over kippers and set aside. In another bowl, combine ⅓ cup mayonnaise, 1 teaspoon any preferred kind of prepared mustard, 2 shakes Tabasco sauce, 1 teaspoon paprika, 2 tablespoons heavy sweet cream, or sour cream, or undiluted evaporated milk, and salt and coarse-ground black pepper to taste. Blend in the kippers and serve with any soft or crisp dark rye or pumpernickel bread.

Cassoulet from Cans

Over medium flame, in a large skillet heat 2 tablespoons olive or vegetable oil. Slice 2 medium-sized yellow onions, and when oil is hot, sauté onions till golden. Add 2 tablespoons flour, stir till smooth, add ½ cup dry white wine, and turn flame as low as possible. Drain and cut into thirds two 9-ounce cans Vienna or "hot" Italian sausages. Add to onions with 1 cup tomato sauce, two 8-ounce cans Boston-style baked beans. Open two 20-ounce cans lamb stew, and with fingers remove all potatoes, then add stew to skillet. Season with 1 teaspoon each dried thyme leaves, marjoram leaves, and crumbled bay leaf. Cover and simmer over two asbestos pads 20–25 minutes. Garnish with fresh or dehydrated parsley before serving.

Sauerkraut Slaw II

Use recipe for Sauerkraut Slaw I on page 137, but for this version add 1 more medium-sized onion and ½ cup sour cream, instead of French dressing and, just before serving, stir in 3 tablespoons caraway seeds.

Blackberry Cobblerettes

Butter well four crockery coffee mugs. Place a rack and 2½ inches water in a large kettle and heat till simmering.

While water is heating, drain one 15-ounce can blackberries, divide fruit evenly among the mugs, and add to each mug 1 teaspoon bourbon, or dark rum, or brandy and 1 teaspoon red or black currant jelly.

In a plastic bag, squeeze into batter 1 cup biscuit mix, ½ cup sugar, 1 slightly beaten egg, and ⅓ cup any kind of liquid milk. Pour over berries, filling each cup ½ full. Tie foil over each cup, set cups on rack in kettle, cover, lower flame, and steam 30 minutes. Serve hot.

Raft-Up Repasts

It's a raft-up when three, four, or five boats assemble by pre-arrangement in fair weather, usually in the mid-afternoon or later. Boat ties to boat, snugly side by side, then everybody moves from one craft to another, mingling, chatting, comparing notes, and in no time there's a party going among the group of friends and acquaintances.

The menus and recipes that follow are planned with this in mind, and take for granted that the only good solution to feeding one and all is for the cooks jointly to come up with a progressive feast, each one taking over as his or her responsibility one course of the repast. Who does what we leave entirely to the organizer of the feed—and there must be one, or chaos will ensue.

Because a raft-up is a sociable occasion involving a number of people, the meal is bound to be of a buffet nature, and the quantities prepared sufficient for at least twelve. So, in this chapter only, we vary the rule that all recipes in the book are for four persons. All herein are for twelve to fifteen.

Each menu includes four different appetizers, one main dish, two satellite dishes, bread and butter of a stated variety, and dessert.

~

CHEDDAR CHEESE SPREAD WITH PISTACHIOS
CANNED PÂTÉ WITH BACON
CLAM DIP CHEZ MOI
GARLIC OLIVES AND CHERRY TOMATOES
TUNA AND CECI SALAD
HOT POTATO CHIPS
CUCUMBER AND HARD-BOILED EGG GREEN SALAD
BUTTERED TRIANGLES OF THIN PUMPERNICKEL
JEANNE'S CHOCOLATE TRIUMPH

Cheddar Cheese Spread with Pistachios

This spread may be fixed a day ahead, refrigerated, and brought to galley temperature before serving.

Grate 2 pounds white cheddar cheese medium-fine and add gradually, while stirring, 1½ cups heavy sweet cream or sour cream. Stir or beat until smooth and of spreading consistency, then work in evenly 1½ cups whole shelled pistachios. Season well with salt and white pepper, stir in 5 tablespoons port wine, and shape the mixture into a mound or a roll. Do not refrigerate if mixed within 2 hours of serving.

Canned Pâté with Bacon

In a medium-sized saucepan, over a low flame, put to melt 4 tablespoons butter. While it is melting, chop finely 2 golf-ball–sized white onions and 1 clove garlic; then sauté until golden and transparent. Remove from stove, stir in 3 tablespoons brandy, or bourbon, or rum and the juice of ½ lemon or 1 tablespoon bottled lemon juice. Season well with salt and black pepper, add ¾ cup cooked, cold, crumbled, crisp bacon or one 1⅝-ounce jar imitation bacon bits. Empty three 5½-ounce cans liver pâté spread into saucepan and combine thoroughly. Refrigerate until ready to serve.

Clam Dip Chez Moi

In a bowl, mash thoroughly two 8-ounce packages softened cream cheese, add ¾ cup cold, cooked, crumbled, crisp bacon or one 1⅝-ounce jar imitation bacon bits, blend in 1½ cups sour cream and 1 tablespoon prepared horseradish. Add ¼ teaspoon

Tabasco sauce, the juice of 3 lemons or 6 tablespoons bottled lemon juice, salt, black pepper, ½ cup chili sauce and blend well. Drain and rinse well two 8-ounce cans minced (not chopped) clams and stir thoroughly into dip. Refrigerate at least 1 hour.

Garlic Olives and Cherry Tomatoes

The olives must be prepared at least a day ahead. Drain well two 1-pound cans each green and black olives. Place in a well-closed container. Mince finely 4 cloves garlic and put in a bowl or sizeable screw-top jar with large mouth. Add 16 crushed peppercorns, the juice of 1 lemon, 4 tablespoons red wine vinegar, and 1 cup olive oil. Beat well and pour over olives. Close container and marinate overnight at galley temperature. After breakfast the next day, put into icebox to chill.

Remove the stems from four 1-pint baskets of cherry tomatoes, wash well, and put into a large bowl or other container. Drain the dressing from the olives into a jar and save. Add olives to tomatoes, toss lightly, and serve with toothpicks.

Tuna and Ceci Salad

Peel and cut into quarters lengthwise 2 fairly large red onions, then slice each quarter thinly (none of the slices should be more than 1 inch long). Put into a large bowl or kettle. Mince finely 5 cloves garlic, add to onions, cover just barely with olive oil, and set aside to soak for 1 hour.

Drain well three 1-pound cans or two 29-ounce cans *ceci* beans (in Spanish, *garbanzos;* in English, chick-peas), and stir into onion-garlic mixture. Drain four 6½-ounce cans, or the equivalent, of tuna, and add in large chunks to the beans. Slice 2 bunches scallions, including green tops, and cut 3 green peppers, pith and seeds removed, into quarters vertically, then crosswise into thin slices. Scrub, clean, and dice coarsely 1 bunch radishes. Add scallions, green pepper, and radishes to salad. Into a bowl, or large-mouthed screw-top jar, put the juice of 2 lemons or 4 tablespoons bottled lemon juice, ½ cup red wine vinegar, salt, black pepper, 2 tablespoons dry mustard, 1½ teaspoons Worcestershire sauce, 1 teaspoon sugar, 3 teaspoons celery seed, and ½ cup olive or vegetable oil or any combination of the two. Beat or shake well, pour over salad, and toss thoroughly.

Cucumber and Hard-Boiled Egg Green Salad

Hard-boil 6 eggs ahead of time.

Wash well, and shake as dry as possible, the broken-up leaves of 2 large heads romaine, 1 large head escarole, 2 medium-sized heads chicory, and 2 large heads Boston lettuce. Set aside on towels or in large colander.

In capacious salad bowl, kettle, or enamel or plastic dishpan or pail, peel and dice 6 cucumbers. Add hard-boiled eggs, cut first into eighths lengthwise, then each eighth cut into thirds crosswise, ½ cup parsley flakes and toss well.

In any suitable receptacle, put 2 teaspoons each salt, coarse-ground black pepper, and dry mustard, 1 teaspoon sugar, 2 teaspoons garlic salt, the juice of ½ lemon, 1 teaspoon Worcestershire sauce, 1 teaspoon capers, 8 green olives, chopped, 1 teaspoon each dried leaves of tarragon, chervil, and thyme, ⅓ cup white wine vinegar, and 2 cups olive or vegetable oil, or any combination of the two that you prefer. Beat or shake well. Pour over cucumber and eggs and stir thoroughly. Just before serving, add the greens and toss well.

Jeanne's Chocolate Triumph

Over a direct flame, bring ½ cup water to a boil in the top of your largest double boiler, dissolve in it 2 teaspoons instant coffee, and cut up and add 3 ounces sweet chocolate and 2 ounces unsweetened chocolate. Place over lower section of double boiler with 1½ inches water in it, and turn flame low.

While chocolate is melting, separate 1 dozen eggs and beat egg yolks thoroughly. When chocolate has melted, stir in egg yolks and cook 1 minute. Remove from stove, separate the two parts of the double boiler, stir ¼ cup dark rum into chocolate mixture, and set aside to cool.

Meanwhile, beat egg whites until light and airy but not stiff; blend into chocolate mixture. Put into a glass or plastic or enamel bowl; chill and serve in cups, with or without whipped cream on top.

PARMESAN-GARLIC SPREAD
SKILLET MUSHROOM CAPS, COLD
PICKLED SHRIMPS
CHIPPED BEEF ROLL-UPS
COLD SLICED TURKEY
RATATOUILLE
POTATO SALAD V
DATE-NUT SQUARES

Parmesan-Garlic Spread

Set aside to soften in a bowl 1½ pounds (6 sticks) butter. Into a bowl or large-mouthed screw-top jar put ¾ cup olive oil and one whole pod, or 10 cloves, finely minced garlic. Add 1 teaspoon each oregano and basil, 3 tablespoons Worcestershire sauce, ½ cup finely chopped fresh, dried, or frozen chives, 3 table-spoons fresh or dried chopped parsley, and 3 teaspoons coarse-ground black pepper.

When butter is soft, blend in thoroughly 3 cups grated Parmesan cheese. Beat dressing well and blend thoroughly into butter-cheese mixture. If not of conveniently spreadable consistency, blend in enough heavy cream, sour cream, or undiluted evaporated milk to make it so.

Let stand at galley temperature for 2 hours to ripen, then chill until ready to serve with any bread or crackers or hard-bread or combination of them that you fancy.

Skillet Mushroom Caps, Cold

After washing and scrubbing 1½ pounds medium to large mushrooms, remove and chop stems and set stems aside. Over medium flames, using two large skillets, in enough olive oil barely to cover the bottom, sauté the mushroom caps, stem side up, for 3–4 minutes, remove from stove and let cool. Slide the mushroom caps from one skillet onto a platter or very large plate and put skillet back on stove over high-medium flame to reheat. When hot, add ¾ cup olive oil, turn flame to medium and, while oil is heating, drain and chop two 2-ounce cans flat anchovy fillets and 3 cloves garlic, and measure out 1½ cups flavored toasted bread crumbs and ¾ cup parsley flakes.

Add garlic and anchovies to oil, stir, and sauté 2 minutes. Stir in chopped mushroom stems and sauté 6 minutes more. Turn off flame, stir in parsley and bread crumbs, and let cool. Put ½ cup mayonnaise in a bowl, stir in 4 tablespoons sour cream, the juice of 1 lemon or 3 tablespoons bottled lemon juice, and salt and coarse-ground black pepper to taste. Blend well with the skillet mixture, and use this to fill the mushroom caps, generously garnishing with paprika.

Pickled Shrimp

Three hours before serving, put into a big bowl 60 cooked and chilled medium-sized shrimp, or 6 well-drained 4½-ounce cans jumbo shrimp. Slice very, very thinly 3 medium-sized white onions, chop finely 3 cloves garlic, and peel, seed, and chop coarsely 6 medium tomatoes. Stir all into shrimp. Mash well 1 small ripe avocado, peel and pit removed; place in a separate bowl and add 2 cups olive or salad oil, 1 cup white wine or tarragon vinegar, 1 teaspoon sugar, 2 teaspoons celery seed, and salt and coarse-ground black pepper to taste. Blend well, pour over shrimp mixture, and toss thoroughly. Place in icebox to chill 1 hour before serving.

Chipped Beef Roll-Ups

Three hours before preparing, soften three 8-ounce packages cream cheese and, when soft, mash until nearly spreadable. Stir in ¾ cup sour or sweet cream or undiluted evaporated milk, ⅓ cup bottled horseradish, ½ cup dehydrated parsley flakes, salt and coarse-ground black pepper to taste, mix well.

Unroll carefully and separate the slices in three 5-ounce jars dried chipped beef and on each slice spread cream-cheese mixture thinly and evenly. Roll into 1-inch rolls and place with care in a heavy plastic bag; close bag tightly and chill. Serve with toothpicks.

Cold Sliced Turkey

Slice thinly and arrange on one or two platters the meat from one 5- to 6-pound roast turkey brought on board from home, or 3 pounds store-bought sliced turkey, or sliced meat from one 3- to 4-pound can boned roast turkey.

Ratatouille

For twelve to fifteen people, you will need two 4-quart pots with covers.

Prepare vegetables first, each in a separate receptacle. Slice thinly 6 large yellow onions; quarter lengthwise 8 green peppers, pith and seeds removed; cut into $\frac{1}{4}$-inch slices 2 unpeeled medium-sized eggplants, 10 zucchini the size of a small cucumber, and 10 medium-sized tomatoes; cut into thirds crosswise $1\frac{1}{4}$ pounds green beans with ends snipped off; and slice thinly 6 cloves of garlic.

Over medium flame, heat in each pot $\frac{1}{4}$ cup olive oil with 8 garlic slices for 5 minutes. In layers, add vegetables, seasoning each layer with salt and coarse-ground black pepper and 3 or 4 slices garlic. Dribble 1 tablespoon more olive oil on the surface, cover, turn flame very low, and cook for 35 minutes; at suitable intervals, stir gently three times during cooking. Remove covers and cook 5–10 minutes longer. Serve hot or cold.

Potato Salad V

Early in the day, boil in one big covered pot 12 medium-sized potatoes and 6 eggs. After 10 minutes, remove the eggs, cook potatoes until tender, and let both cool.

To prepare salad, chop coarsely 2 medium-sized red onions, dice coarsely 2 green peppers, pith and seeds removed, chop up one 2-ounce can flat anchovy fillets, slice thickly 24 pitted black olives, and put them all into a large salad bowl. Slice peeled potatoes and eggs fairly thinly, add, and toss.

Mix $\frac{2}{3}$ cup each mayonnaise and sour cream, then stir in juice of 1 lemon, 1 tablespoon prepared horseradish, salt and coarse-ground black pepper to taste. Pour dressing over salad and toss again. Garnish with one $1\frac{5}{8}$-ounce bottle imitation bacon bits. The salad need not be refrigerated.

Date-Nut Squares

On the assumption that two 12-inch dome-lidded heavy aluminum skillets are a rarity in any one galley, we suggest that this dessert be cooked in two batches in one skillet, dividing the batter evenly between two 8-inch-square cake pans.

Place your heavy skillet with a rack in it on high flame to preheat for 10 minutes. Butter cake pans well and set aside. Prepare two boxes date muffin mix as directed, using a stout plastic bag as mixing bowl. Add ¾ pound chocolate bits, sweet or semi-sweet and shake bag to mix well. Squeeze half the batter into each cake pan, spreading smooth. Put one cake pan on rack in skillet, cover, and cook 30 minutes without removing cover.

Remove cake pan, set aside to cool, and repeat with second pan. Cut into squares and serve.

JEANNE'S HOT NIBBLES

SMOKED SALMON ROLLUPS

AVOCADO-FILLED RAW MUSHROOMS

STUFFED DILL PICKLE SLICES

HAM HASH

SKILLET SWEET POTATOES

CREAMED ONIONS AND CELERY WITH

WATER CHESTNUTS

WILD RICE MUFFINS

SKILLET LIMELIGHT PIE

Jeanne's Hot Nibbles

Many different kinds of dry cereals may be used such as Corn or Rice Chex, Quisp, Alpha-Bits, Cheerios, or Mini Shredded Wheat, as well as unsalted nuts (almonds, pecans, walnuts, Brazil nuts, hazelnuts), and also popcorn, potato chips, and corn chips, or a mixture of any or all.

Heat two large skillets over medium flame, and melt 2 tablespoons butter in each. Stir in ½ tablespoon A-1 Sauce or other bottled steak sauce (for instance, Sauce Robert, Sauce Diable, or Sauce Escoffier). Add to each skillet 4 cups cereals, or nuts, or chips, or mixture of these and stir to coat with sauce. Sprinkle each skillet's contents with ½ teaspoon chili powder and ⅛ teaspoon cayenne, and stir again. Cover, turn flame as low as possible, and cook no more than 5 minutes. Drain on paper towels or newspaper, and serve warm.

Smoked Salmon Rollups

Two or three hours before preparing, soften three 8-ounce packages cream cheese. When soft, put in bag or bowl and blend in ½ cup sour cream, ¼ cup mayonnaise, juice of 1 lemon or 3 tablespoons bottled lemon juice, 1 teaspoon orange extract, and 1 tablespoon curry powder.

Cut slices of Nova Scotia or Irish smoked salmon into 3-by-4-inch pieces, spread each slice with cream cheese mixture, roll up, chill 1 hour, and serve with toothpicks.

Avocado-Filled Raw Mushrooms

Scrub well 50 medium-sized fresh mushrooms; remove and discard stems. With top surface uppermost, drain on paper towels or newspaper and sprinkle with lemon juice to prevent discoloration.

Peel and pit 1 large avocado, dice into a bowl, and mash until smooth. Add 1½ teaspoons onion salt, 1 teaspoon celery salt, 2 tablespoons tomato purée, the juice of 1 lemon or 3 tablespoons bottled lemon juice, salt and coarse-ground black pepper to taste, and stir well.

Turn mushroom caps over and fill with avocado, mounding filling in each cap. Dust with paprika and serve on platters.

Stuffed Dill Pickle Slices

Drain a 1-quart jar of large dill pickles into a bowl and save liquid. Cut each pickle in half crosswise and with an apple corer carefully scoop out and discard the center.

Drain and mash smooth one 4½-ounce can shrimp and blend in ¼ cup mayonnaise and 1½ tablespoons chili sauce. Carefully stuff shrimp mixture into each pickle half, place in plastic bag, close tightly, and chill 1 hour or more. When ready to serve, cut stuffed pickles crosswise into ½-inch slices.

Ham Hash

Mince finely 1 golf-ball–sized white onion and 1 green pepper, pith and seeds removed. Add ½ pound medium-sized mushrooms (or four 3-ounce cans chopped mushrooms, drained). Measure out separately ⅔ cup undiluted condensed beef broth and 1 tablespoon Worcestershire. Chop (not too small) enough canned or any other kind of cooked ham to make 3½ cups.

Over a medium flame, heat a large heavy skillet for 7 minutes, and in it melt 4 tablespoons butter. Stir in minced onion, sauté til lightly browned, add green peppers and mushrooms, and cook for 4 minutes. Stir in bouillon, Worcestershire sauce, 1 tablespoon paprika, and salt and coarse-ground black pepper to taste. Add chopped ham and ½ cup grated Parmesan cheese; mix thoroughly. Set flame low, cover, and cook 15 minutes.

Skillet Sweet Potatoes

Line a 12-inch heavy aluminum skillet with foil, keeping foil away from rim of skillet to allow for snug-fitting cover, and over high flame, preheat for 10 minutes.

Use 8 medium-sized precooked yams or sweet potatoes, or two well-drained 2-pound cans unsweetened whole or sliced yams or sweet potatoes, or two 29-ounce cans unsweetened mashed yams or sweet potatoes. Cut all but the last of these into pieces and, in any large receptacle or strong plastic bag, mash well. If you are using previously mashed potatoes, simply empty into any large receptacle or strong plastic bag.

Beat or knead into potatoes ½ cup each softened butter and undiluted evaporated milk or heavy cream, 2 tablespoons sherry, ½ teaspoon ground nutmeg, 1 teaspoon ground cinnamon, and salt and coarse-ground black pepper to taste.

Turn or squeeze potatoes into heated foil-lined skillet, dot with ½ cup butter, sprinkle with 1 teaspoon cinnamon and cover. Turn flame to medium low, and cook 30 minutes without lifting cover.

Creamed Onions and Celery with Water Chestnuts

Drain over a large bowl two 1-pound cans each whole small boiled onions and celery stalks, leaving onions in the cans. Cut celery diagonally into ¾-inch slices and return to cans. Put 2 inches water in the bottom of your largest double boiler and place double boiler over medium flame to heat. Put ¼ cup (½ stick) butter in the top of the double boiler, along with 1 teaspoon salt, ½ teaspoon white pepper, 2 teaspoons dry mustard, and 1 tablespoon Worcestershire sauce. While butter is melting, measure out 4 tablespoons flour; open two 10½-ounce cans condensed cream of celery soup and one 10½-ounce can condensed cream of mushroom soup.

When butter is melted, add flour, blend till smooth, and stir in undiluted soups. Put into sauce ⅓ soup can each white wine wine, reserved vegetable liquid, and undiluted evaporated milk or heavy cream. Stir to blend, and cook until thickened.

When sauce has thickened, stir in onions and celery, cover, set flame very low, and keep hot until ready to serve.

Wild Rice Muffins

Once more, on the assumption that two 12-inch heavy dome-lidded skillets are a rarity in any one galley, we suggest that these muffins be cooked in two batches, one after the other, in one skillet. Divide the batter evenly between two 8-inch square cake pans; after removing from the pan, and cutting into squares, keep the first batch warm in the top of your largest double boiler, with 2 inches water, just off the boil, in the bottom.

Early in the day, or the day before, cook as directed on the package enough wild rice to make 2 cups, cooked.

Butter both cake pans well, and then place your covered, heavy dome-lidded, 12-inch skillet, with a rack in it, on a high flame to preheat for 10 minutes. While skillet is heating, into a heavy plastic bag put 4 cups flour, 2 tablespoons baking powder, 1 teaspoon salt, and cooked rice. Close bag and knead and squeeze to mix well. In any suitable container, combine 3 eggs, 2 cups (16 ounces) undiluted evaporated milk, and 4 tablespoons (¼ cup) vegetable oil. Beat or shake well to blend, add to dry ingredients, reclose bag tightly, and knead and squeeze to mix thoroughly and form a smooth batter.

Divide batter evenly between the cake pans, spreading smooth, place one pan on rack in skillet, lower flame to high-medium, cover, and cook 30 minutes without lifting cover. If muffins do not test done, cook 10 minutes longer.

Remove cake pan, set aside to cool for 10 minutes, and repeat with second pan. After 10 minutes, cut muffins in first pan into squares, and keep warm as directed above.

Skillet Limelight Pie

This dessert should be made early in the day.

Put into a heavy plastic bag 28 each of gingersnaps and vanilla wafers or the equivalent, close bag tightly, and roll with a filled quart bottle till cookies are crushed finely. Over two low flames, set two 8-inch pie pans with 3 tablespoons butter in each. When butter is melted, remove pans from heat, tilt each from side to side to coat pan sides and bottom, and then pour excess butter into bag with crushed cookies. Squeeze to blend well, add crumb mixture to the pans, dividing evenly, press mixture in smooth, even layer over bottom and sides of each pan, and set aside.

Over a high flame, put a 12-inch covered heavy dome-lidded skillet, with a rack in it, to preheat for 10 minutes. Then place one pie pan on the rack, cover, and bake for 10 minutes without lifting cover. Remove pan, set aside to cool, and repeat with second pie pan, cooking that in turn when done.

While crusts are cooling, over a medium flame put to heat the bottom of a large double boiler with 2 inches water in it. Separate 4 eggs, putting the yolks into the top of the double boiler, off the stove. Add ½ cup fresh lime juice or bottled unsweetened lime juice, ½ cup sugar and stir well. Measure out a second ½ cup sugar and set aside, put 1 envelope unflavored gelatin into ½ cup water to soften.

Cook egg-yolk mixture over simmering water for 10 minutes or until somewhat thickened, and dissolve gelatin-water mixture into it. Remove top of double boiler at once from stove and let cool, then put into icebox to chill until syrupy. Meanwhile, beat egg whites until foamy but not stiff, gradually stir in the second ½ cup sugar, beating all the while, and, lastly, 3 tablespoons dark rum. Fold into syrupy lime mixture, pour into crusts, and chill several hours.

TAPENADE
CHICKEN APPETIZERS
DILLED RAW CARROTS
EGGPLANT CUBES MARINARA
FRENCH BREAD
DELPHIC PASTA PIE
SALAD OF THREE GREEN VEGETABLES
BREAD STICKS
WATERMELON SHERRY COMPOTE

Tapenade

Into a bowl, put two 6½-ounce cans tuna fish with oil, and mash finely. Drain into same bowl the oil from six 2-ounce cans flat anchovy fillets. Chop anchovies, then mash finely and stir into tuna fish. Crush ½ cup capers; drain, chop, and crush one 1-pound can pitted black olives; mince finely 3 large cloves garlic; and add all to the tuna fish. Pour in the juice of 4 lemons or ½ cup bottled lemon juice. Stir to blend thoroughly, then add, while stirring constantly, 1 cup olive oil. Blend in ½ cup brandy. Mixture should be the consistency of mayonnaise. Chill until ready to serve.

Chicken Appetizers

Put the contents of three 5-ounce jars zesty cheese spread, or the equivalent amount from a large jar, into a roomy bowl, and beat until creamy, then beat in ½ cup sour cream or undiluted evaporated milk. Pull apart and dice finely the meat from two 13-ounce cans boned chicken or turkey. Stir into cheese along with salt and coarse-ground black pepper to taste, ¼ teaspoon cayenne, and 1 teaspoon Worcestershire sauce. Serve at galley temperature.

Dilled Raw Carrots

These should be prepared 4 to 5 days ahead.

From two 1-quart jars dill pickles, remove all pickles, leaving brine. Reserving 6 pickles, put balance into one or two large jars filled with half and half water and mild vinegar, cover tightly, shake well, and put aside for future use. Chop finely the reserved pickles and put half in each jar of brine.

Scrape 2 bunches raw carrots, slice lengthwise into thin sticks, divide evenly between the two jars of brine, and set aside to ripen till ready to serve.

Eggplant Cubes Marinara

Prepare these a day ahead. Cut 2 large unpeeled eggplants into ½-inch cubes, put into a large saucepan, cover with cold water, bring to a boil over high flame, and cook uncovered 5 minutes. Remove from stove, drain very well, and put at once into a salad bowl or strong plastic bag. In any suitable receptacle combine ¾ cup white wine vinegar, ¼ cup dry white wine, 4 finely minced cloves garlic, 1 tablespoon salt, 1 teaspoon coarse-ground black pepper, 2 tablespoons parsley flakes, 1 cup sliced pimiento-stuffed green olives, and 1 teaspoon each dried oregano and basil. Pour over eggplant, cover tightly, cool, and let stand in icebox overnight. Before serving, add 1½ cups Italian olive oil, and toss or shake lightly. Serve in a bowl with toothpicks.

Delphic Pasta Pie

Over a high flame bring to a vigorous boil a very large kettle three-quarters full of water, add two 1-pound boxes fettuccini, or green noodles, and dribble over the water about 3 tablespoons oil to prevent boiling over. Half cover, cook 9 minutes, remove from stove, drain, return to kettle and set aside.

Slice thinly two large white onions. Remove meat from four 1-pound cans hamburgers, and break into small pieces. Reserve sauce in cans.

Over medium flames, melt 2 tablespoons butter in each of two large skillets, divide onions between the skillets, and sauté until a light brown. Stir meat into the onions, dividing evenly between skillets, and cook 5 minutes. Add to each skillet one 8-ounce can tomato sauce, half a 6-ounce can tomato paste, half the reserved meat sauce, 1 teaspoon salt, ½ teaspoon coarse-ground black pepper, and 1 teaspoon cinnamon. Stir well, lower flame, and cook uncovered for ½ hour, or until sauce is greatly reduced.

Toss pasta in kettle with ½ cup soft butter and 12 ounces (1½ cups) grated Parmesan or Romano cheese, or a mixture of the two in any proportion. Turn meat mixtures into the pasta, stir thoroughly, put kettle over low flame, cover, insert flame-tamer or two or three asbestos pads, and heat till ready to serve.

Salad of Three Green Vegetables

Prepare the dressing in advance in the following manner:

Into any suitable receptacle or a large-mouthed screw-top jar, pour 1 cup olive, vegetable or salad oil, ¾ cup white wine vinegar or, for a milder flavor, the same amount of half-and-half dry white wine and any non-wine mild vinegar. Add a scant ½ teaspoon sugar and 1 teaspoon each celery salt, onion salt, garlic salt, dry mustard, and salt. Shake or beat well, then stir in 1 tablespoon minced parsley, fresh or dried, 1 teaspoon Worcestershire sauce and ¼ teaspoon each dried leaves of thyme, marjoram, and tarragon. Shake or beat once more. Refrigeration is not necessary.

This non-lettuce salad uses 2 pounds (or the equivalent) each of green beans, asparagus tips, and peas (fresh, frozen or canned or a mixture thereof) marinated, after cooking and draining, in the dressing for at least an hour. In a large vessel, mix them well, add dressing, and toss thoroughly. It may, before serving, be garnished in several ways or not at all.

Watermelon Sherry Compote

Two to three hours before serving, cut ½ watermelon into large but manageable chunks, remove seeds, and scoop out the flesh into balls with a vegetable cutter. Put into any very large vessel, sprinkle with ⅔ cup superfine sugar, toss gently until sugar is dissolved, pour 1 pint sherry over, and toss gently again. Ladle the fruit into three 1-quart airtight containers, distributing the juices as evenly as possible, and chill.

Variation: Use ¼ watermelon and 1 fresh pineapple or two 1-pound drained cans cored whole pineapple, cut into balls, and toss together gently before seasoning.

INDONESIAN COCONUT
CUCUMBER SPREAD
CHILI SPREAD, EXTRA-HOT
MÜNSTER CHEESE AND RAW ONION CANAPÉS
SKILLET TAMALE PIE
TIJUANA SALAD
FRIJOLES REFRITOS II
TORTILLAS
BANANA-PINEAPPLE COMPOTE

Indonesian Coconut

Pierce the eyes of a small fresh coconut; drain off and discard the liquid. With a hammer, break the coconut into three or four pieces, remove flesh from shell by levering with the point of a strong knife, grate the coconut flesh coarsely, and set aside.

Open one 2-ounce can shrimp paste, chop coarsely 2 large white onions and ½ cup Macadamia nuts, mince finely 3 cloves garlic, and measure out 3 tablespoons brown sugar, ¼ cup ground hot red peppers, and ⅓ cup soy sauce.

Over a medium flame, in a large skillet, heat 3 tablespoons peanut oil, add onions and garlic, sauté till golden, turn flame low, and stir in grated coconut, shrimp paste, and all other ingredients except Macadamia nuts. Cook gently, stirring constantly, until fairly dry and lightly browned. Over a medium flame, on the other burner, put your largest double boiler with 2 inches water in the bottom; cover and heat.

When skillet mixture is done, stir in Macadamia nuts, turn mixture into top of double boiler, and keep hot. Serve as "finger food."

Cucumber Spread

In any suitable vessel, soften three 8-ounce packages cream cheese and mash till smooth. Stir in 3 tablespoons sour cream, 1 tablespoon each paprika, celery salt, and Worcestershire sauce, and salt and coarse-ground black pepper to taste.

Peel, seed and grate coarsely 4 medium-sized cucumbers, add, with their juice, to cream cheese mixture, and stir until well blended, then chill.

Chili Spread, Extra-Hot

Into any suitable large vessel, empty two 12-ounce cans chili (the kind without meat), and mash well. Grate medium-fine 2 large white onions, and stir into chili with 1 tablespoon chili powder, 1 tablespoon celery salt, ¼ teaspoon Tabasco sauce, and juice of 1 lemon or 2 tablespoons bottled lemon juice. Chill.

Münster Cheese and Raw Onion Canapés

Cut into 1-inch squares 1½ pounds sliced Münster cheese. Peel and slice very thinly 4 golf-ball–sized white onions, put 1 slice onion on half of the cheese squares, spread onion slices thinly with Dijon-style prepared mustard, cover with another cheese square, spear with toothpick, and dust with salt and paprika. Serve on any flat, portable surface.

Skillet Tamale Pie

Chop coarsely 2 large yellow onions and 2 large green peppers, pith and seeds removed. Remove meat from three 1-pound cans hamburgers and break meat into small chunks. Reserve sauce in cans. Over a medium flame, in your largest skillet, heat 3 tablespoons oil, add onions and green peppers, and sauté till brown. Meanwhile, over a medium flame, put 5 cups water on to boil in a large saucepan. Measure out 1½ cups cornmeal, open one 29-ounce can whole tomatoes, and add meat to onions and green peppers. Stir into skillet the sauce from the meat cans, with 1 tablespoon Worcestershire sauce, 2 tablespoons chili powder, 2 tablespoons salt, ½ teaspoon coarse-ground black pepper, 4 or 5 drops Tabasco sauce, 2 tablespoons parsley flakes, and the tomatoes. When heated, turn off flame and pour into any suitable vessel, returning emptied skillet to stove.

When water boils, add cornmeal gradually to it, stirring to prevent lumps. Cover, and cook 9 or 10 minutes. One package of instant-cooking cornmeal also may be used. Follow directions on package.

Into a heavy plastic bag, empty one box corn muffin mix and add one 12-ounce can corn kernels, ⅓ cup undiluted evaporated milk, 1½ teaspoons onion salt, 3 or 4 drops Tabasco sauce, 2 tablespoons parsley flakes, and 2 egg yolks. Close tightly, and squeeze to form a lumpy batter. Beat 2 egg whites and fold batter into them.

Line the skillet in which the meat mixture was cooked with buttered foil, cover foil surface smoothly with cornmeal mush, and fold foil in and away from rim of skillet so that cover will fit tightly. Turn meat mixture into mush, spoon corn muffin batter over it, sprinkle liberally with paprika, cover snugly, insert flame-tamer or two or three asbestos pads under skillet, and cook over medium-low flame for 30 minutes without lifting cover.

Tijuana Salad

Dice coarsely into a bowl the flesh of 4 large or 6 medium avocados, toss gently with the juice of 2 lemons or 6 tablespoons bottled lemon juice, and chill.

Slice thinly 2 small white onions and put in a bowl. Peel 3 medium oranges and remove all white pith on surface and membranes between sections; dice coarsely, and add to onions with whatever juice you can save. Slice pimiento-stuffed olives drained from one 2-ounce jar, and add to oranges and onions. Pour over the mixture 4 tablespoons each olive oil and white wine vinegar, season to taste with salt and coarse-ground black pepper, and toss well.

Line a large salad bowl with the leaves of any salad greens, pile avocado cubes in center, pour orange-onion dressing over and toss gently.

Frijoles Refritos II

In any large receptacle, to two well-drained 29-ounce cans red kidney beans, add 2 tablespoons chili powder, 1 tablespoon salt, 1 teaspoon coarse-ground black pepper, one $1\frac{5}{8}$-ounce jar imitation bacon bits, and 1 cup oil, bacon fat, meat drippings, or lard. Stir all together, then mash until smooth.

Over medium flame, heat a large heavy skillet for 5 minutes. Turn bean mixture into it and cook, stirring frequently, until all fat is absorbed. Stir in $\frac{1}{2}$ cup grated cheddar cheese and cook until cheese is melted. Keep hot.

Tortillas

Use three 10-ounce cans tortillas, and cook according to directions on cans. Keep hot in the top of your largest double boiler over simmering water and serve as a bread.

Banana-Pineapple Compote

Drain syrup from two 29-ounce cans pineapple chunks into a saucepan, and put fruit aside. Put 6 peeled and thinly sliced bananas into a bowl; toss gently at once with juice of 2 lemons or 4 tablespoons bottled lemon juice. Add 1 cup grated coconut, 2 teaspoons ground cinnamon, ½ teaspoon each ground nutmeg and cloves, and the pineapple chunks. Toss again and set aside.

Over medium-high flame, bring syrup to a boil in an uncovered saucepan and cook till reduced by half. Let cool, stir in ½ cup dark rum, and pour over fruit. Stir gently and chill until ready to serve.

CANTALOUPE CUBES AND CHIPPED BEEF

MUSTARDY SHRIMP

RADISHES AND SCALLIONS

VINE LEAVES

CHICKEN ORIENTALE—HOT CHINESE NOODLES

CHINESE VEGETABLES IN OYSTER SAUCE

BRANDIED PEACHES AND KUMQUATS

FORTUNE COOKIES

Cantaloupe Cubes and Chipped Beef

Dice into ¾-inch cubes the flesh of 2 large cantaloupes, seeds removed. Unroll slices from two 5-ounce jars dried beef, and cut into ½-by-1-inch picees. Roll a piece of beef around each cantaloupe cube, fasten with toothpick, chill, and serve.

Mustardy Shrimp

Into a bowl, put well-drained shrimp from three 4½-ounce cans, mash thoroughly, and add juice of 1 lemon or 3 tablespoons bottled lemon juice, 2 tablespoons Dijon-style prepared mustard, salt, coarse-ground black pepper, and 4 tablespoons sour cream. Mix until of spreadable consistency. Chill before serving.

Radishes and Scallions

Use 8 bunches fresh radishes and snip radishes from leaves. Place in colander, and run cold water over, to remove surface dirt. Spread several thicknesses of newspaper or paper towels on handiest surface. Scrub radishes well and remove roots, stem ends, and any imperfections on surface. Place each radish, as done, to drain on paper towels or newspapers.

Cut root ends off scallions, peel off outer layer, cut to desired length, wash well, and lay out to drain on newspaper or paper towels in same manner as radishes.

Wrap each variety of vegetable in its own paper or cloth towel, and refrigerate until ready to serve.

Vine Leaves

Drain liquid from three 14-ounce cans stuffed grape leaves into a saucepan, and place leaves into a bowl. Heat liquid over low flame until just ready to simmer; add to it ¼ cup each white wine and tarragon vinegar. Turn off flame, pour liquid over vine leaves, and set aside to cool.

Chicken Orientale

Into a 4-quart pot, empty one 1-pound jar orange marmalade and add two 13¾-ounce cans undiluted condensed clear chicken broth, the juice of 6 lemons or ¾ cup bottled lemon juice, 1½ teaspoons salt, 1½ cups dry sherry, 6 tablespoons thinly sliced crystallized ginger, and 4 tablespoons (¼ cup) soy sauce. Stir well and simmer 5 minutes over low flame. Blend 6 tablespoons cornstarch with 6 tablespoons water, stir into sauce, and keep stirring until it thickens.

Pull apart the meat from three 13-ounce cans cooked chicken, dice coarsely, add chicken to sauce, heat till bubbling, cover, and keep hot over lowest possible flame until ready to serve.

Hot Chinese Noodles

Put over low flame the top of your largest double boiler and empty into it four 3-ounce cans crisp Chinese noodles. Cover, heat through, then put over bottom of double boiler, with 2 inches water in it to keep hot.

Chinese Vegetables in Oyster Sauce

Drain into any suitable receptacle the liquid from 3 medium-sized cans each bean sprouts, whole water chestnuts, and bamboo shoots, leaving the vegetables in the cans. Empty 3 packages dried mushrooms into the liquid and soak 45 minutes. When mushrooms are nearly ready, over a medium flame, in a large saucepan or skillet heat 4 tablespoons vegetable oil. While oil is heating, take mushrooms out of liquid, and cut into bite-sized pieces. When oil starts to smoke, put in vegetables and stir. Then add mushrooms and mix well into vegetables.

Stir in ¾ cup bottled oyster sauce, cover, and cook gently 5 minutes. Turn off flame, pour into top of your largest double boiler, with 2 inches water in the bottom, and keep hot until ready to serve.

Brandied Peaches and Kumquats

Into a saucepan, drain the syrup from 3 large jars brandied peaches and 4 medium-sized cans kumquats. Put fruit into any suitable vessel. Put saucepan over low flame and cook syrups, uncovered, until reduced by half. Remove from stove, add 3 tablespoons brandy or dark rum, and let cool.

Meanwhile, cut fruits into large dice. Return to bowl and toss gently. Pour syrup over fruit and chill.

Cockpit Cooking

Outdoor cooking, on any boat, should only be done at anchor in calm waters or in the gentlest of swells, and precautions against the danger of fire must be taken. The charcoal-grill menus and recipes that follow are all planned for dinners. They rarely require lighting the galley stove except for making coffee.

The safest and most efficient arrangement for cockpit cooking is to mount on the taffrail a platform, made to fit your grill or hibachi, with 1 inch to spare all around, and fitted with fiddles, thus setting the fire over the water. Lash or hook the platform securely to the rail. If the fiddles are made to fold flat and the grill is also foldaway, storage is easy. That's why, though used by some, hibachis are not really practical.

An alternative arrangement is to have made an asbestos-padded three-sided foldaway shield of plywood or metal, modeled on those with which many camp stoves are equipped, and designed to fit your grill, with 2 inches to spare all around. The back and hinged side walls should extend at least 8 inches above the grill itself, and eyeholes should be provided on sides and back to which the four corners of the grill can be hooked with a light coil spring. This moveable device can be placed on any spot in the cockpit that is most workable and convenient, and stows flat.

Bag your charcoal in heavy plastic, the starter fluid likewise, and stow wherever practical, even in the bilge.

~

HAM AND GREEN OLIVE SPREAD
MY OWN GRILLED CHICKEN
MISTO RUSTICA
THREE-BEAN SALAD
CANNED FRUITS GRILLED IN FOIL
ASSORTED COOKIES

Ham and Green Olive Spread

Into a bowl put 1 cup sour cream and stir into it two 3-ounce cans deviled ham, or ½ cup finely chopped ham of any other kind, as well as ¼ teaspoon Tabasco sauce and 2 teaspoons prepared horseradish. Chop finely enough pimiento-stuffed green olives to make ½ cup (1 small bottle), or mix ⅓ cup prechopped green olives with 1 small jar of chopped pimientos, blend well into ham mixture, and chill at least an hour. Serve with rye-flavored crackers, hard bread, or Melba toast.

My Own Grilled Chicken

Bring on board, unfrozen, 1 quartered frying chicken of about 2 to 2½ pounds, dressed, and 1 extra chicken breast. Before grilling, lay chicken pieces in one layer on a sheet of foil and, with fingers, smear one side of each piece liberally with vegetable or olive oil, season with salt and coarse-ground black pepper, and strew with dried thyme leaves or dust well with powdered thyme. Turn chicken pieces over, and repeat the oiling and seasoning procedure.

Put juice of 1½ lemons or 4½ tablespoons bottled lemon juice into a pipkin, and set on grill, near edge, to warm. Grill chicken skin side down till brown, then turn and finish cooking. Baste frequently with lemon juice.

Misto Rustica

Prepare three or more hours before serving.

Chop coarsely 2 tennis-ball–sized yellow onions; slice diagonally into ½-inch pieces 4 outside stalks celery, tops and leaves removed, scrub and stem ½ pound mushrooms. Slice thinly 3 cloves garlic, and put aside separately.

Put a 9- or 10-inch heavy skillet over medium flame to heat. Meanwhile, cut into ¼-inch slices one medium-sized eggplant. When skillet is hot, add 4 tablespoons salad or olive oil, or a combination of the two, and the slices from 1 clove of garlic. When garlic is starting to turn color, add one layer of eggplant slices, sauté till lightly browned on both sides, and remove; then sauté balance of eggplant and remove. Add 1 more tablespoon oil, the onions, and the slices from a second clove garlic; sauté till golden and remove. In the same way, sauté the celery, remove, then sauté mushroom caps, adding more oil if needed, and the slices of the last clove of garlic. Remove.

Turn flame low, add a little more oil to the empty skillet and place one layer of eggplant in the bottom of it. Season with salt, coarse-ground black pepper, and a light sprinkle of basil, then add a thin layer each of the sautéed mushrooms, onions, and celery. On top of celery, sprinkle another light dusting of basil. Repeat until all vegetables are used. Drain well one 1-pound can whole tomatoes, saving the liquid, if you want, dump tomatoes over the vegetables and add 1 cup red wine. Cover and cook ½ hour, stirring gently once or twice. Let cool and serve from skillet.

Three-Bean Salad

Drain one 8-ounce can each baby green lima beans, cut green beans, cut wax beans, and corn kernels. Put all into a salad bowl and mix well.

In a large-mouthed screw-top jar, put 1 small finely chopped onion, 1 finely minced clove garlic, 1 teaspoon salt, ½ teaspoon coarse-ground black pepper, ½ teaspoon dry mustard, ¼ teaspoon sugar, the juice of ½ lemon or 1 tablespoon bottled lemon juice, 1 tablespoon chili sauce, ¼ cup or 4 tablespoons olive oil, and 1 tablespoon red wine vinegar. Close jar and shake well. Pour over vegetables, toss well, and chill or not, as you prefer.

Canned Fruits Grilled in Foil

Drain one 8-ounce can apricot halves and one 8-ounce can prunes or plums, and put fruit into a bowl. Add 1/3 cup coarsely chopped pitted dates and 3 tablespoons raisins, and mix well. Divide between four squares of foil, each large enough to enfold fruit loosely, and add to each portion of fruit 2 teaspoons brandy or apricot liqueur. Seal each foil package tightly, and cook around edge of grill for no more than 20 minutes after chicken has been turned over. Remove from fire when ready, open bundles to let steam escape, and serve in foil in individual bowls, passing a pitcher of heavy cream and a plate of assorted cookies.

SHAD ROE-AND-BACON SQUARES

GRILLED FOLDOVER HAM

GRILLED SWEET POTATOES

CARROTS IN FOIL

GRILLED APPLE SLICES

Shad Roe-and-Bacon Squares

Chill well one 7¾-ounce can shad roe. When ready to prepare, open can and cut roe into ¾-inch pieces. Cut uncooked chilled bacon into ½-inch squares and sandwich roe between bacon pieces, holding together with a toothpick. Place all sandwiches on a large square of foil, fold up loosely but with tight closure, leaving a space above the sandwiches, place at outside edge of grill, and cook 15 minutes.

Grilled Foldover Ham

This dish may be prepared ahead of time, wrapped, and kept cool until grill is ready for cooking over hot ashes. Use any ready-cooked ham—baked or boiled, canned or store-bought or home-cooked. It should be sliced thinly, each slice at least 4-by-6-inches in dimension, 3 slices allowed per person.

Drain well three 3-ounce cans mushroom stems and pieces, open one 6-ounce can tomato paste, mince finely 2 cloves garlic and 1 small white onion. Mix 1/3 cup fine, dry, flavored bread crumbs, 2 tablespoons parsley flakes, and 1½ teaspoons paprika.

Over medium flame, in a saucepan melt 2 tablespoons butter, stir in garlic and onion, sauté till golden, then stir in half the can of tomato paste and all the mushrooms. Heat through, remove skillet from stove and blend in bread-crumb mixture. If needed, add enough additional crumbs or tomato paste to make stuffing spreadable.

Spread each ham slice with stuffing, fold in half, and wrap in buttered foil, closing tightly.

Bury packages in hot ashes to cook for 20 to 25 minutes.

Grilled Sweet Potatoes

Peel 4 good-sized yams or sweet potatoes and cut into ¾-inch slices. Reassemble each potato, insert a small dab of butter between slices, sprinkle each slice with salt, coarse-ground black pepper, ground nutmeg, and allspice. Wrap each potato carefully in heavy-duty foil. Bury in hot ashes and cook for 1 hour.

Carrots in Foil

For each serving, allow ½ cup shoestring strips scraped raw carrots. Put each serving on a square of heavy-duty foil, add 1 tablespoon butter, sprinkle with salt, coarse-ground black pepper, and dried marjoram leaves. Wrap snugly and cook 35 minutes on the grill over hot coals.

Grilled Apple Slices

An hour or two before cooking, drain over a saucepan 1 large can pie-apple slices, leaving the slices in the can. Over a high flame, reduce apple syrup by two-thirds, let cool, and then stir in 4 tablespoons apricot preserves.

Divide apple slices into four even portions and put each on a square of heavy-duty foil. Pour even amounts of preserve mixture over fruit, wrap closely, and bake over hot coals for 10 to 15 minutes. Set aside and keep warm. Serve with sour cream or fresh heavy cream.

POIVRONS GRILLÉS

OR

CANNED TOP-GRADE PÂTÉ

GRILLED FISH WITH SPECIAL SAUCE

SLICED POTATOES AND CHEESE IN FOIL

SKEWERED CUCUMBERS AND MUSHROOMS

PEACHES, RUM, AND COCONUT IN FOIL

Poivrons Grillés

Poivrons Grillés (Toasted Peppers) can be prepared early in the day or as late as 2 hours before serving, or can be brought aboard in an airtight container.

Cut 4 or 5 sweet green, red, or yellow peppers, or a mixture of all three, into three or four vertical sections, remove pith and seeds, coat each piece lightly on both sides with olive oil, and set aside for 1 hour.

Over a medium flame, heat your largest skillet or 2 medium-sized skillets. Wipe the pepper sections with paper or cloth towel, sauté till lightly browned on each side, and let cool. Cut each section crosswise into thirds and put into any suitable container.

Into a large-mouthed screw-top jar or a bowl, put 2 tablespoons olive oil, 1 tablespoon red wine vinegar, salt, coarse-ground black pepper, 3 good shakes each of garlic salt and onion salt, and ½ teaspoon dry mustard. Shake or beat well, pour over peppers, toss, and serve at galley temperature.

Canned Top-grade Pâté

This is an excellent alternative to Poivrons Grillés in this menu, if for any reason fresh sweet peppers are not on hand or readily available.

One-half pound of any kind of pâté that you like, either bought or prepared at home and frozen, will serve four persons. Canned pâté will, of course keep indefinitely on board if not opened, and one 8-ounce can of any kind is sufficient for four. Be sure to buy the best, in a delicacy shop with a wide assortment.

Grilled Fish

A hinged broiler, buttered, which encloses fish between twin racks, allows the fish to be basted and turned without danger of the fish breaking. Therefore, it is a must for cockpit-cooked fish. As a substitute, two buttered cake racks may be used, with strong tongs, or even a pair of pliers from the ship's tool chest, as a means of turning handily the racks containing the fish.

Any fresh-caught fish tastes delicious with Special Sauce. Small fish should be grilled whole, large fish split, and in either case heads, bones, and scales, if necessary, should be removed before cooking. Thawed frozen fish in the form of steaks or fillets may also be used. Do not overcook any fish, and baste frequently with sauce.

Special Sauce

Chop finely 1 large white onion. Over medium flame, heat a medium-sized skillet and, when hot, put in 2 tablespoons butter and 2 tablespoons olive oil. Add onion and sauté till golden.

While onion sautés, put into a bowl the juice of 1 lemon, or 2 tablespoons bottled lemon juice, 1 tablespoon Worcestershire sauce, ¼ cup honey, 2 tablespoons catsup, ¼ cup white wine, and 1 teaspoon each salt and dried basil leaves. Mix well and blend with onions. Simmer 5 minutes, stir in 4 tablespoons parsley flakes, remove from stove, put into a small pot, and set on edge of grill for basting.

Sliced Potatoes and Cheese in Foil

Peel 4 large Idaho potatoes and cut into ¾-inch slices. Butter well one side of each slice, season that side with salt and coarse-ground black pepper, reassemble each potato, and put on a square of heavy-duty aluminum foil. Cut processed cheddar or swiss cheese slices into pieces to fit between the potato slices and insert slices of cheese between slices of potato. Carefully wrap each potato securely, bury in hot coals, and roast for about 30 minutes.

Skewered Cucumbers and Mushrooms

Peel 3 large, firm cucumbers and cut into 1-inch slices. Scrub and stem 16 medium-to-large mushrooms and drain on paper towels or newspaper. Arrange cucumbers and mushroom caps alternately on four skewers. Over medium flame, melt 5 tablespoons butter in a large skillet and dip skewers in, to coat with melted butter. Grill over hot coals for 8 minutes. Let each person season his own when served.

Peaches, Rum, and Coconut in Foil

Use fresh or good-quality canned whole or halved peaches, allowing 1 large peach, or the equivalent, per person. Peel and remove pits from fresh peaches. Drain canned peaches well before preparing.

Put each serving on a square of buttered heavy-duty aluminum foil. Turn up the sides of the foil to prevent sauce from leaking out. On top of each serving, put 1 tablespoon butter, 1½ tablespoons prepared or freshly grated coconut, 1 tablespoon slivered almonds, and 2 tablespoons dark rum. If you are using fresh peaches, add a little sugar as well. Wrap each foil package carefully and cook at edge of grill while vegetables are cooking and for the same length of time (8 minutes).

CRABMEAT SPREAD MARQUISE

SKEWERED BEEF CUBES

SMALL ONIONS IN FOIL

CORN KERNELS IN FOIL

CHOCOLATE-MINT CREAM PIE

Crabmeat Spread Marquise

Drain and empty into container one 7¾-ounce can crabmeat, pick over to remove all bits of bone and sinew, then flake well. Mix in lightly 3 tablespoons mayonnaise and add ½ teaspoon Worcestershire sauce, 1 tablespoon catsup or chili sauce, the juice of ½ lemon or 1 tablespoon bottled lemon juice, salt, paprika, a dash of cayenne, and 1 small pickle of any kind, minced or finely sliced. Mix again and chill. Serve with any bread or crackers or suchlike on hand.

Chocolate-Mint Cream Pie

The pie should be prepared at least 3 hours before serving.

Empty into a saucepan one package powdered chocolate pudding, add any kind of liquid milk as directed on package, cook over a medium flame until thickened, stirring constantly, and remove from stove. Stir in $\frac{1}{8}$ teaspoon peppermint extract, $\frac{1}{2}$ teaspoon ground cinnamon, 2 tablespoons rum, and set aside to cool.

Into a heavy plastic bag, put 28 cookies (chocolate, chocolate chip, or vanilla, or a combination of any of the three), close bag tightly and roll with a heavy bottle or pound with flat edge of a hammer until finely crumbed. To butter the sides and bottom of an 8-inch pie pan, put 3 tablespoons butter in bottom, set over very low flame to melt butter, remove pan from stove, and tilt from side to side to coat well. With fork, stir crumbs into remaining butter until evenly blended, and press mixture in an even layer over bottom and sides of pan. Chill.

When filling is cool, spoon evenly into chilled crust and keep as cold as possible. Just before serving, top with fresh or pressure-canned whipped cream.

Skewered Beef Cubes

The raw meat and sauce may be put together at home and brought aboard if desired or prepared from scratch in the galley.

Into any medium-sized airtight container pour the juice of 2 lemons or one-third cup bottled lemon juice. Mince finely 1 clove garlic and 2 golf-ball–sized white onions, and add to lemon juice with 1 teaspoon each dry mustard, ground ginger, and turmeric, $\frac{1}{2}$ teaspoon each ground cinnamon and cloves, and 2 tablespoons honey. Cover and shake thoroughly.

From $1\frac{1}{2}$ pounds tender beef, remove fat, gristle, and bones, if any, and cut meat into $1\frac{1}{2}$-inch cubes, place in a covered mixing bowl, pour the sauce over it, and mix thoroughly. Let stand at least 30 minutes or as long as overnight.

Remove meat from sauce, thread on four skewers and grill over hot coals, turning occasionally, until cooked to the desired degree of doneness. Sauce may be discarded or kept for another occasion. Ham steak, for instance, is good cooked in the sauce, after browning the meat. Pork chops, too, after browning. In their case, 40 minutes over a low-medium flame is needed.

Small Onions in Foil

Use raw or canned boiled small whole white onions. Raw onions will take 50 minutes to grill, canned onions only about 20 minutes.

Drain two 1-pound cans boiled small whole white onions or peel 20 small raw white onions. Cut four large squares heavy-duty aluminum foil and put onions on them, dividing evenly. Season each portion with salt, pepper, paprika, a liberal sprinkling of parsley flakes and any grated cheese, then dot generously with butter.

Fold the packages securely and cook around the edge of the grill.

Corn Kernels in Foil

Use four ears cooked corn on the cob or two 12-ounce cans or 2 packages thawed frozen corn kernels. Scrape kernels from corn on the cob, drain canned corn, or open thawed frozen corn. Cut four large squares heavy-duty aluminum foil and place corn on them, dividing evenly. Season each portion with coarse-ground black pepper, ¼ teaspoon sugar, a good sprinkling of salt, and 2 teaspoons imitation bacon bits, then dot generously with butter.

Fold packages securely and cook for 20 minutes around the edge of the grill.

CANNED HOT TAMALES

CHILIBURGERS

COLESLAW V

APRICOT-LIME COMPOTE

Canned Hot Tamales

Drain, reserving the sauce, two 1-pound cans tamales. Remove outside wrapping around each tamale and divide tamales evenly among four squares heavy-duty foil. Close foil securely and heat over charcoal at edge of grill.

Chiliburgers

Mix into 1½ pounds ground round steak 2 teaspoons each salt and chili powder, 1 teaspoon each garlic salt and coarse-ground black pepper, 3 teaspoons celery salt, and sauce reserved from the tamales. Form into patties and put over hot coals to grill.

While the meat is cooking, open one 1-pound can chili without meat, and chop coarsely, or slice thinly, 2 large yellow onions. Put open can of chili at edge of grill to heat. Split hamburger rolls, toast briefly, and put on a piece of foil under the grill to keep warm.

To serve, put a meat patty on half of a roll, spoon chili over it, add a generous amount of onions, and cover with other half of roll.

Coleslaw V

This may be store-bought or made at home and brought aboard, or made fresh for today.

To make this version, remove outer leaves from one small cabbage, and shred, after first cutting out and discarding stem and heavy stalks, and place in any suitable receptacle. Toss with enough French dressing to moisten and set aside. In a separate container, mix into ½ cup mayonnaise 1 cup sliced pitted black olives, 2 tablespoons chili sauce, 1 tablespoon prepared mustard, 1 teaspoon garlic salt, 1 tablespoon paprika, and 1 finely chopped onion. Add dressing to cabbage, toss well, and keep cool.

Apricot-Lime Compote

Drain into a saucepan two 1-pound cans or one 29-ounce can apricot halves. Slice thinly 1 unpeeled lime, add to apricot juice with ¼ teaspoon vanilla, put over medium flame, boil until reduced by half, and let cool.

Put fruit into a bowl, sprinkle generously with ground ginger, and pour over it 2 tablespoons rum, brandy, or bourbon. Add cooled syrup and lime, and stir gently to mix.

CATSUP CREAM CHEESE SPREAD
GRILLED KNOCKWURST WITH SPICY SAUCE
FIXED-UP SAUERKRAUT
LENTIL HOT-POT
ORANGES WITH LIME MARMALADE

Catsup Cream Cheese Spread

In any suitable receptacle, soften two unwrapped 3-ounce packages cream cheese, then mash and mix in 2 tablespoons French dressing. Grate over cheese 1 very small white onion, add 2 teaspoons anchovy paste, 1 tablespoon catsup, salt, coarse-ground black pepper, and 1 tablespoon parsley flakes. Mix well and chill.

Grilled Knockwurst with Spicy Sauce

Slice 8 knockwurst into thirds crosswise and thread onto four skewers. In a pipkin, put 2 tablespoons butter, and in a separate container blend 4 tablespoons catsup, 2 teaspoons each Worcestershire sauce and dry mustard, and 2 tablespoons red wine. Melt butter over coals at edge of grill, stir in other ingredients, and use to baste knockwurst as they cook.

Fixed-Up Sauerkraut

Drain well one 29-ounce can sauerkraut, saving the can. Rinse sauerkraut thoroughly, drain again, and squeeze out any remaining liquid. Put back in can and stir in 1 teaspoon salt, 1/2 teaspoon coarse-ground black pepper, 2 white onions finely chopped, and 2 tablespoons bacon fat, then put 1 bay leaf on top.

Fill can with dry white wine, cover can with foil, and pierce foil in three or four places to allow steam to escape. Cook at edge of grill for 45 minutes.

Lentil Hot-Pot

Into a saucepan over a medium flame, put the liquid from two 20-ounce cans lentil soup, leaving the lentils in the cans, then combine lentils in one can and set aside. Mince finely 1 clove garlic and stir into the liquid with contents of 4 envelopes dehydrated chicken or beef broth, 1/4 teaspoon ground cloves, 1/2 teaspoon coarse-ground black pepper, 1 teaspoon ground turmeric, and 1 tablespoon curry powder. Simmer uncovered until reduced by two-thirds. Put 3 tablespoons butter on top of lentils, fill can with reduced soup, cover with foil, pierce foil in three or four places to allow steam to escape, and cook at edge of grill for 30 minutes.

Oranges with Lime Marmalade

Into a saucepan over a medium flame, put the syrup from one 29-ounce or two 16-ounce cans orange sections, leaving fruit in cans. Simmer orange syrup til reduced by half. Stir into syrup ¼ cup lime marmalade, the juice of ½ lemon or 2 tablespoons bottled lemon juice, two 1½-ounce jiggers light or dark rum, let cool, and then pour over oranges in cans and chill till ready to serve.

HILLARY'S CHEESE SPREAD
GRILLED FRESH-CAUGHT FISH
CELERY AMANDINE IN FOIL
HOT PICKLED BEETS IN FOIL
OR
ARTICHOKE HEARTS IN FOIL
HOT FRUITCAKE WITH RUM

Hillary's Cheese Spread

This will keep for several weeks in the icebox and can be brought aboard in an airtight container, or made fresh in the galley, then chilled in any tightly closed container.

Into any convenient receptacle, put ¾-pound sharp cheddar cheese spread and into it grate 2 medium-sized white onions. Stir in 5 tablespoons catsup, 2 teaspoons Worcestershire sauce, 1 tablespoon dehydrated parsley flakes or finely chopped fresh parsley, ¼ teaspoon coarse-ground black pepper, and ½ teaspoon each dried leaves of tarragon, basil, dill weed, and thyme. Add ¼ cup (2 ounces) sherry or Madeira or dry vermouth, and 2 good dashes Tabasco. Blend all together thoroughly.

Grilled Fresh-Caught Fish

The preparation of charcoal-grilled fresh fish is given on page 203, and any variety may be used for this dinner. However, if fresh salmon is being cooked, the substitution of *Artichoke Hearts in Foil* for *Hot Pickled Beets in Foil* is recommended, for much better flavor and color harmony.

Celery Amandine in Foil

Use fresh or canned celery. Fresh celery will require no previous cooking, so the flavor and texture of the dish will be different from that using canned celery.

Remove tops and leaves of 1 bunch fresh celery, or drain well two 1-pound cans celery stalks. Cut celery crosswise into 2-inch pieces, divide evenly on four large squares of heavy-duty foil, season with salt and coarse-ground black pepper, and dot generously with butter. Strew over each portion 1 tablespoon slivered toasted almonds and pour over each 1 tablespoon heavy cream or undiluted evaporated milk. Wrap securely, arrange around edge of grill, and cook over hot coals for 15 minutes.

Hot Pickled Beets in Foil

These can be pickled at home and brought on board or bought already pickled. They keep for at least 2 weeks in the icebox or a very cool place. To prepare unpickled canned beets, in a saucepan over medium flame, put ½ cup malt or tarragon vinegar, 4 tablespoons brown sugar, 1 teaspoon salt, 1 teaspoon onion salt, ¼ teaspoon garlic salt, and 2 teaspoons mixed whole pickling spices. Simmer, uncovered, for 3 minutes.

While sauce is simmering, drain well one 1-pound can plus one 8-ounce can sliced or small whole beets. After 3 minutes, turn off flame, add beets to sauce, and let cool.

Cut heavy-duty aluminum foil into four good-sized squares, remove beets from sauce and divide evenly among the foil squares, add 1 tablespoon sauce to each portion, and dot generously with butter. Wrap packages, place around edge of grill, and cook over hot coals for 15 minutes.

Artichoke Hearts in Foil

Drain one 1-pound can artichoke hearts, rinse well, and drain again. Cut four sizeable squares heavy-duty foil, divide artichoke hearts evenly among them, and over each portion sprinkle liberally onion salt, celery salt, and fresh or bottled lemon juice. Dot with butter, sprinkle generously with grated Parmesan cheese, wrap packages securely, place around edge of grill, and cook for 15 minutes.

Hot Fruitcake with Rum

Cut 8 thin slices from a loaf-shaped or round fruitcake and spread one side of each slice with orange marmalade, then pair with one uncoated slice. On each of four squares of heavy-duty foil, put two slices cake. Douse with plenty of rum or bourbon or brandy, wrap packages securely, place around edge of grill, and cook for 20 minutes.

CAPONATA

SKEWERED SCAMPI

FETTUCCINI PARMIGIANA

ZUCCHINI IN FOIL

RAW APPLES OR PEARS WITH

A MILD SEMISOFT CHEESE

Caponata

This canned appetizer is often labeled "Eggplant Appetizer" and comes in 8-ounce cans. For four persons, empty 2 cans *Caponata* into a bowl and serve with sea biscuits.

Skewered Scampi

Use fresh raw or thawed frozen raw shrimps. In either case, the shrimp should be large enough for 1 dozen to serve four persons. Shell and devein shrimp, split lengthwise almost through, and spread out into butterfly shape.

In a wide shallow dish put ⅔ cup olive oil, the juice of 2 lemons (or 4 tablespoons bottled lemon juice), mince finely 3 medium-sized cloves garlic and add to oil, along with ⅓ cup dehydrated parsley flakes, 2 teaspoons salt, and 1 teaspoon coarse-ground black pepper. Stir to blend, place shrimp in dish, spoon sauce over them, and set aside for 1 hour or more. When ready to cook, thread shrimp on four skewers, transfer sauce to a small saucepan and place near edge of grill. Cook shrimp for 8 minutes over hot coals, turning three times and basting with sauce at each turning.

Fettuccini Parmigiana

In plenty of vigorously boiling water cook, uncovered, $\frac{1}{2}$ pound fettuccine for 9 minutes, stirring occasionally to make sure none sticks to the bottom of the kettle.

While fettuccine are cooking, cut $\frac{1}{2}$ stick ($\frac{1}{4}$ cup), butter into $\frac{1}{4}$-inch slices or into chunks roughly the same size, and measure out 1 cup grated Parmesan cheese. When pasta is done, drain well and return to kettle.

Put butter on fettuccine and toss thoroughly. Add cheese and salt and coarse-ground black pepper to taste, toss again and cover. Turn flame as low as possible, and insert a flame-tamer or two or three asbestos pads under kettle to keep the pasta warm till ready to serve.

Zucchini in Foil

Wash well but do not peel 4 very small zucchini, or 2 somewhat larger ones, and cut into $\frac{1}{2}$-inch-thick slices. On four sizeable squares of heavy-duty foil, place equal portions of zucchini, season with salt and coarse-ground black pepper, dot generously with butter, wrap packages securely, arrange around edge of grill, and cook for 10 to 12 minutes.

Ten Days between Landfalls

LUNCHES AND DINNERS ONLY

Long passages require solving beforehand a number of galley-related problems that don't exist on shorter hauls. Fresh water is one, a good supply of cooking fuel another, refrigeration a third. Unpredictability of weather must be reckoned with, and calls for menu flexibility. Stocking up for a long run is like starting your own grocery store, and stowage is consequently much more of a headache, especially in any boat under 40 feet with four aboard.

But the goal is worth it: freedom from all shore-based irritations for ten days or many.

The menus and recipes in this chapter are based on certain presuppositions: First, a fresh-water tank adequate for cooking, drinking, and washing for four people, to be supplemented by sea water for washing dishes, shampooing hair, and rinsing out clothes and towels. Second, a carefully computed fuel supply with an ample surplus. Third, an icebox well-stocked with ice before casting off, with small packages of dry ice surrounding the water ice and a reserve of 25 to 30 pounds of cut-up dry ice kept in a separate styrofoam ice chest; plus, finally, an informed awareness of what does, and does not, really need to be refrigerated.

No rough weather menus are included here, though many can be translated into those terms if need arises. Should a prolonged stormy spell hit, lockers should be stocked knowingly enough in the beginning to provide the makings for any simple heated-in-a-few-cans meals that must be produced. Perhaps the special later chapter devoted entirely to rough-weather menus and recipes will give you some ideas.

Breakfasts also are omitted, despite the well-known early-morning hunger of all sailors. Depending on the weather, the provisions, and the crew's preferences, the resourceful cook will come up with breakfasts to delight them all, either culling from the menus elsewhere in this book or following known breakfast habits, or both.

One more word: if the planned run is longer than the ten days covered here, the simplest thing to do is to repeat menus from the third day on, making sure that before you leave land behind, your provisions are sufficient—with overage to take care of unlooked-for sudden changes in wind, weather, or compass course.

~

LUNCHES

SIAMESE CORNED BEEF SANDWICHES
COLESLAW—MUSTARD PICKLES
FRESH CANTALOUPE

Siamese Corned Beef Sandwiches

Over a medium flame, put two opened 12-ounce cans of corned beef into a large or medium-large saucepan one-third full of water to heat for 10 minutes. On the other burner, over a medium flame, put to heat your largest double boiler, with 2 inches water in the bottom. When water boils, remove double boiler and place a large heavy skillet over the same flame. In it melt 2 tablespoons butter, toast 16 slices rye bread four at a time, until brown on both sides, and remove to top of heated double boiler. Repeat, adding butter as needed, until all slices have been toasted.

Meanwhile, slice 2 or 3 large yellow onions and set aside. Remove hot corned beef from cans and slice thickly or crumble coarsely.

For each sandwich, put one slice each of corned beef and onion on one piece of toast, season with salt and coarse-ground black pepper, and sprinkle with ½ teaspoon fresh or unsweetened bottled lime juice. Cover with another slice of toast, and serve as ready.

Coleslaw — Mustard Pickles

Both are brought aboard ready-prepared at home or store-bought, the coleslaw in any suitable container and the pickles in a jar.

Fresh Cantaloupe

Cut into quarters lengthwise 1 large cantaloupe. With dessertspoon, remove seeds and all flesh adhering to them. Squeeze fresh or unsweetened bottled lime juice over each portion and serve.

POT ROAST SALAD RITZ
FRESH FRENCH BREAD
MIXTURE. OF FRESH BERRIES

Pot Roast Salad Ritz

Before preparing, boil, cook, peel, and dice finely 4 medium-sized potatoes, and hard-boil 2 eggs.

Into a large bowl, put 1- to 1½-inch-long shoestring strips of beef, cut from four ½-inch-thick slices cold cooked pot roast. Add 2 quartered ripe tomatoes, 3 thinly sliced scallions, 2 thinly sliced sweet or sour pickles, 1 teaspoon finely chopped fresh or frozen chives, 1 teaspoon dried tarragon leaves, and mix well. Add potatoes and 1 teaspoon freshly chopped or dried flakes of parsley, and mix again. Toss well with French dressing, made as follows:

Into any suitable airtight container, put ½ teaspoon Dijon-style prepared mustard, ½ teaspoon Worcestershire sauce, 1 tablespoon salt, 1 teaspoon coarse-ground black pepper, a scant ¼ teaspoon sugar, 2 tablespoons red wine vinegar, and 3 tablespoons olive oil; shake well.

Line a salad bowl with leaves of any mild-flavored salad

greens, turn salad into bowl, and garnish with the hard-boiled eggs, peeled and cut into eighths lengthwise.

Mixture of Fresh Berries

Use 1 pint each of any two varieties of fresh berries in season. Wash well, and mix in a bowl. Sprinkle with 2 tablespoons superfine sugar, add 3 tablespoons Cointreau, stir to blend, and chill.

CHICKEN AND OYSTER SKILLET CASSEROLE
CORN DOLLARS
BRIE AND RAW APPLES

Chicken and Oyster Skillet Casserole

Open one 13-ounce can boned chicken, one 8-ounce can whole oysters, and one 10½-ounce can condensed cream of chicken soup.

Separate chicken meat from jellied broth in can, put meat into any fairly large receptacle, break into sizeable pieces, and leave jellied broth in can. Drain liquid from oysters into chicken can, leaving oysters in their own can.

Over a medium flame, in a large or medium-sized skillet, melt 2 tablespoons butter. When butter has melted, add chicken meat, and cook until tinged with brown on all sides. While chicken is cooking, empty soup into any convenient container, put jellied chicken broth and oyster liquid into emptied soup can, and fill the can with fresh or canned heavy cream or undiluted evaporated milk. Mix well with undiluted soup.

When chicken has tanned, turn flame low, add drained oysters, and cook until edges of oysters begin to curl. Add soup mixture, cover, simmer 10 minutes, and keep warm till ready to serve.

Corn Dollars

Into a heavy plastic bag, put 1 cup cornmeal, ½ cup flour, ½ teaspoon salt, and 1 teaspoon each baking soda, ground cinnamon, and superfine sugar. Reserving liquid, drain one 12-ounce can corn kernels, and add corn to bag. In a bowl, beat 2 eggs well, add corn liquid, the juice of ½ lemon or 2 tablespoons bottled lemon juice, 3 tablespoons salad oil, and 1¼ cups undiluted evaporated milk. Beat again lightly. Add to dry ingredients, close bag tightly, and knead and squeeze to form a smooth batter.

Over a high flame, heat a large heavy skillet, rub with oil or butter, and put in batter by large spoonfuls. Cook until top surface is covered with little holes, turn, and cook till brown on the underside. As each is done, remove to a plate and repeat, adding butter as needed, until all batter is utilized. Serve under, or alongside, chicken and oyster skillet casserole.

Brie and Raw Apples

Wash and dry 4 sharply flavored red apples. Two hours before serving, put 1 pound Brie on a plate, remove all wrappings, and let stand to soften. Serve apples with knives for cutting into sections and for spreading Brie on them.

SKILLET MUSHROOMS AND NOODLES
WITH TINY MEAT BALLS
APRICOTS WITH PORT WINE

Skillet Mushrooms and Noodles with Tiny Meat Balls

Saving the liquid, drain four 3-ounce cans button mushrooms. Over a high flame, in a medium-sized skillet, melt 2 tablespoons butter, add mushrooms, cover, and cook for 3 minutes, shaking from time to time to make sure the mushrooms cook evenly, and set aside in skillet.

Over the same flame, put a large pot or kettle three-fourths full of water. When boiling vigorously, add one 8-ounce package, or half of a 1-pound package, of any kind of noodles. Cook, uncovered, for 9 minutes, drain, and set aside.

Meanwhile, over a medium flame on the other burner, in a skillet melt 4 tablespoons (½ stick) butter, add 3 tablespoons flour, turn flame low, and blend well. Gradually add reserved mushroom liquid and 1¼ cups undiluted evaporated milk, stirring constantly, and then blend in the contents of 2 envelopes powdered chicken broth. Next add juices and butter from skillet containing mushrooms, and ⅓ cup dry sherry or Madeira. Season well, then stir mushrooms into sauce. Add the drained noodles, stir again, cover, and insert flame-tamer, or two or three asbestos pads, under skillet. Turn flame as low as possible.

Drain four 8-ounce cans cocktail meat balls. Over a medium flame, heat 2 tablespoons olive oil, add the drained meat balls, and sauté, turning frequently, until browned. Stir into mushroom-noodle mixture and keep hot.

Apricots with Port Wine

Drain syrup from one 29-ounce can apricot halves into a saucepan. Boil syrup until reduced by two-thirds. Add 2 tablespoons apricot jam, ½ cup port, and 1 tablespoon rum. Pour over the apricots and serve hot or cooled.

DEVILED CREAMED EGGS MORNAY
ON CANNED PUMPERNICKEL
CANNED PICKLED PEARS

Deviled Creamed Eggs Mornay

Early in the day, hard-boil 8 eggs and cool.

When ready to prepare, shell eggs and split lengthwise, then remove the yolks to any suitable receptacle and mash finely. Add one 3-ounce can smoked ham spread and 1 tablespoon each dehydrated parsley flakes or finely chopped fresh parsley and finely chopped fresh, dried, or frozen chives. Season well, bind with just enough mayonnaise to make into eight balls for filling half of the egg whites. Cover each filled egg white with an unfilled egg white, and press together to give the effect of whole eggs.

Over medium flame, put your largest double boiler, with 2 inches water in the bottom, arrange eggs in the top, and cover. Set flame as low as possible to heat eggs until Sauce Mornay has been prepared.

Canned Pickled Pears

These are available at many gourmet food shops. The label reads "Petit Pickled Pears," and they are delicious. Drain off and discard at least half the juice in the can, pour remaining juice over pears and serve hot or cool as you prefer, with or without cream of any kind.

Sauce Mornay II

Over a medium flame, put a medium-sized double boiler with 1 inch water in the bottom, and into the top, empty one 10½-ounce can undiluted condensed cream of asparagus soup. Fill the emptied can one-third full of dry white wine, and add a second one-third of undiluted evaporated milk or fresh or canned heavy cream. Stir into the soup, and then stir in the contents of 3 envelopes dehydrated chicken broth. When sauce is hot, add 3 tablespoons each grated Parmesan cheese and grated or finely diced Swiss cheese. Stir until well blended and pour over eggs. Keep warm until ready to serve.

CROÛTE DE MÜNSTER

ORANGE AND OLIVE SALAD

BUTTERSCOTCH-CITRON COOKIES

Croûte de Münster

In any suitable receptacle or bowl, beat well 1 dozen eggs, cut 4 slices rye bread into ¼-inch dice and put bread into a sizeable heavy plastic bag. Add 1 cup beer to bag, close tightly, and shake to blend. Dice enough sliced Münster cheese to make 2 cups.

Over a medium flame, put a large heavy skillet with ½ cup (1 stick) butter in it. While butter is melting, add eggs to bread mixture, reclose bag, and shake to combine.

When butter has melted, set flame low, pour egg mixture into butter, and stir in cheese. Cook until the bottom of the mixture is set, turn over, and set the other side. Cut into wedges.

Orange and Olive Salad

Drain well one 1-pound can Belgian endives, cut into 1-inch slices, and put into a salad bowl. Remove skin, pith, and seeds from 2 large or 3 medium-sized oranges, reserving the skin for use in the cookies. Slice oranges thinly, then cut the slices in half and add endive. Slice thinly and separate into rings 1 small onion, then slice 12 pitted black olives, and add both to the salad.

Into any suitable container, put ¼ cup (4 tablespoons) salad oil, and add the reserved orange juice, the juice of ½ lemon or 1½ tablespoons bottled lemon juice, 1 teaspoon ground ginger, ¼ teaspoon garlic salt, and salt and coarse-ground black pepper to taste. Shake or beat well, add to salad, and toss before serving.

Butterscotch-Citron Cookies

Cut reserved orange skin into shoestring strips, and break up 12 hard butterscotch candies.

Butter a heavy 12-inch dome-lidded skillet, line it with heavy-duty foil, and butter foil. Fold foil away from skillet rim to allow the lid to fit snugly. Over a medium flame, preheat skillet for 10 minutes.

Meanwhile, in a heavy plastic bag, mix, according to directions on package, 1 box plain or spice cookie mix. Close bag tightly and squeeze or knead to form a fairly stiff dough, add orange-skin strips and broken-up candies, reclose bag, and knead again to blend.

When skillet is hot, drop cookie dough by rounded teaspoonfuls into foil liner, about 1 inch apart. Cover skillet, insert flame-tamer or three asbestos pads over flame, and cook 25 minutes without lifting cover. If cookies do not test done at that time, re-cover and cook 8–10 minutes longer.

SHRIMP CREOLE WITH RICE

GREEN BEAN SALAD IV

CRÈME CARAMEL

Green Bean Salad IV

Prepare this first, after breakfast dishes are done. Over medium flame, heat together, without draining, the contents of one 1-pound can whole green beans and one 8-ounce can cut wax beans. When hot, remove from stove and drain well. Marinate the hot beans in 4 tablespoons (¼ cup) tart French dressing. Serve chilled or cooled.

Shrimp Creole with Rice

Use 1 pound large precooked shrimps, or 2 packages thawed frozen large precooked shrimps, or three 4½-ounce cans jumbo shrimps, well drained. Over a medium flame, sauté shrimp in 4 tablespoons (½ stick) butter for 2 minutes, and turn off flame. Remove shrimps from skillet and set aside.

Chop finely 1 large white onion, mince 1 clove garlic, dice small 1 green pepper with pith and seeds removed (or substitute ½ cup sliced green olives), and drain well one 3-ounce can sliced mushrooms and one 1-pound can whole tomatoes, leaving all solids in the cans. Open one 8-ounce can tomato sauce and one 10½-ounce can undiluted condensed consommé. Over a medium flame, add 3 tablespoons butter to skillet, stir in garlic and onions, sauté for 5 minutes, and add green pepper (or olives), mushrooms, and 2 whole tomatoes from the 1 pound can. Season with salt and coarse-ground black pepper to taste, ¼ teaspoon each dried basil and oregano, and a good dash of cayenne. Blend well and sauté 5 minutes more. Put into any suitable container, half the can of tomato sauce, thin with 1 cup consommé and add to skillet. Simmer for 10 minutes, stir in shrimp, and then stir in 3 tablespoons sherry, or Madeira, or Marsala, turn flame as low as possible, insert flame-tamer or two asbestos pads, and keep warm until rice is ready to serve. Prepare rice according to recipe for Robinson Rice on page 63.

Crème Caramel

Into the bottom of a 4- or 6-egg poacher, put enough water just to clear the bottom of the egg cups.

Off the stove, mix, in a heavy 5-inch frying pan, ⅔ cups sugar and 3 tablespoons water. Over a high-medium flame, cook without stirring (but watching carefully) until mixture becomes syrupy and turns a golden brown, tilting the pan from side to side as it cooks. Remove from stove, pour into four egg cups in the poacher, and roll the syrup around each cup to coat the sides.

Over a medium flame, in the top of your smallest double boiler, with ½ to ¾ inches water in the bottom, heat 3 cups diluted evaporated milk or reconstituted powdered milk. While milk is heating, in any suitable container, beat 4 whole fresh eggs just enough to blend, or use ½ cup powdered eggs to which ¾ cup water has been added gradually. Stir in ¼ cup sugar, remove milk from stove, pour slowly over eggs, stirring to keep smooth, and add 2 teaspoons vanilla extract. Pour into the four caramelized egg cups, cover, and, over a low flame, steam gently for 15 minutes or until custard tests done.

BROCCOLI AND POTATO SOUP

SAUTÉED REUBEN SANDWICHES

LEMON FROTH

Broccoli and Potato Soup

Over a medium flame, put your largest double boiler, with 2 inches water in the bottom. Pour into the top two 12-ounce cans cream of broccoli soup and stir in one 10½-ounce can undiluted condensed cream of potato soup. Season highly with 2 teaspoons each onion salt and celery salt, ½ teaspoon white pepper, and 1 teaspoon salt. Stir in the contents of 3 envelopes dehydrated chicken broth, and 3 tablespoons dehydrated parsley flakes. Set flame very low, cover, and cook for 20 minutes.

Sautéed Reuben Sandwiches

Early in the day, put one 12-ounce can of corned beef to chill well, either in the icebox or some cool part of the boat.

When ready to prepare, cut corned beef into ¼-inch slices and from a large piece of Swiss cheese, cut enough medium-thin slices to match the beef in size and number. Drain well one 8-ounce can sauerkraut, rinse, and drain well again.

Over a medium-low flame, put a large heavy skillet to heat. While skillet is heating, cut in half 12 slices dark rye bread, canned or fresh, and cover 12 half-slices with slices of corned beef and cheese, strew each with sauerkraut, and cover with the other half-slices of bread. Butter generously both outer sides of each sandwich, put in heated skillet, raise flame somewhat, and cook until cheese begins to melt and bread is lightly toasted—about 4 minutes on each side.

Lemon Froth

After the breakfast dishes are done, put over a medium flame the bottom of a medium-sized double boiler with 1 inch water in it. Separate 4 eggs, putting the whites into a bowl and the yolks into the top of the double boiler. Beat egg yolks till light, then stir in the juice of 2 lemons or 6 tablespoons bottled lemon juice and 1/2 cup sugar. Put over double boiler bottom and cook, stirring constantly, until thickened. Remove double boiler from stove, set aside, and turn off flame.

Beat egg whites until stiff, then beat in gradually 1/4 cup (4 tablespoons) sugar. Fold hot yolk mixture into whites, blending well. Chill till ready to serve.

THICK-AND-THIN OXTAIL SOUP
WITH TOASTED SHIP'S BISCUITS
WINTER SALAD
RICE PUDDING WITH CHERRIES

Thick-and-Thin Oxtail Soup

Over a medium flame, put your largest double boiler, with 2 inches water in the bottom, pour into the top one 15½-ounce can each thick oxtail soup and clear oxtail soup, and heat for 10 minutes.

Toasted Ship's Biscuits

Over a medium flame, heat a medium-sized double boiler with 1 inch water in the bottom, and when water boils, remove from stove. Split carefully 12 ship's biscuits, and butter the split sides. Over a low flame, heat a 12-inch heavy skillet for 5 minutes. Fill bottom with one layer of biscuits, split side down, and cook till tan. Remove as done to top of heated double boiler. Repeat until all biscuits have been toasted. Serve hot.

Winter Salad

Drain well and put into any suitable container or vessel, the contents of one 8-ounce can each lima beans, cut green beans, speckled pinto beans, and thinly sliced water chestnuts. If only whole water chestnuts are in your locker, slice thinly after draining and before adding to beans. Chop coarsely 1 small red onion and add, then mix all together. In a separate container, put 3 tablespoons red wine vinegar, 1 finely minced clove garlic, 6 tablespoons olive oil, salt and coarse-ground black pepper to taste, and 3 tablespoons dehydrated parsley flakes. Shake or beat well, pour over vegetables, toss, and serve cooled or chilled.

Rice Pudding with Cherries

Drain well, discarding the juice, one 8-ounce can pitted black cherries, and open one 15-ounce can rice pudding. Over a medium flame, put a small double boiler with ¾ inch water in the bottom, and into the top put one layer of cherries, without crowding. Pour rice pudding over them and add the rest of the cherries on top. Cover, cook over low flame for 15 minutes, and serve hot.

TOMATO AND CELERY BROTH

RUSSIAN SALAD

HOT CANNED SCONES

BROWNIES

Russian Salad

Shred into a salad bowl 1 head iceberg lettuce. Cut into shoe-string strips enough precooked ham, canned chicken (jellied broth discarded), canned tongue slices, and any kind of cheese to make ½ cup of each. Add to lettuce and mix well.

In a separate container, stir into ½ cup mayonnaise 4 table-spoon chili sauce, 5 tablespoons garden relish, 1 finely minced small white onion, 1 small jar chopped pimiento, and 3 table-spoons sliced green olives. Add dressing to salad, toss well, and serve cool or chilled.

Brownies

Prepare according to recipe given on page 113. Use one burner for the brownies while you use the other for the Tomato and Celery Broth, and heat the scones after the brownies are done.

Tomato and Celery Broth

In a saucepan over a low flame, put the liquid drained from one 1-pound can cut celery, and cook until reduced by half. Remove from stove and over the same flame put a medium-sized double boiler with 1¼ inches water in the bottom. Into the top, pour one 18-ounce can tomato juice. Add celery liquid and season with ¼ teaspoon ground thyme, a good dash of cayenne, salt, and coarse-ground black pepper.

Set a sieve over the top of the double boiler, add celery pieces from the can, and press them through into broth. Remove sieve and stir in contents of 2 envelopes dehydrated beef broth. Cook 10 minutes and remove from stove until ready to serve in mugs.

Hot Canned Scones

Over a medium flame put your largest double boiler with 2 inches water in the bottom. Into the top empty 1 large can scones. Cover and heat for 15 minutes.

DINNERS

FROMAGE BOURSAULT
ON FRESH FRENCH BREAD
VEAL CHOPS À LA RITZ
GREEN NOODLES—GREEN SALAD
STRAWBERRIES AND CANTALOUPE WITH
PINEAPPLE SHERBET
OATMEAL WAFERS *

Fromage Boursault

This is a semisoft mild rich cheese carried by most cheese stores and gourmet specialty groceries. Open and unfold wrapping as soon as you bring it aboard with your other provisions, and put in a somewhat warm place to soften well. Serve with ½-inch-thick slices of French bread.

Veal Chops à la Ritz

Use four 1-inch-thick shoulder, rib, or loin veal chops, trimmed of fat. Chop coarsely 4 fairly large white onions and mix 4 tablespoons grated Parmesan cheese with ½ cup (8 tablespoons) flavored bread crumbs. Over a medium flame, in a heavy 12-inch skillet, melt 4 tablespoons (½ stick) butter. Meanwhile, on the other burner, over a medium flame, put your smallest double boiler with ¾ inch water in the bottom, and an additional 4 tablespoons butter in the top. When this butter has melted, turn flame very low, but not off.

When butter in skillet has melted, add onions and sauté till golden. While onions are sautéing, spread one side of the chops with the cheese-and-crumb mixture. When onions are cooked, put the chops on the bed of onions in the skillet, with the crumbed side uppermost. Dribble melted butter from the small double boiler over the chops, pour around the meat (but not over it) 1½ cups dry white wine, cover, set flame low, and cook for 1 hour, or a little longer if chops do not test done.

Green Noodles

While chops are cooking, on the other burner cook one-half of a 1-pound box of green noodles, following the directions on page 212 for Fettucini Parmigiana, omitting the cheese. Return well-drained noodles, after adding butter called for, to kettle. Re-cover and insert three asbestos pads under kettle, to keep noodles warm and allow the butter to melt through them, over a very low flame. Toss thoroughly before serving.

Green Salad

Use any combination of three or four varieties of mild- and sharp-flavored salad greens. Tear into bite-sized pieces, wash well in a colander, shake as dry as possible, put into any suitable receptacle, and toss with a French dressing made with 2½ parts oil, 1 part lemon juice (fresh or bottled), 1 part white wine vinegar, and seasoning to taste.

Oatmeal Wafers*

The recipe for these is given on page 309.

Strawberries and Cantaloupe with Pineapple Sherbet

Pick over and hull 1 pint strawberries, and set aside in a sizeable receptacle or heavy plastic bag. Cut in half lengthwise 1 medium-sized cantaloupe, scoop out seeds and the flesh adhering to them, and with vegetable cutter scoop out the melon into small balls. Mix with strawberries, add 3 tablespoons any variety of fruit liqueur, and stir or shake gently but thoroughly.

When ready to serve, divide fruit evenly into four individual bowls and top with even amounts from 1 pint pineapple sherbet, brought aboard along with other provisions and kept cold.

RADISHES AND SCALLIONS WITH SALTINES

SMOTHERED BEEF, PROVENÇALE STYLE

CORN ON THE COB

SALADE DU MIDI

RASPBERRY MOUSSE WITH LADYFINGERS

Radishes and Scallions

The technique for preparing these is given on page 87.

Smothered Beef, Provençale Style

A fine solid 4-or-5-pound eye round, top round, or rump of beef is required to make this dish successful. Also a pot or kettle deep enough to allow plenty of room around the meat for all the vegetables and the pigs' feet. If you do not have aboard anything big enough, do not attempt this dish; substitute something else as main dish for this menu.

In the morning, even before breakfast if you are up to it, take the meat from the icebox, unwrap, and put to warm to galley temperature. Right after the breakfast dishes are done, put the meat into a pot or kettle that will fulfill the necessary size requirements. Chop 6 shallots finely, strew over meat, add 2 cups red wine, cover, and set aside to marinate for 2 hours, turning meat every half-hour.

Around noon, or a half-hour earlier, slice 4 medium-large white onions, 5 scraped carrots, and 3 cloves garlic. Dice ¼ pound salt pork finely, scrub and slice ½ pound fresh mushrooms, drain one 4-ounce bottle pimiento-stuffed green olives, and cut the olives in half crosswise.

Over a high-medium flame, put a large heavy skillet with the diced salt pork in it. When the fat begins to run, add the onions, carrots, and garlic, lower flame and sauté over this gentle flame until the onions begin to tan a little. Meanwhile, remove the meat from its marinade and dry it well all over with paper towels or a cloth towel or a clean rag.

With a slotted spoon, remove the vegetables from the skillet, put in the meat, brown lightly on all sides, and then pour in ½ cup brandy or bourbon, let it bubble awhile, and turn off flame.

Put the meat back into pot and add marinade. Stir up the brandy in the skillet to bring into it the browned bits in the bottom, add ½ teaspoon dried thyme leaves, and pour over meat. Put the carrots and onions around the meat, next the mushrooms, then the olives, and last 2 pigs' feet. Add one 10½-ounce can undiluted condensed beef bouillon, and if meat is not covered, add enough more wine to do so. On top of meat, put 1 large bay leaf, and cover pot.

Mix 2 cups flour or prepared biscuit mix with enough water to form a stiff dough, shape it into a long thin roll and use it to seal together pot and cover. Put pot on the lowest possible flame, with three or four asbestos pads under it, and cook until ready to serve, or for at least 6 hours, when it should be fork-tender. Serve from pot, slicing meat generously on the horizontal and spooning vegetables and sauce over each portion.

Corn on the Cob

The procedure for cooking corn is given on page 75.

Salade du Midi

Two hours before serving, hard-boil 3 eggs, plunge into cold water, drain, and set aside.

Peel, seed, and chop very coarsely 4 medium-sized tomatoes and 2 medium-sized cucumbers, and put into a sizeable heavy plastic bag. Dice 1 fair-sized white onion and 1 medium-sized green pepper, pith and seeds removed, and add. In any convenient container, mash the yolks of the hard-boiled eggs, then chop the whites as finely as you can, along with 1 large or 2 medium cloves garlic. Mix 4 tablespoons olive oil with the yolks and season to taste with salt, coarse-ground black pepper, and ½ teaspoon sugar. Stir in chopped whites and garlic, along with 2 tablespoons dehydrated parsley flakes or finely chopped fresh parsley. Pour the juice of 1½ limes or 3 tablespoons bottled unsweetened lime juice over vegetables, add olive oil mixture to bag, close bag tightly, shake gently to mix, and chill well.

Raspberry Mousse

Three hours before serving, put 1 envelope unflavored gelatine in ⅓ cup cold water to soften. Drain well over any suitable airtight container 1 package thawed frozen raspberries, and set the fruit aside. Mix into the raspberry juice 1 tablespoon fresh or bottled lemon juice, ½ teaspoon salt, and ½ cup sugar. Over a low flame, put the softened gelatine in the top of your smallest double boiler with ¾ inch water in the bottom and melt. Stir gelatine into juice mixture and chill till it begins to set around the edge, which should not take more than 15 minutes if container is placed next to the ice, then remove from icebox, and beat until frothy.

In a large container, whip 1 cup heavy cream, then fold in the gelatine mixture and the drained fruit. Divide evenly among four snap-top plastic refrigerator dishes, and chill until ready to serve.

CANNED CHICKEN LIVER PÂTÉ

SAUERKRAUT WITH SAUSAGES

POTATO PANCAKES

BEET SALAD

BAKED APPLES

Canned Chicken Liver Pâté

There are several pâtés on the market, and they can be found in most gourmet grocery stores and sometimes on the gourmet shelves of supermarkets. In provisioning for this long passage, since this food is equally useful either for an appetizer, as planned here, or for sandwiches, with chopped hard-boiled eggs worked in, our suggestion would be to lay on at least six 7- or 8-ounce cans. As an appetizer, 1 can is sufficient for four.

After opening, squeeze over the pâté the juice of 1 lemon or 3 tablespoons bottled lemon juice.

Sauerkraut with Sausages

This classic dish may be bought imported from France in 14-ounce cans, ready to heat and serve, and 3 cans are enough for four persons. To prepare, empty the cans into the top of your largest double boiler, with 2 inches water in the bottom, drain well one 8-ounce can cut green beans, and stir in thoroughly. Taste for seasoning and add if needed, then heat over a medium flame for 20 minutes.

Choucroute Garnie, the French name for this skillet casserole, is likely to be more satisfying and flavorful when prepared in the galley especially for this meal, and is not difficult to put together, but should be cooking on the stove a good 3 hours before dinnertime, over the lowest flame possible.

When provisioning ashore for this passage, buy ½ pound sliced hot sausage, usually designated as "peperoni," and a picnic ham weighing around 2 to 2½ pounds. The dish itself will use only 1 pound, so figure on slicing some of the balance of the ham for sandwiches and turning the rest into a fine ham hash for breakfast some morning. If the ham is kept in a cool place, it need not be refrigerated.

Cut 1 pound of the ham (or a little less than half the entire piece) into 1-inch cubes, and set aside. Drain well two 8-ounce cans or one 1-pound can cut green beans and one 8-ounce can each sliced carrots and whole small boiled white onions. Drain well three 1-pound cans sauerkraut, rinse thoroughly, drain, and rinse again, then squeeze hard with your hands to remove as much water as possible. Peel 1 large white onion and fasten to it 2 bay leaves, each held to onion by 4 whole cloves.

Over a low flame, put a large, deep, heavy pot or saucepan containing 2 tablespoons bacon fat or 2 slices diced uncooked bacon. When fat has melted, or fat of bacon is running, spread over it one-third of the sauerkraut, lay the clove-stuck onion on top, strew over kraut half of the diced ham and half of the "peperoni" slices, then half of the drained green beans. Add another third of the kraut, the rest of the ham and sausage and green beans. Add canned carrots and onions, then the balance of the kraut. Pour in one 13¾-ounce can undiluted condensed clear chicken broth and enough dry white wine to bring liquid not quite to cover the top layer of sauerkraut. Cover pot and, over lowest possible flame, cook for 3 hours.

For a meatier dish, 4 sliced frankfurters may be added 15 minutes before serving. When ready to serve, remove clove-stuck onion, and ladle from pot into bowls.

Potato Pancakes

Use three 14-ounce cans ready-to-serve potato pancakes, available at many gourmet groceries, or one box prepared potato pancake mix, or 4 medium-sized raw potatoes.

If you are using canned potato pancakes, drain and heat as directed on can.

For potato pancake mix, prepare as directed on the box. Fry over medium flame in a heavy 12-inch dome-lidded skillet in plenty of melted butter, turning once, and sprinkling each side with salt and coarse-ground black pepper. As done, remove to top of medium-sized double boiler with 1 inch water in the bottom, and, when all are cooked and removed, take skillet from stove and, without changing flame, use burner to heat double boiler over two asbestos pads for 15 minutes, then remove with asbestos pads to keep warm until ready to serve.

If you use raw potatoes, peel and grate them coarsely into a bowl or pan, cover with cold water, and soak for 5 minutes. Meanwhile, put into a heavy plastic bag 2 tablespoons flour or 4 tablespoons fine dry bread crumbs, add 1 tablespoon heavy cream (fresh or canned or sour), 1 egg lightly beaten, 1 grated small white onion or 2 teaspoons onion salt, 1 teaspoon salt, and ½ teaspoon coarse-ground black pepper. Close bag tightly, and knead and squeeze until all ingredients are well blended. Drain grated potatoes, then squeeze with both hands to remove any remaining liquid and add to plastic bag. Close and shake, then knead and squeeze to blend thoroughly. If too dry, or not dry enough, to form into pancakes, spoon in more cream or flour or crumbs as needed. Cook in the same manner as pancakes made from prepared mix, omitting the added seasoning.

Beet Salad

Use one 14-ounce can ready-to-serve beet salad, available at gourmet food shops, or make salad from one 1-pound can shoe-string beets, drained well. Mix the plain beets with cream mustard dressing, made by mixing together 1 teaspoon Dijon-style prepared mustard, ½ teaspoon fresh or bottled lemon juice, 2 tablespoons mayonnaise, and 6 tablespoons undiluted evaporated milk, added little by little while stirring. Season to taste with salt and coarse-ground black pepper. Cool well or chill, if possible.

Baked Apples

Use one can ready-to-serve baked apples containing 4 apples, or 4 tart raw apples. Sprinkle ground ginger generously over each portion of canned baked apples before serving.

To prepare raw apples, core, but do not peel, them, then dice finely enough crystallized ginger to make 1 tablespoon. Into the hollow of each apple, put 1 teaspoon honey and one-fourth of the diced ginger. Put apples in any saucepan or pot into which they will fit snugly, pour ½ inch water in the bottom, cover, and steam over low flame for 15 minutes or until they test done.

Serve canned or fresh-cooked apples hot or cold, with or without cream.

SKEWERS ROLAND

BURGUNDY BEEF WITH WALNUTS

GARLIC SAUTÉED POTATOES

ARTICHOKE AND MUSHROOM SALAD

STRAWBERRIES AND COOKIES

Skewers Roland

This appetizer comes from Spain in a can, ready to serve. Two cans should serve four. It is to be found under the Roland brand name in many fine food stores, and it keeps indefinitely unopened. It consists of assorted pickles, pimientos, olives, and other sharp-flavored bits strung on 6-inch skewers, and should be served with bland crackers as an accompaniment.

Burgundy Beef with Walnuts

Use three 15-ounce cans ready-to-serve *Boeuf Bourguignon*, sold in gourmet departments under that title, or two 1½-pound cans good-quality beef stew. If you use the latter, discard all potatoes, or reserve them for use some other time.

Over a medium flame, put your largest double boiler, with 2 inches water in the bottom; into the top, empty the cans. To beef stew, add ½ cup red wine, season either *Boeuf Bour-guignon* or stew with salt and coarse-ground black pepper to taste, and turn flame low.

On the other burner, over a medium flame, in a heavy 5-inch skillet or saucepan, melt 2 tablespoons butter. When it foams, add ¾ cup walnut meats, and sprinkle lightly with salt. Sauté, shaking occasionally, till nuts are crisp, and add to meat mixture in top of double boiler. Cook for 15 minutes.

Garlic Sautéed Potatoes

Use two 1-pound cans sliced cooked potatoes or 4 medium-sized raw potatoes. The cooking procedure is the same for both, but the timing is quite different.

Peel raw potatoes, slice thinly, put in cold water to cover, and soak for 10 minutes; drain canned potatoes well, and leave them in the cans.

Meanwhile, over a medium flame, in a large heavy skillet, put 3 tablespoons butter to melt, and add immediately 1 large or 2 medium-sized whole cloves garlic, each stuck with a toothpick. Set flame low, and cook until butter has browned and garlic is turning color. Remove garlic and add potatoes—the raw potatoes well-drained and patted dry on paper towels, the canned potatoes directly from the can. Stir to coat potatoes with butter, insert a flame-tamer or three asbestos pads under skillet, cover, and cook slowly, allowing 20 minutes for canned potatoes and 50 minutes for raw potatoes.

Artichoke Heart and Mushroom Salad

Drain well one 1-pound can artichoke hearts and two 3-ounce cans button mushrooms. Put into a heavy plastic bag, close tightly, and shake to mix. In any suitable container, mix ½ cup mayonnaise and 2 tablespoons undiluted evaporated milk. Grate into it 1 small clove garlic and add juice of ½ lemon or 1½ tablespoons bottled lemon juice, 2 tablespoons parsley flakes, ½ teaspoon dried basil, salt and coarse-ground black pepper to taste, and stir well. Mix in thoroughly 1 teaspoon anchovy paste, turn dressing into the bag with the vegetables, close tightly, and shake till well blended. Chill.

Strawberries and Cookies

Early in the day, put two 15-ounce cans strawberries to chill. One hour before serving, drain syrup from the cans into a saucepan, put fruit into a heavy plastic bag, and put bag in icebox. Over high-medium flame, bring syrup to a boil, uncovered, and cook until reduced by half. Flavor with 3 tablespoons rum or brandy, or bourbon, or any fruit liqueur. Cool, then add syrup to fruit. Chill. Serve with any cookies you like.

PETIT MÜNSTER DE FRANCE

ON BREMNER WAFERS

BRAISED CHICKEN TARRAGON

CREAMED SPINACH—GOLDEN CUBED POTATOES

MACAROONS AND PEPPERMINTS

Petit Münster de France

Among the several cheeses that do not need refrigeration until opened, this one is unusual and delectable in flavor. One cheese will serve four persons comfortably. As with all semisoft cheeses, it is best unwrapped early and served at galley temperature. Bremner wafers are superior and delicious crackers sold in tins that seal them from dampness, and are readily available at stores that make a big point of stocking gourmet specialties and in the delicacy shops of department stores with a discerning assortment of cheeses on hand.

Braised Chicken Tarragon

Use 1 can whole cooked chicken. Drain all can liquid into any suitable container, then dry outside of chicken with paper towels or cloth towel or clean rag.

If not trussed, truss well. Into the cavity put ½ tablespoon butter and 3 teaspoons dried tarragon leaves.

Over high flame in a heavy 12-inch dome-lidded skillet, melt 4 tablespoons butter and, when foamy, add chicken and brown on all sides, remove and set aside. Put into the skillet all liquid drained from can, stir up into it all the browned bits, and simmer for 2 minutes. Return bird to skillet, cover, set flame low, and heat for 10 minutes. Uncover, sprinkle 2 more teaspoons dried tarragon leaves on chicken, pour over the chicken ¾ cup undiluted evaporated milk, re-cover, and cook 10 minutes more. Carve and serve in skillet, spooning sauce over each portion.

Creamed Spinach

On the other burner, while chicken is browning, put a medium sized double boiler, with 1½ inches water in the bottom, over a medium flame. In the top, put 2 tablespoons butter and, when melted, add 1 teaspoon flour and stir till smooth. Drain well two 1-pound cans chopped spinach, with your hands squeeze out all remaining liquid, and put in top of double boiler with ¼ teaspoon ground nutmeg, ½ teaspoon salt, and ¼ teaspoon coarse-ground black pepper. Remove bottom of double boiler and, over low direct flame, cook spinach until all moisture has evaporated (about 5 minutes). Mix in ⅓ cup undiluted evaporated milk, bring to a boil, put over bottom of double boiler, and replace on same flame to heat for 10 minutes. Then remove and put over two asbestos pads to keep warm, and to free burner for potatoes.

Golden Cubed Potatoes

Drain well two 1-pound cans whole cooked potatoes, and cut into ¼-inch cubes. Over a medium flame in a heavy skillet melt 3 tablespoons butter, add potatoes, stir to coat with butter, set flame low, and cook, uncovered, for 20 minutes.

Macaroons and Peppermints

Since both of these keep well on board if stored in airtight containers kept in a reasonably cool place, a combination of the two, served as "finger food," will make a good finishing touch to this menu.

SEVICHE OF SHRIMP ON LARGE CORN CHIPS

BEEF ENCHILADAS

MEXICAN RICE

CLAMS MÉXICAINE

SLICED MANGOES

Seviche of Shrimp

This should set to "cook" (it's the acid in the lime juice that, in accordance with an historically ancient chemical discovery, does the "cooking," magically transforming the raw shrimp into succulently softened and pink "cooked" morsels) so, early in the day, drain well two $4\frac{1}{2}$-ounce cans jumbo shrimp. Into any airtight container large enough to hold shrimp, put 1 large white onion, thinly sliced, 2 bay leaves, 1 minced clove garlic, $\frac{1}{8}$ teaspoon dried hot red pepper, $\frac{1}{4}$ teaspoon coarse-ground black pepper, and $\frac{1}{2}$ teaspoon dried tarragon leaves. Add the juice of 2 limes or 4 tablespoons unsweetened bottled lime juice and 1 tablespoon chili sauce; mix well. Add slowly 2 tablespoons olive oil and mix again.

Stir in shrimp, cover, and chill until ready to serve.

Beef Enchiladas

These are available in cans in any shop with a good selection of Mexican specialties. Four 16-ounce cans will serve four generously. Empty cans into top of your largest double boiler with $1\frac{1}{2}$ inches water in the bottom, set over high-medium flame, and heat for 15 minutes, then set aside over two asbestos pads to free burner.

Mexican Rice

Chop finely 1 small white onion and 1 medium-sized clove garlic, slice thinly 1 medium-sized carrot, and open one 8-ounce can each tomato sauce and tiny peas, but do not drain cans.

Directly over a low flame, into a big skillet that will nest into a pot, put 1½ tablespoons salad oil and, when hot, add 1 cup raw noninstant white rice. Stirring often, sauté rice until opaque and golden. Stir in onion, garlic, and tomato sauce, put two asbestos pads under the pan, and cook about 20 minutes. Drain liquid from peas into rice, add one 13¾-ounce can undiluted condensed clear chicken broth and the carrot. Mix well, remove asbestos pads, bring to a boil, cover, replace asbestos pads, and cook 30 minutes, or until all liquid is absorbed. Remove asbestos pads, nest into a pot that fits it, stir in peas, cover, and, over same low flame, heat for 10 minutes. Remove and put on hot asbestos pads to keep warm. Before serving, garnish with 1 tablespoon ground coriander and 2 tablespoons parsley flakes.

Clams Méxicaine

Drain well over a saucepan one 8-ounce can Italian plum tomatoes and two 8-ounce cans minced clams, and add to liquid 2 teaspoons chili powder, 1 teaspoon paprika, and a good dash Tabasco. Over a medium flame, bring liquid to a simmer, and cook, uncovered, until reduced by half. Meanwhile, over a high-medium flame on the other burner, put to heat a heavy 5-inch skillet with 2 tablespoons olive oil in it. While oil is heating, chop finely 1 large white onion, and slice thinly 1 cup pitted black olives. When oil is hot, add onions and olives and sauté until onions are golden, then stir in tomatoes and drained clams. Bring to a simmer, cook 3 minutes, add reduced sauce, and season with salt and coarse-ground black pepper. Stir once more, to blend well the clams and the sauce, cover, and remove from the burner to two asbestos pads to keep hot. Serve with a ladle over the rice, preferably in a shallow bowl.

Sliced Mangoes

Mangoes may not be everyone's favorite fruit, but in a menu like this the slices are most suitable in flavor and consistency. If, at first, you find them too mild, add a good squeeze or dollop of fresh or bottled lime juice, or a sharp-flavored liqueur to each serving.

Drain well, discarding the syrup, two 1-pound cans sliced mangoes, put into a plastic bag, close tightly, and chill. Serve with coconut sprinkled over each portion.

STUFFED VINE LEAVES

CRABMEAT AND MUSHROOMS

IN WINE SAUCE AMANDINE

ON FINN-KRISP

COOKED VEGETABLE SALAD

CHOCOLATE NUT ROLL

Stuffed Vine Leaves

This canned appetizer is imported from Greece, and can be found in delicacy or gourmet food shops. It should be chilled, or kept in a cool place, until ready to serve, then opened and the packages of stuffed leaves arranged in a bowl or on a plate, with toothpicks or forks provided to spear them. One 14-ounce can will serve four persons generously, and the accompaniment should be any bland cracker.

Crabmeat and Mushrooms in Wine Sauce Amandine

Drain well, rinse, and then slice thinly the contents of one 5-ounce can whole water chestnuts, and return to can. Drain over any suitable container two 3-ounce cans sliced broiled-in-butter mushrooms, leaving mushrooms in cans. Drain two 7¾-ounce cans crabmeat, put into any container, pick over carefully to remove any bits of bone and sinew, and pull apart into fair-sized pieces. Into a 1-pint measuring cup or pint-sized jar, put ½ cup undiluted evaporated milk, ¾ cup dry white wine, and ¼ cup reserved mushroom liquid, discarding the balance.

Over a medium flame, put a medium-sized double boiler with ¾ inch water in the bottom, and into the top put 3 tablespoons butter, ½ teaspoon dry mustard, ¼ teaspoon dried tarragon leaves, 1 teaspoon salt, and ½ teaspoon ground white pepper. While butter is melting, measure out 3 tablespoons flour.

On the other burner, toast ½ cup almonds in a small skillet with 2 tablespoons butter in it. Set aside when golden tan.

Stir flour into butter in double boiler until smoothly mixed, then add liquid and blend well. Remove top of double boiler to direct high flame, and stir constantly until sauce thickens. Turn off flame and remove from stove.

Put hot water from double boiler into the bottom of your largest double boiler, and add enough water to bring to a depth of 2 inches, cover and put over medium flame.

Off the stove, into the top of this double boiler, put the crabmeat and water chestnuts, strew the mushrooms over them, and top with toasted slivered almonds, then pour the sauce over this mixture, put over double boiler bottom, cover, lower flame somewhat, and cook for 20 minutes. Serve over broken-up Finn-Krisp.

Cooked Vegetable Salad

Use one 8-ounce can each of any three varieties of well drained canned vegetables. Put into a heavy plastic bag, add 1 teaspoon each onion salt and celery salt, $\frac{1}{4}$ teaspoon garlic salt, and 2 tablespoons parsley flakes. Add 4 tablespoons oil-and-vinegar dressing, close bag tightly, shake well, and chill.

Chocolate Nut Roll

This can be purchased in gourmet food shops in 1-pound cans and may be served hot or cold.

To heat, place unopened can in a deep saucepan with sufficient water to come two-thirds of the way to the top of the can, cover, and steam over low flame for 20 minutes. Remove can from water, wrap a towel around it to avoid burning your fingers, open, turn out onto a plate, cut into four even slices, and serve with bottled hard sauce or bourbon sauce.

To serve cold, slice evenly into four portions, and dribble a little brandy over each portion before serving.

HOT SHRIMP-AND-CHEESE ''WAFFLES''
BEEF WITH CHINESE VEGETABLES
SWEET AND PUNGENT CHICKEN
BOILED RICE
KOWLOON COMPOTE

Hot Shrimp-and-Cheese "Waffles"

These delicious morsels come from England, tightly packed in a can, and so will keep indefinitely. They can be found in gourmet food shops under the name given above, among the various dry snacks and crackers. Though excellent cold, they are even more satisfying when heated. Over a medium flame, put your small double boiler with ½ to ¾ inches water in the bottom, fill the top with the "Waffles", cover, and heat for 15 minutes.

Boiled Rice

For the way I prefer to cook raw non-instant rice, see recipe for Robinson Rice, page 63.

Beef with Chinese Vegetables

Drain well two 8-ounce can roast beef and cut into shoestring strips. Drain one 5-ounce can water chestnuts and one 8½-ounce can bamboo shoots, and slice thinly, if not already sliced. Drain well the smallest can of bean sprouts you can find (if larger than 8 ounces, reserve the extra for use in a salad some other time). Cut in half lengthwise 1 large white onion, and then slice thinly; mince finely 1 large clove garlic. In ¼ cup cold water, mix 2 tablespoons cornstarch, ½ teaspoon each ground ginger and dry mustard, and 2 tablespoons soy sauce. Open one 10½-ounce can condensed beef bouillon.

Over a high flame, in a heavy 12-inch skillet, heat 3 tablespoons vegetable oil, put in onion and garlic, and cook 3 minutes, then add beef, vegetables, bouillon, and all other ingredients except soy sauce mixture. Stir, cover, and cook 5 minutes. Add soy sauce mixture and stir constantly until sauce thickens smoothly. Turn mixture into the top of your largest double boiler, with 2 inches water in the bottom; cover and set over low flame. Bring water in bottom to a boil, then remove and put over three asbestos pads until ready to serve. Use same skillet, without washing, to cook *Sweet and Pungent Chicken.*

Sweet and Pungent Chicken

Remove meat from one 13-ounce can boned chicken, and pull apart into sizeable pieces. Open and drain one 8-ounce can each pineapple chunks and Italian plum tomatoes leaving all solids in the cans. Over a high flame, put the big, heavy skillet with 2½ tablespoons vegetable oil in it and, when hot, add chicken. Brown quickly, remove meat, and set aside. Put 1 cup undiluted condensed clear chicken broth, or the contents of 2 envelopes dehydrated chicken broth and 1 cup water, into the hot skillet; lower flame somewhat, add pineapple chunks, 2 tablespoons each sugar and catsup, the juice of ½ lemon or 1 tablespoon bottled lemon juice, ¾ teaspoon salt, and ½ teaspoon white pepper. Stir in 2 tablespoons cornstarch, mix well, bring to a boil, and add chicken and tomatoes. Stir again, bring to a boil, set flame low, cover, and cook for 3 minutes.

Kowloon Compote

Drain over a saucepan one 20-ounce can lichee fruit in syrup and one 8-ounce can crushed pineapple, and put fruit into a heavy plastic bag. Add to the syrups the juice of 1 lime or 2 tablespoons unsweetened bottled lime juice, and 2 tablespoons finely diced crystallized ginger. Cook, uncovered, over a medium flame until reduced by half. Let cool, pour over fruit in bag, close bag tightly, and chill if possible. Sherry or rum may be poured over when serving if desired.

MUSSEL CANAPÉS

TONGUE HEATED IN SAUCE MADÈRE

POTATOES WITH CARAWAY AND DILL WEED

CELERY KNOBS FERMIÈRE

GOOSEBERRY AND RASPBERRY COMPOTE

Mussel Canapés

Over a medium flame, put a heavy 5-inch skillet to heat and drain into it the oil from two 3¾-ounce cans smoked mussels. Mince finely two medium-sized cloves garlic, and add to oil with ½ tablespoon parsley flakes and salt and pepper to taste. Sauté 5 minutes. Meanwhile, mince mussels very finely, add to skillet, set flame low, stir gently, and sauté for 1 minute. Remove skillet from fire, stir in juice of 1 lemon or 3 tablespoons bottled lemon juice, and let cool. Serve with sea biscuits or any kind of bland crackers.

Tongue Heated in Sauce Madère

Drain well two 8-ounce cans sliced tongue or thinly slice the equivalent from a whole canned tongue, saving the jelly around it.

Over a medium flame, put a medium-sized skillet with 2 tablespoons butter in it. While butter is melting, chop finely one medium-sized white onion and one small dill pickle, open one 10½-ounce can brown gravy, and have ready 3 envelopes dehydrated beef broth and jelly from around the tongue. Sauté onion till tan and add gravy, tongue jelly, and dehydrated broth. Bring to a boil and simmer until reduced by half. Stir in ⅓ cup Madeira or sherry, add chopped pickle, turn off flame, and remove from stove.

Over a medium flame, put your largest double boiler, with 2 inches water in the bottom, and place tongue slices in the top. Pour sauce over tongue, cover, set flame low, and heat for 20 minutes, then remove so as to free burner and place over the three hot asbestos pads to keep warm.

Potatoes with Caraway and Dill Weed

Drain well two 1-pound cans whole boiled potatoes with dill, and put in the top of a medium-sized double boiler with 1¼ inches water in the bottom. Add 3 tablespoons caraway seed, 3 tablespoons butter, and salt and coarse-ground black pepper to taste. Cover and cook over low flame for 10 minutes, then insert three asbestos pads under pot, raise flame to medium, cook 15 minutes longer and set aside with asbestos pads to free burner and to keep warm.

Celery Knobs Fermière

Drain over any suitable container two 1-pound cans celery knobs, dice celery very coarsely and return to cans. Chop finely one large white onion.

Over a medium flame in a heavy saucepan or skillet, melt 2 tablespoons butter, add onion along with 1 teaspoon each onion salt and celery salt, and sauté. Meanwhile, measure out 2 tablespoons flour and open one 10½-ounce can condensed consommé. When onions are golden, add flour, mix together till smooth, then cook a few minutes. Add 1 cup undiluted condensed consommé, celery knobs, 1 bay leaf, ¼ teaspoon dried thyme leaves, and 1 tablespoon parsley flakes. Stir and cook until thickened, cover, and cook over very low flame for 20 minutes, then discard bay leaf. Set flame as low as possible, insert flame-tamer or two asbestos pads under skillet, and keep hot until ready to serve.

Gooseberry and Raspberry Compote

Both these fruits, imported from England in 15-ounce cans, are to be found in fine food stores. Drain over saucepan the syrup from 1 can of each fruit, and mix. Put fruit into a heavy plastic bag, close tightly and put to cool. To the syrup, add 2 tablespoons currant jelly, put uncovered over a medium flame, bring to a boil, cook until reduced by half, and let cool. Pour syrup over fruit in bag, reclose bag tightly, and chill if possible. Serve any kind of cookies as an accompaniment.

COCONUT CHIPS

OYSTERS, SHRIMPS, AND CAVIAR TSARINA

RICE COOKED IN CLAM JUICE

TWO-TONE ASPARAGUS SALAD

WHITE PEACHES

Coconut Chips

Shipped from Hawaii, these are widely distributed in cans. They keep indefinitely, even after being opened, and one can will serve four persons adequately. A reserve of three or four cans is recommended for the many uses to which these chips can be put.

Oysters, Shrimps, and Caviar Tsarina

Drain well three 8-ounce cans whole oysters, one 4½-ounce can tiny shrimp, and set aside solids. Open 1 very small jar Beluga or lumpfish caviar, and set aside. Chop finely 1 small white onion.

Directly over low flame, in the top of your largest double boiler, melt 1 tablespoon butter, add onion and 1 teaspoon onion salt, and sauté for 2 minutes, or until pale gold. Pour ½ cup dry white wine over onion and reduce until wine only barely covers the bottom of the pan, but take care not to scorch. Add

1⅓ cups sour cream, stir well, season generously with pepper (but no salt), and stir in ½ teaspoon dried tarragon leaves, a good dash each ground nutmeg and cloves, and 1 tablespoon fresh or bottled lemon juice. Bring to the boiling point, but do not boil.

Put over bottom of double boiler with 2 inches water in it, bring water to a boil, and stir in oysters, shrimp, and caviar. Dust with paprika, cover, and heat for 15 minutes.

Rice Cooked in Clam Juice

Chop finely 1 large white onion and, over a low flame, in a heavy skillet with cover, melt 3 tablespoons butter. Add onion, sauté until just transparent, then add ⅔ cup raw rice and stir to coat rice with butter. Next, add two 8-ounce bottles or one 15-ounce can clam juice, cover, set flame as low as possible, insert three asbestos pads or a flame-tamer under skillet, and cook 20 to 25 minutes, or until all liquid is absorbed and rice tests done.

Two-Tone Asparagus Salad

Drain well one 1-pound can each green asparagus spears and white asparagus spears, put into a shallow dish, and mix gently with fingers to distribute colors evenly. Pour over asparagus a simple oil and white wine vinegar dressing, seasoned with ¼ teaspoon sugar, salt and white pepper, 1 teaspoon onion salt, and ¼ teaspoon garlic salt.

White Peaches

These are available in 29-ounce cans in many gourmet food stores, and are so superior to any other canned peaches that we suggest you stock up on them (one can will serve four persons). The peaches should be chilled if possible. When ready to serve, divide fruit evenly among four bowls and put a small amount of syrup from can on top of each, discarding the rest.

Food for Frostbiters

MENUS AND RECIPES FOR EIGHT VERY COLD DAYS

There is quite a population of hardy sailors who find it exhilarating to cruise around Maine and Alaska and other northern waters in wintry weather. It may not be for the thin-skinned and timorous, but it does hold a lot of satisfaction for many. A little snow or ice on the deck and shrouds, a frosty but not very rough sea, the pretty look of snow-dusted buildings at all your ports of call, the almost total lack of aquatic traffic, and, as a result, the excellent chances of getting acquainted with the year-round residents—who don't, somehow, take up much with summer folk—are all worth the doing. At least, you'll have no refrigeration problems. Even ice cubes, if they are a sine qua non of your lifestyle aboard, can be made on deck, if you carry along an ice-cube tray or two, and rig some way to keep the trays, in the cockpit or over the stern lazarette, from tipping (another place that shock cords can be used).

A different frostbiting contingent enthusiastically go in for day races during the cold weather in the same waters on which they race with equal fervor during the summer. Their feeding requirements vary somewhat from those of the cold weather cruising people, but both need plenty of very warm clothes, and careful planning. For frostbite racers, stowage of the vitally necessary fragile thermos bottles is, of course, a problem, but, in the interests of sheer sustenance, it is one that has to be solved—before casting off.

For cruising at leisure in cold waters, the requirements are something else—if not in essentials, then in long-passage arrangements.

First and foremost is a snug, warm cabin. This is the heart of the ship. The warmth can be achieved without installation of a pot-bellied wood- or charcoal-burning stove, or any stove necessitating chimney and pipe. Two ordinary red clay house bricks, salvaged perhaps from a handy demolition site or asked for sweetly at a brickyard, heated on the galley stove over a medium fire for one hour in the morning and a second hour in the evening will not only warm the cabin effectively around the clock, but also combat condensation. The cabin's snugness, in terms of wind-and-chillproofing, is up to the boatbuilder and the orders of the skipper to those who fit out the boat for this kind of a cruise.

Sandwich-making and salad bowls depart with the first frost. Hot meals and ample quantities are the thing. An assortment of wide-mouthed thermos bottles of differing sizes, capacities and end-purposes cannot be dispensed with, and the stowage of them, handy for day-in-day-out usage but safely disposed to prevent knockabout breakage, must be well thought out beforehand. Brackets, specially made and installed to fit each one neatly, is one possible solution. A shelf protected by shock cords, with ordinary quilted pot holders or doubled-over pieces of cut-up towels put between each bottle, is another. In any case, carry spare liners for all the thermoses—two for each, if feasible from a stowage point of view, since replacements may be hard to come by at ports of call.

Food will keep warm in thermoses for many hours, especially if stowed near a running engine. Two more suggestions: hot drinks of all kinds, including toddies and their relatives, are welcome after or during a cold watch above, and almost any kind of flavored crackers or quick snacks are a boon.

As for the outside personnel, battery-operated pocket hand-warmers are a big help for long turns at the helm, but a headache when actually engaged in working on the deck. They also serve admirably inside the bedclothes at the bottom of the bunk, to warm cold feet. In this regard, let's mention that the warmest bunk sheets in these waters are those made of cotton flannelette, which can be bought from the large mail order companies.

Given a good strong battery and plenty of gasoline for the planned run, a turning engine also provides a lot of warmth for the cabin.

The menus and recipes that follow are specifically planned for cold weather. Many of them can be translated into thermos-bottle meals, and all aim to warm the vitals, and satisfy the ravenous appetites, of the somewhat frozen skipper and crew.

~

BREAKFASTS

HOT CANNED FIGS
PANADE WITH CELERY AND CROUTONS

Hot Canned Figs

Over a medium flame, put your largest double boiler, with 2 inches water in the bottom, and in the top, put the contents of one 29-ounce can whole figs. Pour 4 tablespoons brandy over the fruit, dust well with ground cloves, cover, and heat for 15 minutes.

Panade with Celery and Croutons

A *panade* is a thick soup, enriched with milk and eggs, and is a usual part of breakfast in provincial France, replacing the hot or cold cereals featured in so many American breakfasts. For cold-weather cruising, it makes a filling and warming intake with which to start the day. If partially cooked the night before, and kept overnight in a wide-mouthed thermos, it will not take long in the morning to finish it in a saucepan over the fire.

Drain well one 1-pound can celery stalks, saving the juice, and dice the celery finely. Cut 6 slices stale white bread in ¾-inch pieces. Over a low flame, in a large saucepan, melt 2 tablespoons butter, add the celery and 3 tablespoons celery juice, and cook slowly over two asbestos pads or a flame-tamer until cooked down by half. Add enough warm water to balance of celery juice to make 3 cups, and put in saucepan, then put in 1 teaspoon salt and the bread. Mix well to soak the bread thoroughly, then bring the mixture to a boil, stirring constantly. Cover and cook for 30 minutes. Remove from stove and put into thermos overnight.

In the morning, beat 1 jumbo or 2 medium eggs lightly, and add 1½ cups fresh, diluted evaporated, or reconstituted dry milk. Put the panade into a saucepan over a medium flame and heat, stirring briskly with a whisk, until smooth. Combine milk and eggs with hot panade and add 1 tablespoon butter. When butter has melted, season well with salt and white pepper and serve in mugs, with plain, rye, or cheese croutons.

EARLY-DAY CONSOMMÉ

FRIED ROLLS WITH SYRUP

FRIED SCRAPPLE

Early-Day Consommé

The night before, put a medium-sized saucepan over a medium flame, and into it pour three 10½-ounce cans undiluted condensed consommé. Add 1½ teaspoons onion salt, 1 teaspoon celery salt, and a liberal sprinkling of parsley flakes. Bring to a boil, cook until slightly reduced, and pour into a thermos. When ready to serve the next morning, put into four mugs, then add 2 teaspoons or 1 tablespoon bourbon or rum, or 2 tablespoons sherry or Madeira, to each mug.

Fried Rolls with Syrup

Open 2 packages frozen crescent dinner rolls. Cut rolls in half, and flatten each half with a spatula. Over a high flame, in a heavy 12-inch skillet, heat 3 tablespoons oil. Lower flame to medium, arrange rolls to cover the skillet bottom, and fry until golden brown on both sides. Meanwhile, on the other burner over a medium flame, heat a medium-sized double boiler with 1 inch water in the bottom. As rolls are done, remove to top of double boiler. Repeat until all rolls are cooked, adding more oil if needed. Serve hot with butter and any syrup.

Fried Scrapple

The recipe for this is given on page 111.

MULLED APPLE JUICE
CODFISH CAKES AND HARD-BOILED
EGGS WITH SAUCE
SAUTÉED ENGLISH MUFFINS
WITH LIME MARMALADE

Mulled Apple Juice

Into a large saucepan, pour one 1-quart can apple juice, or the equivalent in smaller cans. Stir in 1 teaspoon ground allspice, one stick (or 1 teaspoon ground) cinnamon, 12 whole (or ½ teaspoon ground) cloves, and ½ cup rum. Put in saucepan over a medium flame, cover, and heat the juice, but do not boil. Pour into a wide-mouthed thermos to keep hot and, when ready to serve, pour into mugs.

Codfish Cakes and Hard-Boiled Eggs with Sauce

The night before, hard-boil 4 eggs. In the morning, over a low flame put a heavy 12-inch skillet with 1 tablespoon butter, in it, and open two 10½-ounce cans or one 29-ounce can codfish cakes and one 10½-ounce can condensed cream of mushroom soup. When butter sizzles, arrange cakes in skillet, raise flame to medium high, and fry until medium-brown on both sides. While cakes are cooking, put to heat on the other burner over a medium flame your largest double boiler with 2 inches water in the bottom, shell and slice the hard-boiled eggs, and split 6 English muffins.

When cakes are cooked, remove to top of double boiler, cover, and then remove double boiler from stove. Leave skillet on stove over low flame for English muffins. On the free burner, over a medium flame, put a medium-sized double boiler with 1½ inches water in the bottom, pour the undiluted mushroom soup into the top, and season with salt, onion salt, and 1 teaspoon Worcestershire sauce or prepared mustard, cover, and heat for 15 minutes. When ready to serve, put two codfish cakes into each of four shallow dishes, cover with egg slices, and pour mushroom soup over the top.

Sautéed English Muffins

The recipe for this is given on page 147. Serve with lime marmalade for a sharp flavor, contrasting well with the codfish cakes.

HOT CRANBERRY JUICE
CREAMED FINNAN HADDIE ON FLATBREAD

Hot Cranberry Juice

The night before, over a medium flame, heat, but do not boil, one 1-quart can cranberry juice, or the equivalent in smaller cans. Pour into a thermos to keep hot and, in the morning, serve in mugs.

Creamed Finnan Haddie on Flatbread

Use two 15-ounce cans flaked finnan haddie or 2 pounds finnan haddie fillets purchased from a fish store. If these are not ready to cook, buy the day before cooking and soak in a saucepan for 2 hours in 2 cups each of water and any kind of liquid milk to remove excess salt, then simmer gently in the same liquid for 15 minutes, drain, cool, and flake.

Over a medium flame, put a medium-sized double boiler with $1\frac{1}{4}$ inch water in the bottom, and into the top put 3 tablespoons butter. While butter is melting, measure out 3 tablespoons flour and $1\frac{1}{2}$ cups any kind of liquid milk. When butter has melted, stir in flour till smooth, add $\frac{1}{2}$ teaspoon white pepper, and the milk. Stir until no lumps are apparent, remove to direct high flame, and cook, stirring constantly, until thickened. Return bottom of double boiler to flame, put over it the double boiler top, stir in the finnan haddie, and heat for 15 minutes. Serve in bowls over Norwegian flatbread, broken up into bite-sized pieces.

HOT TOMATO AND SAUERKRAUT JUICE
HAM WITH WHITE WINE SAUCE
FRIED CORNMEAL MUSH

Hot Tomato and Sauerkraut Juice

The night before, pour one 18-ounce can tomato juice and 1½ cups canned sauerkraut juice into a saucepan. Put over a medium flame to heat, but do not boil. Pour into a thermos. When ready to serve in the morning, slice ½ lemon, pour juice mixture into mugs, and float a lemon slice on top of each.

Ham with White Wine Sauce

Prepare the sauce first, and set aside in medium-sized double boiler to keep warm.

Over a medium flame, put your largest double boiler with 1¾ inches water in the bottom, and 4 tablespoons butter in the top, add salt and coarse-ground black pepper to taste, cover, and heat. Meanwhile, measure out 4 tablespoons flour, ¾ cup any kind of liquid milk or cream, and ¾ cup dry white wine. Have ready 4 opened envelopes dehydrated chicken broth. When butter has melted, stir in flour until smooth, add milk and wine and dehydrated chicken broth, stir to remove any lumps, remove top of double boiler to direct medium flame, and cook, stirring constantly, until thickened. Replace over bottom of double boiler, cover, lower flame, and keep hot.

Slice thinly ½ pound cured or canned ham, or use ½ pound presliced store-bought boiled ham. Over a medium flame, put a large heavy skillet with 2 tablespoons butter in it. When butter has melted, add the ham slices, turn flame high, and cook until browned on both sides. Add to sauce in top of double boiler. Turn off flame under skillet but leave on stove.

Fried Cornmeal Mush

Cook the mush the night before. Put 1½ quarts water into a saucepan or pot, set over a high flame, and bring to a boil. Meanwhile, mix 1½ cups yellow cornmeal with 2 teaspoons salt, and add enough cold water to make a batter thin enough to run off a wooden spoon (this prevents lumping). When water in saucepan boils, spoon batter into it gradually, stirring, and continue stirring for 10 minutes, or until mush thickens. Set flame low, cover, and cook for 1 hour. Remove to a flat-bottomed, not too shallow, pan of a suitable size, and let cool overnight.

In the morning, cut the mush into ½-inch slices, put a medium flame under the skillet in which the ham was fried, add 2 tablespoons butter, and, when melted, cover the bottom of the skillet with slices of mush. Fry on both sides till a light brown. Remove as done to a shallow dish fitted into the top of the double boiler. Repeat, adding butter as needed, until all mush is cooked. Serve in bowls, with ham and sauce poured over the mush.

CHICKEN CONSOMMÉ BELLEVUE

PAN-FRIED STEAK II

HASHED BROWN POTATOES II

STEWED TOMATOES II

Chicken Consommé Bellevue

The night before, put in a saucepan one 13¾-ounce can undiluted condensed clear chicken broth combined with two 10½-ounce cans (or two 8-ounce bottles) clam juice. Set over a high flame and bring to a boil, then stir in the contents of 2 envelopes dehydrated chicken broth, season with salt and white pepper, set flame low, simmer 5 minutes, and then pour into a quart-sized thermos.

For breakfast, serve in mugs with a good squirt of pressure-canned whipped cream on top of each.

Hashed Brown Potatoes II

This recipe is given here instead of following menu order because this dish takes the longest to cook.

Use one package prepared dried hashed brown potatoes or 4 cooked medium-sized potatoes, peeled and cubed. Prepare mix according to directions on the package, and keep warm in the top of a medium-sized double boiler with 1½ inches water in the bottom.

If using diced fresh cooked potatoes, over a medium flame

melt 3 tablespoons butter, or any other fat, drippings, or shortening, in a heavy 12-inch skillet. When fat has melted, add the potatoes; stir and lift until coated with fat. Set flame low and cook, uncovered, until potatoes are brown on all sides, adding more fat if needed. They will take about 20 minutes to cook. Remove from skillet, as for prepared mix, and keep warm.

Pan-Fried Steak II

Use ½-inch-thick individual portions of any available tender beefsteak, fresh or thawed frozen. Be sure to bring meat to galley temperature before cooking.

The cooking procedure is the same as for Pan-Fried Steak I, the recipe for which is given on page 87, with these exceptions: the heat is not as high; 2½ tablespoons fat of any kind must be melted, but not scorched, before adding the meat to the pan; and the cooking time is just half that for an inch-thick, full-sized steak.

Fry the steaks after the potatoes are done and removed from the skillet, using the same pan.

Stewed Tomatoes II

Drain well two 1-pound cans whole tomatoes, reserving the juice to use some other time. Over a low flame, put a medium-sized heavy skillet, and in it melt 3 tablespoons butter. Put in tomatoes and season with 1½ teaspoons onion salt, 1 teaspoon each celery salt and paprika, a dash of Tabasco, and salt and coarse-ground black pepper to taste. Cover and cook for no more than 10 minutes.

HOT COOKED PRUNES IN PORT WINE

THICK BREAKFAST SOUP

COFFEE CAKE II

Hot Cooked Prunes in Port Wine

The recipe for this is given on page 158.

Thick Breakfast Soup

This is another of the filling soups very commonly served for breakfast in provincial France, adapted here for galley preparation, to be made the night before if desired.

Over a medium flame, in a large saucepan, put the undiluted contents of one 10½-ounce can each condensed consommé, chicken soup with rice, and any chunky-style vegetable or beef soup. Season to taste, stir well to mix, and heat to a boil.

If soup is made the night before, with slotted spoon remove all solids to one quart-sized wide-mouthed thermos, and pour clear soup into another thermos. In the morning, spoon an even amount of solids into each of four mugs, then fill each mug with clear soup. If soup is made in the morning, simply ladle it into mugs, distributing solids evenly. Serve with chunks of bread to dip into soup and also to eat as "fist food".

Coffee Cake II

Over a high flame, put to preheat for 10 minutes a 12-inch covered dome-lidded skillet with a rack in it. Meantime, put 3 tablespoons butter in the bottom of an 8-inch-square cake pan and place in skillet to melt butter. When butter has melted, remove pan from skillet, rotate and tilt pan to distribute melted butter over sides of the pan, sprinkle the bottom with ⅓ cup brown sugar, and over the sugar strew one 8-ounce can or jar mincemeat. In a heavy plastic bag, put 1 package prepared biscuit mix, add any kind of milk or fresh water as directed on package, close tightly, and blend by squeezing and kneading. Spread batter over sugar and mincemeat, smoothing evenly, put into preheated skillet, cover, and cook 20–30 minutes without lowering flame or lifting cover. When it tests done, turn onto a plate, cut into squares, and serve hot with butter.

HOT BISHOP
CHICKEN LIVERS IN MUSHROOM GRAVY I
CRACKED-WHEAT PILAF
SKILLET CHERRY CAKE

Hot Bishop

The night before, over a low flame, put 1 cup water in the bottom of a fair-sized saucepan; add to it 1 rounded teaspoon each ground cloves, mace, ginger, cinnamon, and allspice. Simmer slowly for 20 minutes, and add 1½ cups fresh, reconstituted frozen, or canned orange juice and the juice of 1 lemon or 3 tablespoons bottled lemon juice, along with 1¼ cups good port wine. Heat to the point of boiling, but do not boil. Pour into a quart-sized thermos and, in the morning, serve in mugs.

Skillet Cherry Cake

Because this takes the longest to prepare and cook, the recipe is given here, rather than following menu order.

Over a high flame, preheat for 10 minutes a covered, heavy, dome-lidded 12-inch skillet with a rack in it. Then put 2 tablespoons butter into an 8-inch-square cake pan and put on rack in skillet. When butter has melted, remove the cake pan and rotate and tilt the pan to coat sides, as well as bottom, with melted butter.

Into a heavy plastic bag put 1½ cups prepared biscuit mix. In any suitable separate container, put ½ teaspoon vanilla extract, ⅛ teaspoon almond extract (optional), ½ cup any kind of liquid milk, and 1 fresh egg or the equivalent of mixed powdered egg and water. Combine, beating lightly, and add to biscuit mix in the bag. Close tightly, and squeeze and knead to form a stiffish dough. Drain well one 1-pound can sour pitted cherries, discarding the juice, add to dough in bag, and knead to distribute fruit well through the dough.

Pour into buttered cake pan, smoothing evenly, put pan on rack in skillet, and bake over medium-high flame for 30 minutes without lifting cover. If at that time it does not test done, re-cover and cook for 5–10 minutes longer. Remove pan from skillet, cut cake into squares, and serve hot with butter.

Chicken Livers in Mushroom Gravy I

Use two 10½-ounce cans ready-to-serve chicken livers in mushroom gravy, or ¾ pound thawed frozen or fresh chicken livers, two 10½-ounce cans plain mushroom gravy, and one 3-ounce can broiled-in-butter sliced mushrooms.

If using canned chicken livers in mushroom gravy, over a medium flame, set your largest double boiler, with 2 inches water in the bottom and into the top, empty both cans, cover, and heat for 15 minutes, then put two asbestos pads under double boiler to heat for 3 minutes. Remove double boiler, with pads, from stove to keep warm and to free burner.

If you are using fresh or thawed frozen livers, over a direct high flame melt 3 tablespoons butter in the top of your largest double boiler and, when butter is sizzling, add chicken livers and sauté briskly until browned, turning often. Stir in mushroom gravy quickly, put top of double boiler over bottom (with 2 inches water in it), lower flame to medium, and heat for 15 minutes. As soon as possible after putting the livers to heat, drain well the 3-ounce can sliced mushrooms and stir mushrooms into livers, re-cover, and continue cooking. When done, insert two asbestos pads under double boiler to heat for 3 minutes; then remove double boiler, with pads, from stove to keep warm and to free burner.

Cracked-Wheat Pilaf

This may be bought in 1-pound cans ready to heat and serve, and one can will serve four. Or it may be made from scratch the day or night before, or a brown rice pilaf, previously made, can be substituted. The procedure and timing is the same for both cracked-wheat pilaf and brown rice pilaf.

Heat the ready-to-serve cracked-wheat pilaf in a medium-sized double boiler, with 1½ inches water in the bottom, over a medium flame for 20 minutes.

To prepare cracked-wheat or brown rice pilaf, chop coarsely 1 large or 2 medium yellow onions. Over a low flame, put a medium-sized heavy skillet with 4 tablespoons (½ stick) butter in it. When butter has melted, stir in onions and sauté until they have taken on some color. Add 1 cup bulgur (cracked wheat) or brown rice and cook, stirring, until the grains are coated. Pour in one 13¾-ounce can undiluted condensed clear chicken broth and ¼ cup water, stir well, cover, insert three asbestos pads or a flame-tamer under the skillet, and cook 45 minutes. Stir well three times at 15-minute intervals. Ladle into a wide-mouthed quart-sized thermos to keep overnight, and heat as for canned pilaf.

LUNCHES

RED FLANNEL HASH
KALE GRUYÈRE
TOPPLED APPLES

Red Flannel Hash

Over a medium flame, put a large heavy skillet with 2 table-spoons butter or fat in it. While fat is melting, open two 15½-ounce cans corned beef hash and open and drain well one 8-ounce can diced beets. When fat has melted, add hash and stir beets through it. Spread evenly, set flame very low, and cook until well browned on the bottom (about 20 minutes). Fold like an omelet to serve.

Kale Gruyère

Drain well two 15-ounce cans kale, then squeeze kale with fingers to remove any remaining moisture and replace in cans. Grate enough Gruyère cheese to make ½ cup. Open one 10½-ounce can condensed cream of celery soup.

On the other burner, over a medium flame, put your largest double boiler with 2 inches water in the bottom, and into the top put the kale, cheese, and soup. Season with salt, coarse-ground black pepper, and ¼ teaspoon ground nutmeg and stir to combine. Cover, and heat for 20 minutes. When hot, remove from stove and keep warm over three asbestos pads.

Toppled Apples

On the free burner, over a high flame, put a heavy 12-inch dome-lidded skillet, covered, with a rack in it to preheat for 10 minutes. Meanwhile, peel and core 5 large green apples and slice ½ inch thick crosswise. Butter an 8-inch-square cake pan, and place in it the apple slices, on their sides, side by side in two rows. Sprinkle 1 cup brown sugar over the apple slices and dot with 4 tablespoons (½ stick) butter, then trickle over them 2½ tablespoons rum or bourbon or brandy.

Put pan onto rack in skillet, cover, and cook without lifting cover for 30 minutes. Serve hot or cold, with or without fresh or sour cream.

EGGPLANT LAYERED WITH HAM
SPAGHETTI WITH WHITE CLAM SAUCE
POOR KNIGHTS OF WINDSOR

Eggplant Layered with Ham

Over a medium flame, put to heat a large heavy skillet, the bottom generously covered with olive or vegetable oil. While it is heating, slice finely 3 large white onions. When oil is hot, turn flame low and sauté onions until golden. While onions are sautéing, peel 2 medium-sized eggplants, cut into ½-inch slices, and season both sides of each slice with salt and coarse-ground black pepper. When onions are done, with slotted spoon remove from skillet and set aside. Put the eggplant slices in the skillet, add 2 tablespoons more oil, raise flame to high-medium, sauté eggplant for 3 minutes on each side, and remove from skillet. In the oil remaining in the skillet, over the same flame, frizzle 8 thin slices cooked ham, and remove from skillet.

Return half the eggplant slices to the skillet, set flame as low as possible, cover each eggplant slice with onions and ham, sprinkle with grated Parmesan cheese, and cover with the remaining slices of eggplant. Cover skillet, and cook for 5 minutes.

Spaghetti with White Clam Sauce

This can be purchased ready to serve, and two 15-ounce cans will serve four. To prepare from scratch, using canned white clam sauce, put a large kettle three-quarters full of water over a high flame on the free burner, cover, and bring to a vigorous boil. Add half of a 1-pound box or one 8-ounce box, spaghetti, and cook uncovered for 9 minutes. Drain well, return to kettle, and set flame low. Stir in two 10½-ounce cans white clam sauce, cover, and heat for 10 minutes. At this point, put two asbestos pads under skillet to heat for 5 minutes, then remove kettle, with pads, to keep warm.

Poor Knights of Windsor

Into a fair-sized shallow dish put ¾ cup dry white wine, and in it soak for 5 minutes 6 slices white bread, stale for preference. Separate 3 eggs; place the yolks in a second shallow dish and, with a fork or whisk, beat till blended. Put the egg whites into an airtight container for use another time, or discard.

Over a medium flame on the free burner, set a medium-sized heavy skillet and put 2 tablespoons butter in it. Dip wet bread into egg yolks, drip off excess yolk, then sauté until golden brown on both sides. Meanwhile, discard wine from shallow dish, and put cooked bread in it, as done, sprinkling each slice with sugar and cinnamon. Put ½ inch water in skillet, put dish with sautéed bread into skillet, cover, and keep hot.

CREAM OF ASPARAGUS BORSCHT

WITH DARK RY-VITA WAFERS

BREAD-AND-BUTTER PUDDING

Cream of Asparagus Borscht

Over a medium flame, put a large saucepan with 2 table-spoons butter in it. While butter is melting, open two 10½-ounce cans condensed cream of asparagus soup and one 8-ounce can whole or sliced or diced or shoestring beets. Drain beets, saving the liquid, chop beets finely and return to can.

When butter has melted, add beets to pan, along with 3 teaspoons sugar and the juice of ½ lemon or 1½ tablespoons bottled lemon juice, stir well and cook for 4 minutes. Add the undiluted soup and 4 tablespoons (¼ cup) beet juice, stir until smooth, and then add ½ cup undiluted evaporated milk or fresh light cream or sour cream, and 2 tablespoons parsley flakes, then stir well again. Season with salt, coarse-ground black pepper, and ¼ teaspoon ground nutmeg. Heat to boiling point, but do not boil. Pour into a quart-sized wide-mouthed thermos until ready to serve in bowls or mugs with buttered dark Ry-Vita wafers, or the equivalent.

Bread-and-Butter Pudding

Over a high flame, put to preheat for 10 minutes a covered dome-lidded 12-inch skillet with a rack in it. Meanwhile, on the other burner, in the top of a small double boiler with ¾ inch water in the bottom, put to heat 1 cup water and 2 tablespoons instant coffee.

Butter lightly 6 slices white or raisin bread, stale for preference, cut into ½-inch squares, and add to heated coffee mixture with ¼ cup raisins.

In any sizeable container, beat 2 eggs, or the equivalent of powdered eggs mixed with water, just enough to blend and stir in ½ cup sugar, ½ teaspoon salt, ¼ teaspoon ground nutmeg, and 1 tablespoon brandy or rum or bourbon. Add hot bread mixture to this, blend well, and pour into an 8-inch-square cake pan. Sprinkle with more nutmeg, put cake pan on rack in skillet, cover, set flame medium low, and cook for 1· hour without lifting cover. Serve hot or cold.

CARAWAY MACARONI RAREBIT ON
TOASTED BOSTON BROWN BREAD
HOT ORANGES

Caraway Macaroni Rarebit

Use two 15-ounce cans macaroni in cheese sauce, or make from scratch. In either case, additional ingredients and seasonings are the secret of the success of this dish.

To make the dish from scratch, put a large covered pot or kettle three-fourths full of water over a high flame, bring to a vigorous boil, add one 8-ounce package or half of a 1-pound package elbow macaroni, boil uncovered for 9 minutes, drain, rinse, and set aside. While macaroni is cooking, grate coarsely 1 pound sharp cheddar cheese and measure out ¾ cup undiluted evaporated milk and 2 tablespoons flour. Over a medium flame put your largest double boiler, with 2 tablespoons butter in the top and 2 inches water in the bottom. When butter has melted, add flour, stir until smooth, then add milk, 1 teaspoon dry mustard, 1¼ teaspoons Worcestershire sauce, 2 teaspoons celery salt, 2 good shakes garlic salt, and 1½ teaspoons paprika. Set over direct flame and cook, stirring constantly, until thickened. Stir in cheese and continue cooking until cheese is well blended into the sauce. Put back over double boiler bottom, mix in macaroni and 2 tablespoons caraway seeds, cover, put over two asbestos pads or a flame-tamer, cook 10 minutes more, and then remove to keep hot and to free burner.

If you are using canned macaroni in cheese sauce, empty cans into the top of your largest double boiler, with 2 inches water in the bottom, stir in all the seasonings listed above, and also ¼ pound coarsely grated sharp cheddar cheese. Cover, put over a medium flame, and heat until cheese has melted. Insert three asbestos pads under double boiler, leave flame on for 5 minutes to heat pads, and remove, with pads, from stove to keep warm and to free burner.

Toasted Boston Brown Bread

Empty and slice ½ inch thick two 1-pound cans Boston brown bread. Over a low flame, put a large heavy skillet with 2 tablespoons butter in it. When butter has melted, cover bottom of skillet with bread slices and toast until lightly browned on both sides, adding more butter if needed. Remove slices as done to keep warm in a covered saucepan over a very low flame and three asbestos pads. Repeat until all bread has been toasted, then remove both the saucepan and the pads under it, to keep warm until ready to serve.

Hot Oranges

Peel 3 large oranges and section them, removing seeds and excess pith. Over a medium flame set a medium-sized double boiler, with 1½ inches water in the bottom, and into the top, put the orange sections. Sprinkle over the fruit ½ cup sugar, ¼ cup sherry or Madeira or Marsala, and ¼ cup raisins, and stir well. Cover and cook for 20 minutes. Serve hot, with grated coconut sprinkled over each portion.

Jeanne's Cock-a-Leekie Soup

This variation of the famous soup of Scotland uses onions instead of leeks, and includes carrots and green beans. Slice thinly 4 medium-sized yellow onions. Over a low flame, put a large pot or saucepan with 2 tablespoons butter in it. When butter has melted, stir in onions and cook till transparent. While onions are cooking, open three 13¾-ounce cans condensed clear chicken broth, one 8-ounce can each of sliced or diced carrots and cut green beans, and one 13-ounce can boned chicken.

When onions are done, pour in two of the cans of chicken broth, reserving one empty can, add 1 large bay leaf, 1 teaspoon poultry seasoning, 2 teaspoons salt, and ¼ teaspoon peppercorns. Cover, raise flame to medium, and bring to a boil. Meanwhile, peel and cube 3 medium potatoes and, when broth boils, add them, re-cover and cook 10 minutes. While potatoes cook, separate chicken meat from its jellied broth, put jelly into the reserved empty broth can, and return meat to their cans. Drain over the jelly the carrots and green beans, leaving vegetables in cans. After potatoes have cooked 10 minutes, add the two cans of liquid to the soup, raise flame somewhat, and cook for 10 minutes more. Stir in carrots, green beans, and chicken pieces. Bring just to the boiling point, stir well and then remove from burner and put over three hot asbestos pads until ready to serve. To serve, ladle into bowls, including plenty of the solids in each portion.

Ham-Filled Skillet Biscuits

Prepare one package biscuit mix dough as directed on box. Roll or pat dough to ½-inch thickness, and cut into twelve squares. Cut 6 thin slices of any kind of precooked ham in half crosswise, or open one 3-ounce can ham spread. Make a large and fairly deep incision in the side of each uncooked biscuit, fold each half-slice of ham in half again and insert, or with a teaspoon push into each incision a level spoonful of ham spread.

Over a medium flame on the free burner, put a large heavy

skillet with 4 tablespoons butter in it. While butter is melting, stir in 1½ teaspoons onion salt, 2 teaspoons celery seed, ½ teaspoon garlic salt, and 2 teaspoons paprika. Arrange biscuits in skillet, turning once immediately to coat with seasoned butter. Cover and cook 6 minutes on one side, turn, and cook 5 minutes more, or until they test done.

Hot Fruitcake Slices

Cut four ½-inch-thick slices fruitcake, douse each liberally with rum or sherry or bourbon or brandy, and arrange in the top of your largest double boiler, with 2 inches water in the bottom. Over a medium-low flame, on the burner freed by removing the soup, put the double boiler, and heat cake slices for 20 minutes.

OYSTER AND NOODLE SKILLET CASSEROLE

LIMA BEAN AND MUSHROOM MÉLANGE

HILLARY'S BUTTERSCOTCH PUDDING

Oyster and Noodle Skillet Casserole

Over a high flame, put a large pot or saucepan three-quarters full of water, bring to a rolling boil, and stir in 1½ cups any kind of plain or fancy noodles, boil for 9 minutes, drain, set aside, and remove pot from stove.

While noodles are cooking, open two 8-ounce cans whole oysters and one 10½-ounce can condensed cream of mushroom soup, chop finely 1 medium-sized white onion, and slice in half crosswise 12 pimiento-stuffed green olives.

Over a direct low flame, put the top of a medium-sized double boiler with 2 tablespoons butter in it. When butter has melted, stir in onions and olives, and sauté till onion is wilted. Meanwhile, put 1¼ inches water in the double boiler bottom. When onions are done, over the same flame, put the double boiler bottom and the top into it. Empty the undiluted mushroom soup over the onion mixture, drain the oyster liquid into the soup, and stir well. Cover and heat for 10 minutes.

Off the stove, put a thin layer of noodles into the top of your largest double boiler, sprinkle with salt, white pepper, and a quick dash of cayenne, put a layer of oysters over it, another layer each of noodles and oysters, seasoning each layer before adding the next, and a final layer of noodles. Pour soup mixture over, cover with mild grated cheese, place double boiler, with 2 inches water in the bottom, on a medium flame, cook for 15 minutes, then remove from stove to free burner for cooking pudding.

Hillary's Butterscotch Pudding

Off the stove, put into a medium-sized saucepan one package butterscotch pudding mix, and stir in 2 teaspoons instant coffee. Cook pudding as directed on the package, but using ¼ cup maple or maple-blended syrup in place of ¼ cup of the milk called for on the package. When pudding is done, stir in ¼ cup each walnut meats and raisins. Serve hot or cooled, with or without cream or whipped cream.

Lima Bean and Mushroom Mélange

Open one 1-pound can or two 8-ounce cans baby green lima beans and two 3-ounce cans or one 6-ounce can sliced mushrooms. Drain all cans over a small saucepan, leaving vegetables in the cans. On the free burner, cook the can liquids until reduced by two-thirds and set aside.

Over a medium flame, put to melt 2 tablespoons butter in a medium-sized heavy skillet. When butter has melted, stir in mushroom slices and sauté until medium brown. Sprinkle with 1 teaspoon each curry powder, onion salt, celery salt, and paprika. Set flame low, stir in lima beans, reduced liquids, and cook for 10 minutes.

SKILLET JAMBALAYA

CHINESE VEGETABLES AMANDINE

NO-COOK NUT AND SPICE NUGGETS

CANNED GREEN GRAPES

Skillet Jambalaya

Cook rice according to the recipe given on page 63. While rice is cooking, open one 5-ounce jar chipped beef, shred meat coarsely, and set aside. Drain well two 4½-ounce cans jumbo shrimp and one 29-ounce can whole tomatoes, saving the tomato liquid for some other use. Chop finely 2 medium-sized white onions, and slice crosswise into thirds 16 pitted black olives. When rice has steamed 10 minutes, remove pot from stove.

Over high flame, put a fairly large heavy skillet with 3 table-spoons butter in it. When butter has melted, sauté chipped beef, onions, and olives till onions are golden. Stir in a good vigorous dash of Tabasco and the tomatoes, lower flame considerably, and add shrimp. Cook for 3 to 5 minutes. When ready to serve, stir in hot rice, sprinkle with parsley flakes, and ladle into bowls.

Chinese Vegetables Amandine

Drain well one 5-ounce can water chestnuts, 1 medium-sized can bamboo shoots, one 3-ounce can sliced mushrooms, and one medium-sized or smaller can of bean sprouts. Slice water chestnuts and bamboo shoots thinly, if not already sliced.

Into a wide-mouthed screw-top jar, put $2\frac{1}{2}$ tablespoons each cornstarch and soy sauce, $1\frac{1}{2}$ teaspoons ground ginger, 1 teaspoon sugar, salt and coarse-ground black pepper to taste, and $\frac{1}{4}$ cup (4 tablespoons) water. Cover tightly, shake well to mix thoroughly, and set aside.

Over a high flame, put a large heavy skillet with 3 table-spoons vegetable oil in it and heat oil. When oil is hot add vege-tables, mix well, and cook, stirring, for 4 minutes. Add soy sauce mixture, blend thoroughly, and then add $\frac{1}{2}$ cup slivered almonds. Cook, stirring, until sauce thickens smoothly. Cover and turn off flame; vegetables will stay hot until ready to serve.

No-Cook Nut and Spice Nuggets

Put into a heavy plastic bag one 12-ounce package small spice cookies, close bag tightly, and crush cookies by rolling with a heavy bottle or pounding with a hammer. Open bag and add 1 teaspoon instant coffee, 1 tablespoon cocoa, $\frac{1}{2}$ cup superfine sugar, 1 cup chopped nuts of any kind or any combination of varieties, and $\frac{1}{2}$ teaspoon each ground ginger, cinnamon, and cloves. Reclose bag tightly, and shake well to mix thoroughly. Empty bag into any suitable rigid container, and blend in 3 table-spoons honey and 4 tablespoons dark rum. Shape into bite-sized ovals. On a sheet of wax paper or plastic or foil, with fingers mix 1 cup confectioner's sugar and ½ cup powdered cocoa. Roll cookie ovals in the mixture. Serve immediately, or store in any tightly covered rigid container.

LÉGUMES PANACHE

SAUTÉED SWEET POTATO SLICES

CRANBERRIED APRICOTS

Légumes Panache

Drain well one 8-ounce can each French-style green beans, baby green lima beans, corn kernels, and cut asparagus. Over a medium flame, put your largest double boiler with 2 inches water in the bottom, and in the top, arrange the vegetables in four distinct layers, in the order listed. Into any suitable container, put ¼ cup undiluted evaporated milk and ½ cup mayonnaise, blend well, and pour over vegetables. Set flame low, cover, and heat for 15 minutes.

Sautéed Sweet Potato Slices

Drain well two 18-ounce cans whole sweet potatoes, cut potatoes into ½-inch-thick slices, and season each slice on both sides with salt and coarse-ground black pepper. Put ½ cup any kind of liquid milk into an 8-inch pie pan, and put ½ cup flour into another. Over a high flame, put a large heavy skillet with 2½ tablespoons oil in it. While oil is heating, dip potato slices in milk and then in flour. When oil is hot but not smoking, lower flame to high-medium, arrange potato slices to fill bottom of skillet, and sauté quickly for about 3 minutes on each side. While potato slices are cooking, empty the milk from the pie pan. Remove cooked potato slices as they are done and put in the pan. Repeat until all potatoes have been cooked, put three asbestos pads under skillet, add to skillet ½ cup water, put a rack in it, and place pan with potato slices on rack. After 3 minutes, remove skillet, with pads, from stove to free burner for the dessert.

Cranberried Apricots

One or two hours before cooking, soak one 1-pound package dried apricots in white wine or water to cover.

When ready to prepare, drain apricots well, and open one 8-ounce can whole cranberry sauce. Put apricots into top of medium-sized double boiler, with 1½ inches water in the bottom, and place over a medium flame. Stir in the cranberry sauce thoroughly, add 2 tablespoons sugar, stir again, and heat for 15 minutes. Serve hot.

DINNERS

LOBSTER SPREAD II
BEEF ROLL SEVILLANA
SAFFRON RICE
SPANISH SPINACH
PEARS WITH ORANGES SMITANE

Lobster Spread II

Drain well two 5-ounce cans lobster meat, chop coarsely, put into any suitable container, pour over it ½ cup sherry or Madeira or sweet vermouth, and set aside for ½ hour.

When ready to prepare, drain well over any suitable container two 3-ounce cans or one 6-ounce can mushroom stems and pieces, leaving mushrooms in the cans, and chop finely 1 small white onion. Over a medium flame, put a medium-sized heavy skillet with 3 tablespoons butter in it. When butter has melted, add onion, sauté till wilted, then add mushrooms and sauté until onion is golden. Sprinkle 2 tablespoons flour over them and blend in half the mushroom liquid. Add contents of 3 envelopes dehydrated beef broth, stir well, and season to taste with salt and coarse-ground black pepper. When thickened, stir in lobster and liquid in which it has marinated, heat for 5 minutes, remove from stove, and serve from skillet with Bremner's oval oat crackers.

Beef Roll Sevillana

Drain over any suitable container three 7½-ounce cans sliced roast beef, or use a ½-inch-thick, 1½-pound piece of fresh or thawed frozen round steak. The preparation is mostly the same in either case; only the timing is different. The uncooked meat will take an hour to simmer, the canned slices need only 15 minutes.

Hard-boil 2 eggs and let cool. When ready to prepare the dish, over a low flame, in a large heavy skillet, fry 4 slices bacon, turning often. Remove from pan, leaving fat in pan, drain and dice bacon. Leave pan on stove, but turn off flame.

Chop coarsely ⅓ cup pimiento-stuffed green olives, or ¼ cup plain olives to which the contents of one very small jar of chopped pimientoes have been added, and set aside. Chop hard-boiled eggs, place into any suitable container, and add diced bacon, olives, 1½ tablespoons parsley flakes, 1½ tablespoons capers, ½ teaspoon coarse-ground black pepper, and 2 teaspoons paprika. Combine well, and bind with a little mayonnaise or sour cream. Spread on the meat and roll up, fastening with string or toothpicks. Add to bacon fat in skillet 3 tablespoons oil or butter or fat or any kind of shortening and over a medium flame heat well. Brown meat rolls on all sides, lower flame, add reserved gravy from canned roast beef, or to uncooked beef add enough water to cover the bottom of the pan. Set flame low, insert flame-tamer or two asbestos pads under skillet, cover, and cook as long as needed, according to the kind of meat used (raw or canned).

Saffron Rice

Over a medium flame, in a small saucepan or the top of a small double boiler, put ½ cup undiluted condensed clear chicken broth from a 13¾-ounce can, leaving the balance of the broth in the can. When broth is steaming, but not at a boil, add ½ teaspoon saffron shreds, remove from stove, and set aside to steep for ½ hour.

When ready to prepare, open a second 13¾-ounce can condensed clear chicken broth, put undiluted into the top of your largest double boiler, then add the balance of the other can of broth. Drain the saffron-steeped broth, discarding the saffron, and add to double boiler top with 1 cup raw noninstant rice and 1 tablespoon salt. Over direct high flame, bring liquid to a boil, cover, set flame low, insert flame-tamer or two asbestos pads under skillet, and simmer for about 25 minutes, or until liquid is absorbed by rice. Put over bottom of double boiler with 2 inches water in it, raise flame, remove pads or tamer, bring water to a boil, and set aside over tamer or pads to free burner.

Spanish Spinach

Drain well one 29-ounce can and one 16-ounce can whole spinach, or use 2 packages frozen spinach leaves. After cooking the frozen spinach, drain well. In either case, after draining, squeeze with your hands to remove any remaining liquid.

Over a low flame, put a saucepan with 3 tablespoons bacon fat or any other salty drippings in it. When fat has melted, add the spinach and cook for 5 minutes, stirring occasionally. Sprinkle with salt and coarse-ground black pepper to taste and add 3 tablespoons piñolas (pine nuts) or pistachios, 1 tablespoon raisins, and 1 chopped hard-boiled egg (optional). Serve at once.

Pears with Oranges Smitane

Drain over a saucepan one 29-ounce can pear halves and one 11-ounce jar orange sections designed for adding to whiskey Old-Fashioneds. Put fruit into a heavy plastic bag and close tightly.

Over a high-medium flame, cook syrups until reduced by half and cool. Stir in 1 tablespoon any kind of preserved fruit peel, or a combination of several. Remove from stove and stir in 3 tablespoons brandy or fruit liqueur of any variety. Add to fruit in bag, reclose tightly, and cool. Just before serving, stir in ½ cup sour cream, if on hand. Otherwise, serve as is.

HOT POPCORN

SMOKED SAUSAGE LYONNAIS

WITH HORSERADISH-AND-WALNUT SAUCE

CANNED RED CABBAGE AND APPLES

POTATO SALAD VI, CANNED, HOT

CHOCOLATE RICE PUDDING

Hot Popcorn

One of the most satisfying predinner appetizers in cold weather is freshly cooked popcorn. The unpopped kernels keep indefinitely, and the method of popping is simple.

Over a low flame, in a deep saucepan melt 4 tablespoons butter. When melted, add 1 cup popcorn kernels, raise flame to medium, cover, and shake constantly until corn starts to pop. Keep shaking until all corn is popped, turn into a bowl, sprinkle with salt, and serve.

Smoked Sausage Lyonnais

Use three 9-ounce cans hotly spiced small smoked sausages, or one hotly spiced whole sausage about 1 pound in weight. Drain canned sausage well. Over a very low flame, put a heavy 8-inch skillet with enough white wine or condensed chicken broth in the bottom to cover to the depth of 1/2 inch. Add sausage or sausages, cover, and poach for 10 minutes. If, when done, you are not yet ready to serve, insert three asbestos pads under skillet to keep meat warm. Drain well, and serve with Horseradish-and-Walnut Sauce.

Canned Red Cabbage and Apples

While sausage is poaching, put to heat over a low flame your largest double boiler, with 2 inches water in the bottom. Empty into the top two 14-ounce cans red cabbage and apples. These are imported from Sweden and may be obtained at many gourmet food specialty stores. Cover, and heat for 15 minutes, then remove and keep warm over three asbestos pads, thus freeing burner for potato salad.

Potato Salad VI, Canned, Hot

Over a low flame, put a deep saucepan, and into it empty two 14-ounce cans potato salad (stocked by a number of fine food shops). Cover and heat for 5 minutes. Insert flame-tamer, heat for 10 minutes more, and remove, with flame-tamer, from stove to keep hot and thus free burner for pudding.

Chocolate Rice Pudding

Over a medium flame, put your smallest double boiler with ¾ inch water in the bottom and 2 ounces broken-up sweet chocolate in the top. Stir in 2 tablespoons undiluted evaporated milk or canned or fresh heavy cream, and heat until chocolate is melted. Empty over the chocolate two 15-ounce cans rice pudding, stir thoroughly to blend chocolate through the pudding, add 1 tablespoon rum or brandy or any fruit liqueur, stir well again, and serve hot in bowls.

Horseradish-and-Walnut Sauce

This sauce, originally described in Escoffier's personal diary, is a delicious change from the usual horseradish–sour-cream sauce.

Into any suitable container, put ½ cup thick sweet cream, fresh or canned. Stir in lightly ¼ cup chopped walnut meats, 1 teaspoon sugar, salt to taste, and 2 tablespoons bottled prepared horseradish.

HOT CLAM SPREAD

CANNED LAMB STEW, EMBELLISHED

CANNED FRENCH-STYLE GREEN BEANS

WINTER COMPOTE

Hot Clam Spread

Drain well, over any suitable container, one 8-ounce can minced (not chopped) clams, and leave clam meat in can. Chop finely 1 small white onion.

Over a medium flame put your smallest double boiler, with ¾ inch water in the bottom and 2 tablespoons butter in the top. When butter has melted, stir in onion and 2 tablespoons parsley flakes. Cook about 8 minutes, add 2 tablespoons flour, mix till smooth, then add the juice from the clams, 1 teaspoon Worcestershire sauce, ¼ teaspoon dry mustard, and salt and coarse-ground black pepper to taste. Put top of double boiler over direct high flame, stir constantly until sauce thickens, add clam meat, and boil, stirring, for 1 minute. Place double boiler top over double boiler bottom, remove from stove and set over three hot asbestos pads to keep warm. Bind the mixture with fine bread crumbs if not thick enough to be of spreading consistency. Serve with sea toast or ship's biscuits or any plain water biscuit.

Canned Lamb Stew, Embellished

Drain well into the top of your largest double boiler the gravy from two 20-ounce cans lamb stew, leaving the solids in the cans. Over direct low flame put gravy to heat slowly and stir in ½ cup dry white wine, 1 tablespoon fresh or bottled lemon juice, 1 garlic clove finely minced, and ¼ teaspoon thyme leaves. Open one 1-pound can whole tomatoes and put 1 tomato in each can of lamb solids, reserving the tomato liquid and the remaining tomatoes for another use. Drain well one 8-ounce can small whole boiled onions, leave onions in the can, and set aside.

Simmer gravy for 10 minutes. Then, if not thick enough, in a small jar put 1½ tablespoons flour and add 2 tablespoons white wine or water or tomato liquid to it, close tightly and shake well to dissolve flour and eliminate all lumps. Pour into gravy, and stir till thickened. Stir in lamb solids, and tomatoes, and onions, and sprinkle generously with parsley flakes, put top of double boiler over bottom, with 2 inches water in it, return to flame, raise flame to medium, and cook for 15–20 minutes.

Canned French-Style Green Beans

Drain well two 1-pound cans French-style green beans and put in the top of a medium-sized double boiler, with 1½ inches water in the bottom. Add salt and coarse-ground black pepper to taste and 2 tablespoons butter, cover and put over a medium flame to heat for 15–20 minutes. When done, remove double boiler from stove and set over three asbestos pads to keep warm, and to free burner for the dessert.

Winter Compote

In a medium-sized heavy skillet, put one 1-pint jar any variety of brandied fruit, peaches for preference, drain well one 8-ounce can each plums, pineapple chunks, and black cherries, add to other fruit, and combine. Stir in 1/4 cup raisins, 1/4 cup sugar, and 1/2 cup any kind of orange juice. Cover and put over low flame to heat. When hot, fit skillet into the top of a large saucepan with 1 1/2 inches water in it, set flame low, and heat.

If brandied fruit is not available, any undrained canned fruit other than plums, cherries, or pineapple may be substituted, with 2 tablespoons brandy or rum stirred in before cooking.

HOT BACON AND CHEESE APPETIZER

MEAT BALLS COPENHAGEN

BOILED POTATOES — CARROTS WITH DILL

CANNED PEACH HALVES STUFFED

WITH CHOCOLATE-CHIP COOKIES

Hot Bacon and Cheese Appetizer

Fry 4 slices bacon until crisp and drain on a paper towel or newspaper or paper napkin or brown paper bag. When cool, crush to bits with fingers.

Grate coarsely enough of any mild cheese to make 1/2 cup. In any suitable container, mix well bacon and cheese, bind with mayonnaise or sour cream, put into the top of your small double boiler, with 3/4 inch water in the bottom, and set over a medium flame to heat. When hot, remove to three asbestos pads to keep warm, and serve as a spread with any rye-flavored bread or crackers.

Meat Balls Copenhagen

Cook these and the potatoes simultaneously. Begin by draining over the top of your largest double boiler two 1-pound cans hamburgers in gravy, leaving meat in cans. To gravy, add 1 teaspoon each dry mustard and paprika, 1 1/4 teaspoons Worcestershire sauce, 1/2 teaspoon dried marjoram leaves, and half of a 6-ounce can tomato paste. Stir well together, put double boiler top over a direct low flame, and bring slowly to a boil, uncovered.

While sauce is heating, peel 8 small or 4 medium-sized potatoes, leaving the small potatoes whole and quartering the larger ones, and put in bottom of double boiler, with 2 inches water in it.

When sauce simmers, stir into it 1⅓ cups canned or fresh sour cream, the meat from the cans, then place over double boiler bottom containing potatoes and water. Cover, cook for 15 minutes, put three asbestos pads under double boiler, allow 5 minutes for pads to heat, and then remove double boiler from stove. Set the top directly over hot pads, drain the water from the potatoes in the bottom, and reassemble double boiler over hot pads to keep warm and to free the burner.

Boiled Potatoes

See instructions in recipe for Meat Balls Copenhagen, above.

Carrots with Dill

Drain well two 1-pound cans whole baby carrots, and off the stove put in top of a medium-sized double boiler with 1 tablespoon butter, 1 teaspoon dill weed, and salt and coarse-ground black pepper to taste. Over a medium flame, set the bottom of the double boiler, with 1½ inches water in it, put top over bottom, cover, and heat for 15 minutes. Put three asbestos pads under double boiler, allow 5 minutes for pads to heat, and remove double boiler, with asbestos pads, from stove.

Canned Peach Halves Stuffed with Chocolate-Chip Cookies

Drain well one 29-ounce can large Elberta peach halves, leaving fruit in can. Soak for 10 minutes in any fruit liqueur or brandy or rum as many broken-up chocolate-chip cookies as there are peach halves. Over a very low flame, put a heavy 12-inch skillet with 1⅓ cups white wine in it, add the peach halves in one layer, their cavities uppermost. Fill cavities with broken-up cookies, allowing one cookie for each, then dab each with butter, cover, and cook for 15 minutes. With slotted spoon remove to bowls and serve hot, with or without fresh or canned cream or pressure-canned whipped cream.

DEVILED SARDINE SPREAD
BEEF ZINGARA
NOODLES
CANNED BABAS AU RHUM

Deviled Sardine Spread

Drain and place into any suitable container three 3¾-ounce cans brisling sardines. Stir in 1 teaspoon each Dijon-style prepared mustard and dry mustard, 3 tablespoons fresh or bottled lemon juice, ½ teaspoon Worcestershire sauce, and 3 dashes Tabasco. Season to taste with salt and coarse-ground black pepper, blend in 1 teaspoon each anchovy paste and capers. Put mixture in top of your smallest double boiler with ¾ inch water in the bottom, place over low flame, bind mixture with mayonnaise, color with 2 tablespoons parsley flakes, and heat 10 minutes. Put two asbestos pads under double boiler for 5 minutes to heat pads and remove from stove, with pads, to keep warm until ready to serve.

Beef Zingara

Drain well over a saucepan two 1-pound cans pot roast. If slices are too big, cut in half. Drain over the same saucepan one 10¾-ounce can chicken livers in mushroom gravy, one 3-ounce can sliced mushrooms, and one 8-ounce can each tiny peas and cut green beans, leaving all solids in cans. Put saucepan with liquids over a medium flame, bring to a boil, season with salt, coarse-ground black pepper, and 1 teaspoon each paprika, onion salt, and celery salt. Cook until reduced by one-third.

While sauce is cooking, arrange the slices of meat in the top of your largest double boiler, strew the chicken livers over the meat, then mushrooms, then peas, and finally green beans. When sauce has reduced, stir into it 1 cup sour cream or 1 cup undiluted evaporated milk into which 1 tablespoon fresh or bottled lemon juice has been thoroughly mixed, and pour over meat and vegetables. Over the same flame on which the sauce has cooked, put the double boiler, with 2 inches water in the bottom, cover, and cook for 15 minutes. On the other burner cook the noodles.

Noodles
See recipe for Fettuccini Parmigiana on page 212.

Canned Babas au Rhum
These are available in most gourmet specialty shops, in cans of various sizes and from various importers. Place the contents, syrup and all, in the top of a medium-sized double boiler, with 1 inch water in the bottom. Heat over a medium flame for 15 minutes during dinner, and serve hot.

HOT CHICKEN AND ALMOND SPREAD

HAM AND APPLES WITH SPICY SAUCE

CABBAGE OR SAUERKRAUT SAVOYARD

DANISH PINEAPPLE CAKE

Hot Chicken and Almond Spread
Open one 5-ounce can cooked chicken, discard all jelly and mince meat finely then, off the stove, put into the top of your small double boiler. Chop enough slivered almonds and any kind of pickle, and grate enough of any mild cheese, to make ½ cup of each, and add to chicken. Season with salt and white pepper to taste and bind with mayonnaise. Put double boiler top over bottom with ¾ inch water in it, and heat over medium flame for 15 minutes, with two asbestos pads under double boiler. Remove from stove, with pads, to keep warm. Just before serving, stir in 1 tablespoon sherry or dry white wine or dry vermouth and 1 tablespoon parsley flakes. Serve with any rye- or oat-flavored crackers or hard bread.

Ham and Apples with Spicy Sauce
Drain well over a saucepan two 1-pound cans pie apples, and remove half the fruit from one can to use for some other purpose. Add to apple syrup one 8-ounce can (1 cup) apple juice.

Use two 1-pound ham steaks cut in half crosswise, or two ½-inch-thick slices taken from a whole or canned ham and also cut in half crosswise, or eight ½-inch-thick slices Canadian bacon.

Over a medium flame, put to heat the saucepan containing apple syrup, and add 1 tablespoon brown sugar, 1 teaspoon ground ginger, ½ teaspoon each dry mustard and ground cinnamon, 1/4 teaspoon ground nutmeg, salt and coarse-ground black pepper to taste, and bring to a boil, then set flame very low and simmer, uncovered for 30 minutes.

Over a direct low flame, put to heat the top of your largest double boiler with 1 1/2 tablespoons meat fat (not butter or oil) in it. When hot, raise flame high, add ham slices, and fry quickly until both sides are well browned. Set flame to low, put apple slices over ham, pour reduced syrup over all, cook 10 minutes, and set over double boiler bottom, with 2 inches water in it, cover, and cook 10 minutes more. Then insert two asbestos pads under double boiler to heat for 5 minutes and remove from stove, with pads, to keep warm and to free burner.

Danish Pineapple Cake

Put into a saucepan of suitable size the contents of one 1-pound can undrained crushed pineapple, add 1/4 teaspoon salt and 1 teaspoon vanilla extract, and cook, uncovered, over low flame for 15 minutes.

Over a high flame, on the other burner, put to preheat for 10 minutes a heavy, covered, 12-inch dome-lidded skillet, with a rack in it. Into an 8-inch-square cake pan, put 4 tablespoons (1/2 stick) butter, put pan on rack in skillet to melt butter. Meanwhile, measure out 4 cups fine dry bread crumbs. When butter has melted, remove cake pan from skillet, pour in 2 cups crumbs, mix thoroughly with melted butter, and smooth over bottom of pan. Spread with half the drained pineapple, and over this spread 1/4 cup (4 tablespoons) gooseberry jam. Spread a third cup of crumbs over fruit and jam, dot with butter, spread balance of pineapple over, add another 1/4 cup jam, and top with balance of crumbs.

Put cake pan on rack in preheated skillet, cover, and cook, without lifting cover, for 10 minutes. Serve hot or cold, with or without canned or fresh cream.

Cabbage or Sauerkraut Savoyard

Use either two 1-pound cans sauerkraut (drained, rinsed, and and drained again) or 5 cups shredded fresh cabbage. The procedure for preparing is the same, but the flavor is different.

Over a medium flame, in a large deep saucepan, cook 4 slices diced bacon until crisp. Add sauerkraut or cabbage, toss well, cover, and cook for 10 minutes. Season well with salt and coarse-ground black pepper, add ½ cup sour cream, or undiluted evaporated milk to which 1 tablespoon fresh or bottled lemon juice has been added, toss again and serve.

CHEESE LOGS
CAPITOLADE OF CHICKEN
HILLARY'S SKILLET SQUASH
ARTICHOKES AND PEAS
GINGERBREAD II RECHAUFFÉ

Hillary's Skillet Squash

Since this dish takes the most time to prepare, we give the recipe for it first, without regard to its place on the menu. Before preparing, toast ½ cup slivered almonds by cooking 5 minutes in 2 tablespoons butter over a low flame.

Open one 1-pound can applesauce and one 29-ounce can cooked mashed squash, and empty into a large, heavy, dome-lidded skillet. Stir in thoroughly ¼ cup (4 tablespoons) brown sugar with 1 tablespoon any kind of syrup added, 4 tablespoons (½ stick) butter, ½ cup undiluted evaporated milk, and 2 eggs (or the equivalent in powdered eggs), beaten. Spread mixture smoothly, sprinkle over it the toasted almond slivers and ½ teaspoon ground or freshly grated nutmeg. Cover, put over a low flame, with flame-tamer under skillet, and cook for 45 minutes.

Cheese Logs

With a sharp knife, cut in half lengthwise 32 oblong hard rye crackers or bread. On half of the half-slices put a strip of soft Swiss, Gruyère, or any other equivalent cheese. Smear the cheese lightly with anchovy paste, and cover with a half-slice of cracker or bread.

Over a direct medium flame, put the top of your largest double boiler with 2 tablespoons butter in it. When butter is foamy, arrange enough sandwiches to cover bottom loosely. Sauté for 3 minutes, turn, and sauté 3 minutes more. Remove from pan, set aside, and repeat until all sandwiches are cooked.

Replace all cooked sandwiches in top of double boiler, set over double boiler bottom, with 2 inches water in it, put over three asbestos pads, raise flame high, and cook until water in double boiler bottom boils. Remove from stove, with asbestos pads, to keep warm and to free burner for the vegetables.

Artichokes and Peas

Drain well one 1-pound can each artichoke hearts and peas, leaving the vegetables in the cans.

Over a low flame, heat 2 tablespoons olive oil in a medium-sized skillet, stir in artichoke hearts, and sauté for 5 minutes. Add 1 teaspoon salt, ½ teaspoon sugar, and peas. Soak a paper towel in water, place over vegetables, cover, and steam gently for 10 minutes. When done, mix lightly and turn into the top of a medium-sized double boiler with 1½ inches water in the bottom. Put over fire, raise flame high, insert three asbestos pads under double boiler, and heat for 5 minutes. Remove from stove, with asbestos pads, and set aside to keep hot until ready to serve.

Capitolade of Chicken

Open two 5½-ounce cans boned chicken, separate meat from jelly, and leave jelly in cans, putting meat into any suitable container.

Chop coarsely one large white onion and mince one medium-sized clove garlic. Drain well one 3-ounce can mushroom stems and pieces or one 3-ounce can sliced or button mushrooms; if either of the latter, chop.

Over a direct very low flame put the top of a medium-sized double boiler, with 2 tablespoons buter in it, and stir in 1 teaspoon onion salt. When butter has melted, stir in onion and garlic, cook till onion is wilted, add mushrooms, and sauté until mushrooms take on color and onion is golden.

Meanwhile, put 1 inch water in the double boiler bottom and open one 10½-ounce can condensed cream of mushroom soup, condensed tomato bisque, or condensed cream of tomato soup. When vegetables are done, stir in undiluted soup and then ¼ cup dry white wine or dry vermouth, cover and heat for 10 minutes. While sauce is heating, pull apart the chicken meat into fairly sizeable pieces and stir in, along with 2 teaspoons parsley flakes. Re-cover and heat 10 minutes more, or until ready to serve.

Gingerbread II Rechauffé

Early in the day, or the day before, make gingerbread from scratch, according to this recipe from my mother-in-law.

In any rigid container, soften to galley temperature 4 table-spoons (½ stick) butter or any bland fat, stir in ¼ cup sugar, ½ cup molasses, 2 teaspoons ground ginger, 1 teaspoon each ground cinnamon and cloves, and blend well. Put a heavy 12-inch dome-lidded skillet, with a rack in it, over a high-medium flame to preheat for 10 minutes.

Butter or grease an 8-inch-square cake pan. Then, in a very small pot or pan, bring ½ cup water to a boil, remove from stove, add 1 teaspoon baking soda, and stir into other ingredients. Add 1¼ cups flour (all-purpose or any other kind) to mixture and beat until smooth. Beat or shake well 1 egg or the equivalent in powdered egg and stir into batter, which will be quite soft. Pour into cake pan, put pan on rack in skillet, cover, and cook for 30 minutes without lifting cover. If at that time it does not test done, cook 10 minutes more. Remove pan and rack from skillet, separate, and set both aside for 10 minutes. Turn gingerbread out of pan onto rack and let cool, then cut into squares and store in any airtight container.

When ready to reheat during dinner, put half the ginger-bread squares into a medium-sized saucepan, cover, and put over the lowest flame possible, with three asbestos pads under the pan. Heat for no more than 10 to 15 minutes. Save the rest of the gingerbread for snacks, midnight nibbling, or another meal.

HOT FRANKFURTER AND CHEESE APPETIZERS

LOBSTER PILAF

BRAISED CANNED CELERY STALKS

HOT DRIED APRICOTS CHEZ MOI

Hot Frankfurter and Cheese Appetizers

Use three well-drained 8-ounce cans small frankfurters or 8 regular-sized frankfurters. Cut each sausage into 1-inch slices, and make a long incision in the side of each piece. Into this, insert an oblong piece of thinly sliced Gruyère (for preference) or swiss or cheddar cheese, cut to fit the dimensions of the piece of sausage, and then insert 1 thin slice any kind of pickle, dill for preference (or ½ teaspoon any kind of chopped relish), and fasten all together with toothpicks.

Over a low flame put a large, heavy skillet with 1 tablespoon any variety of fat or shortening or drippings in it. While skillet is heating, on the other burner over a moderate flame put to heat over two asbestos pads or flame-tamer a medium-sized double boiler, with 1½ inches water in the bottom. When skillet is moderately hot, arrange appetizers closely, but without crowding, in the bottom. Sauté until meat takes on some color and cheese is running, turn into the double boiler top, cover, and remove from stove, with asbestos pads or flame-tamer, to keep hot until ready to serve.

Lobster Pilaf

Use three 5-ounce cans lobster meat or two 1-pound fresh lobsters, boiled, shelled, and cooled.

Chop finely 1 large white onion, and mince finely 1 large clove garlic. Over a medium flame, put a heavy 12-inch dome-lidded skillet with 1 tablespoon each butter and oil (olive oil for preference) in it, stir in onion and garlic, and sauté until onion is golden. While onion and garlic are cooking, measure out 1⅓ cups uncooked noninstant rice and open one 13¾-ounce can condensed clear chicken broth and one 8-ounce can or bottle clam juice.

When onion and garlic are done, stir rice in thoroughly, season with salt, white pepper, and 1 bay leaf, then add broth and clam juice, set flame low, cover, and cook for 20 minutes or until all liquid is absorbed.

Meanwhile, use the other burner to cook lobster and sauce. If canned lobster meat is used, drain cans well, pick meat over carefully and cut up coarsely. Fresh-cooked lobster should be prepared the same way. Without washing it, put over a medium flame the skillet in which the appetizer was cooked, with 2 tablespoons butter in it. While butter is melting, measure out ½ cup heavy fresh or canned cream or sour cream, and mix into it 2 teaspoons paprika and 1 tablespoon grated Parmesan cheese. When butter has melted, stir in lobster meat, and sauté, stirring occasionally, until lobster turns a little tan on all sides. While lobster sautés, set up your largest double boiler with 2 inches water in the bottom. When lobster is done, stir in cream mixture and 2 tablespoons parsley flakes, season with salt and white pepper. Heat, uncovered, for 10 minutes and remove from stove, replacing with double boiler bottom; put the latter on a flame-tamer or three asbestos pads to heat for 5 minutes.

When rice is done, turn off flame, and stir in 3 tablespoons grated Parmesan cheese. Off the stove, into the top of the double boiler, put half the cooked rice, spread over it the lobster and sauce, top with the balance of the rice. Cover, set over double boiler bottom, turn flame low, cook for 5 minutes, and remove from stove with asbestos pads or flame-tamer.

Braised Canned Celery Stalks

Use the skillet in which the rice was cooked, without washing it. Drain well into the skillet the liquid from two 14-ounce cans celery stalks (available at specialty food stores), leaving the vegetable in the cans, and stir into the liquid the contents of 3 envelopes dehydrated chicken broth, salt and white pepper, and 1 teaspoon onion salt. Put over a medium flame, bring to a boil, and cook, uncovered, until reduced by half. Add the celery stalks, set flame low, and heat through—about 7 minutes.

Dried Apricots Chez Moi

Three or four hours before preparing, in any suitable saucepan, soak 1 pound dried apricots in 2 cups dry white wine or dry vermouth, with water added, to cover fruit if necessary.

When ready to prepare, add ⅓ cup sugar and a few drops vanilla extract to liquid and, over a medium flame, cook fruit for 30 minutes, or until soft, in the same liquid in which they have soaked. Drain well, return to saucepan, turn flame very low, stir in 2 tablespoons any fruit liqueur (peach or cherry for preference), and keep hot until ready to serve.

When the Going Is Rough

MENUS AND RECIPES FOR EIGHT FOUL DAYS

By far the best way to cope with cooking in nasty weather and a heavy sea is at anchor in a snug harbor. Your craft may be bouncing around, all right, but at least your battle with the elements has diminished to a manageable level.

Make no mistake about it—when you're under way and the going gets rough, the cook is in for a trying experience. All hatches are closed, of course, all fiddleboards and shock cords in front of shelves are in place to keep things from richocheting around the cabin, the bad-weather locker is well-stocked, and galley strap, rubber boots, mitten-shaped pot holders and silicone-coated apron (made ashore from an ironing-board cover by removing drawstring or elastic and sewing on tape at strategic points) are ready to hand, but even so life below can be hot, damp, and unpleasant especially for you who must not only get some hot food into everybody else (I might mention that the cook comes last in this particular hierarchy) but replenish energy, morale and courage to go back topside with food that is *interesting*. The more unpleasant the cook's situation, the rougher the chances of mere survival may be to skipper and crew. Even if precious little may find its way into your own insides, remember this maxim. To tide you over, take a shot or two of what helps you most, force-feed yourself if necessary, when and as you can,

283

and above all carry on so as to be ready for the next invasion of the hungry.

In this kind of sailing, forget your frying pans and drip coffeepot. Nobody should be expected to do much more than boil water and stew up the contents of a few cans, in as deep a pot as possible and making sure that no pot is more than half full.

Ingenuity, adroitness, and, above all, tenacity are called for when it comes to producing restorative hot meals for the weary sailors who come below for sustenance and morale after fighting wind and waves. Still, in this kind of going, interesting concoctions can be put together for a main dish, with a dessert involving little or no cooking, served separately.

The only feasible foul-weather meal is one wherein the main course is served all at once in a deep heavy bowl and eaten with a spoon. Under the circumstances, the amenities must give way to prudence.

If your stove is not gimballed, we urgently recommend that before embarking on any passage when rough weather may be a hazard, a fairly large gimballed one-burner Sterno stove be installed, hung near the companionway if possible, and 'that an ample supply of fuel for it be laid on. With sufficient wide and small-mouthed thermos bottles, well stowed and protected, this little number will provide the heat for coffee, soup, stews, hot water and broth, day and night, until the weather ameliorates. And be sure to have aboard plenty of fancy cookies and cakes that keep well.

When it is literally impossible to prepare a meal on either stove, a stock of instant breakfast mixes, kept in the bad-weather locker, may tide everybody over, but, along with freeze-dried foods and pemmican, these are a very, very last resort.

The menus and recipes in this chapter endeavor to take full cognizance both of the formidable conditions under which the heavy-weather cook must operate and of the fatigue factor assailing skipper, crew, and cook alike, yet they provide the departure from the ordinary that should interest and restore tired abovedeck hands sufficiently to give them zest to return to the fray.

BREAKFASTS

FRESH GRAPEFRUIT IN SECTIONS
HOT CREAM OF WHEAT WITH
RAISINS, DATES, AND MILK

Fresh Grapefruit in Sections

Cut 2 large grapefruit in half crosswise, and, without peeling, cut each half into sections. This is "finger food".

Hot Cream of Wheat with Raisins, Dates, and Milk

Cook instant Cream of Wheat as directed on package, using a pot twice too large for the amount of cereal and water. While cereal is cooking, cut into quarters 8 or 10 dates. When cereal is done, stir in dates and a goodly amount of raisins. Serve in deep bowls with any kind of liquid milk. No additional sweetening should be necessary, but, if you have to, accommodate the sweet-tooths on board with sugar spooned over the milk.

FIXED-UP FIGS
OATMEAL
SOFT-BOILED EGGS ON
BROKEN-UP CRISP HARD RYE

Fixed-Up Figs

Open one 29-ounce can whole figs and pour off half the syrup. Set can into a deep kettle one-third full of water, over a medium flame. Pour into can of figs ½ cup claret and 1 teaspoon bottled lemon juice. Put 8 eggs in kettle around the can of figs. Heat until eggs are soft-boiled. Remove eggs to prevent their cooking further, turn off flame, and let figs keep hot until ready to serve.

Soft-Boiled Eggs on Broken-Up Crisp Hard Rye

Into each of four deep bowls, break up 2 sizeable pieces crisp hard rye bread. Over each serving break two soft-boiled eggs, season with salt, black pepper, and a good sprinkle of imitation bacon bits.

ONE-KETTLE BREAKFAST
(PRUNES, CODFISH CAKES, AND
BOSTON BROWN BREAD)

One-Kettle Breakfast

Open one 29-ounce can prunes or plums, and pour off half the syrup. Add 2 tablespoons rum or bourbon or brandy, and set can in large kettle one-third full of water, over a medium flame. Open one 1-pound can Boston brown bread, and set can in kettle with can of fruit. Open one 26-ounce can codfish cakes, and put can in kettle also. Finally, wedge in one opened 8-ounce can tomato sauce. Cover kettle, tie down lid, and cook for 15 minutes. Serve fruit first, in deep bowls; re-cover kettle, set flame low, and when fruit has been consumed, serve codfish cakes in same bowls, with tomato sauce spooned over each serving. Protecting your fingers from the heat with a towel or pot holder, remove the can of brown bread from the kettle, slide out bread, and slice thickly. Butter generously and serve as "fist food".

V-8 JUICE AND CONSOMMÉ
BUBBLE-AND-SQUEAK
ON CORNMEAL MUSH

V-8 Juice and Consommé

The night before, in a pot twice too large for the amount of liquid, heat the contents of one 16-ounce can V-8 juice and one 10½-ounce can undiluted condensed consommé. Add 1 tablespoon bottled lemon juice and 2 tablespoons sherry. Pour into a heated thermos bottle to keep hot overnight.

Bubble-and-Squeak

Into a pot twice too large for the amount of food, empty three 8-ounce cans Vienna sausages and two 1-pound cans sauerkraut. Stir in one 10½-ounce can undiluted condensed cream of mushroom soup and heat over low flame till bubbling.

Cornmeal Mush

In a pot twice too large for the food, cook four portions of white or yellow cornmeal as directed on the package. Serve in deep bowls, with Bubble-and-Squeak on top.

SPICED HOT SAUERKRAUT JUICE
SALAMI AND EGGS
PUMPERNICKEL

Spiced Hot Sauerkraut Juice

Pour contents of one 29-ounce can or two 1-pound cans sauerkraut juice into a saucepan twice too deep and large for the liquid. Stir in 1 teaspoon each onion salt, celery salt, and bottled lemon juice and ½ teaspoon Worcestershire. Put over a medium flame, and when it boils, pour into a wide-mouthed thermos bottle to keep warm until ready to serve.

Salami and Eggs

Over a low flame, melt 2 tablespoons butter in a deep pot, add 8 slices salami, torn into large pieces with fingers, and cook briefly.

Into a separate deep receptacle, break 8 eggs, add salt, pepper, and ½ cup any kind of liquid milk and beat slightly. Turn into pot with salami in it and cook, stirring, until done.

Pumpernickel

Open two 15-ounce cans sliced pumpernickel, butter each slice, and serve as "fist food" with salami and eggs.

HALF-AND-HALF CHICKEN BROTH
AND TOMATO JUICE
PENNY'S CHIPPED BEEF ON
BROKEN-UP SHIP'S BISCUIT

Half-and-Half Chicken Broth and Tomato Juice

Into a saucepan or pot twice too large for the amount of liquid, pour one 13¾-ounce can undiluted condensed clear chicken broth and one 18-ounce can tomato juice, and heat over a high flame to the boiling point. Stir in 4 tablespoons (¼ cup) sherry and serve in mugs.

Penny's Chipped Beef

In a deep saucepan or pot twice too large, over a low flame, put 2 tablespoons butter and, while it is melting, pull apart the contents of one 5-ounce package or jar chipped beef. Stir into melted butter, then stir in the undiluted contents of one 10½-ounce can each undiluted condensed cream of celery and condensed cream of mushroom soup. Season with white pepper, a dash of cayenne, and ½ teaspoon ground nutmeg. Raise flame to medium and cook, stirring, until mixture begins to bubble. Serve in deep bowls over broken-up ship's biscuit, or any hard bread or biscuit.

WHOLE ORANGE

BEAN-AND-POTATO SOUP

WITH CANADIAN BACON

Whole Orange

Allow as many oranges per person as desired, and cut each orange into quarters lengthwise without peeling. Serve in deep bowls, as "fist food".

Bean-and-Potato Soup with Canadian Bacon

Into a saucepan or pot twice too large and deep for the amount of soup, over a medium flame, empty, undiluted, one 10½-ounce can each condensed bean soup and condensed cream of potato soup, reserving one empty can. Pour into empty can the contents of one 5⅓-ounce can of undiluted evaporated milk, add water to fill soup can, and stir into soup. While soup is heating, cut or tear into bite-sized pieces 10 slices Canadian bacon, and stir into soup. When soup bubbles, ladle into mugs and serve with buttered pumpernickel—canned or fresh or stale.

HOT APPLE JUICE AND APRICOT NECTAR
CHICKEN LIVERS IN MUSHROOM GRAVY II
OVER HOMINY GRITS

Hot Apple Juice and Apricot Nectar

Over a high flame, into a saucepan or pot twice too large and deep for the liquid, pour one 18-ounce can apple juice and one 12-ounce can apricot nectar. Add 1 tablespoon rum or bourbon or sherry, and heat to a boil. Remove from stove and place where it won't spill until ready to serve in mugs.

Chicken Livers in Mushroom Gravy II

Into a saucepan or pot twice too large and deep for the amount of food, empty two 10¾-ounce cans chicken livers in mushroom gravy, season well, and heat over a low flame until it bubbles. Then remove from stove to a damp towel on the counter, or put pot into sink, until grits are done.

Hominy Grits

Using a large saucepan or pot, cook instant hominy grits as directed on package. When done, ladle into four deep bowls, pour chicken livers over the grits, and serve.

LUNCHES

CLARET BOUILLON
MACARONI BOLOGNESE
APRICOTS IN HONEY

Claret Bouillon

Into a saucepan twice too large and deep for the amount of liquid, empty two 10½-ounce cans undiluted condensed beef consommé and 1¼ cups claret or light red wine. Add 2 sticks cinnamon, 1 tablespoon sugar, and 1 tablespoon bottled lemon juice. Bring to a boil and set aside on a damp towel to prevent toppling over. When ready to serve, heat to drinking temperature and serve in mugs.

Macaroni Bolognese

Over a low flame, into a saucepan or pot twice too large and deep for the amount of food, empty the contents of one 8-ounce can sliced tongue, two 15-ounce cans macaroni in cheese sauce, and one 10½-ounce can Sauce Bolognese (rich tomato and meat sauce). Stir to mix, cover, and heat for 10 minutes. Serve with bread sticks.

Apricots in Honey

Over a medium flame, put into a deep saucepan (1½-quart or larger) 4 tablespoons (¼ cup) bottled lemon juice, 4 tablespoons (¼ cup) water, 1 cup or one 8-ounce bottle honey, and a few drops vanilla. Bring to a boil. While mixture is heating, drain well one 29-ounce can apricot halves, add fruit to honey mixture, and when mixture starts to simmer, turn off flame and leave until ready to serve.

PSEUDO-PISSALADIÈRE

HOT CRUSHED PINEAPPLE WITH

BROKEN-UP CHOCOLATE COOKIES

Pseudo-Pissaladière

This galley adaptation of the French cousin to a pizza is equally good and filling served over either broken-up hardtack or Syrian bread.

Over a low flame, into a deep 4-quart saucepan or pot, empty one 29-ounce can plus one 1-pound can whole tomatoes, two 3-ounce cans or one 6-ounce can tomato paste, ½ teaspoon dehydrated minced garlic, 1 teaspoon rosemary, and 1 tablespoon anchovy paste. Stir well, mashing tomatoes while stirring, and cook for 15 minutes. Stir in contents of two 3½-ounce cans French-fried onion rings. Drain well one 8-ounce can pitted black olives, add to pot, and heat until mixture bubbles. When serving, spoon over hardtack and sprinkle each portion generously with grated Parmesan cheese.

In calmer weather, this dish may be made with 4 large yellow onions, sliced, and then sautéed in ½ cup olive oil until beginning to take on color and with 6 fresh ripe tomatoes, peeled, seeded, and chopped coarsely, omitting canned French-fried onion rings, canned tomatoes, and tomato paste, and cooking over a low flame for 30 to 40 minutes.

Hot Crushed Pineapple with Broken-Up Chocolate Cookies

Over a low flame, put a deep saucepan (2½-quart capacity or larger). Drain well one 29-ounce can crushed pineapple, put fruit into saucepan, and heat through. While fruit is heating, with your fingers break up 16 chocolate cookies into bite-sized pieces. Strew over each serving of pineapple.

BAKED BEANS WITH
FRANKS AND SOUR CREAM
FIG NEWTONS AND
CHEDDAR CHUNKS

Baked Beans with Franks and Sour Cream

Drain well three 8-ounce cans cocktail frankfurters or two 1-pound cans regular-sized frankfurters. Cut small franks crosswise in half, and regular-sized franks crosswise into four pieces.

Over a medium flame, into a deep saucepan of at least 3-quart capacity, empty one 29-ounce can or two 1-pound cans baked beans in tomato sauce (without pork). Season well with salt, coarse-ground black pepper, and garlic salt; then mix in ½ cup sour cream, canned or fresh. Stir in cut-up frankfurters and heat until bubbling. After ladling into deep bowls, spoon more sour cream over each portion. Serve with any kind of heavy, flavorful rye or pumpernickel bread, canned or fresh.

CLEAR TOMATO SOUP
VIENNA SAUSAGES AND SAUERKRAUT
FIXED-UP RICE PUDDING

Clear Tomato Soup

Over a low flame, into a deep saucepan or pot of at least 2½-quart capacity, empty one 10½-ounce can each undiluted condensed consommé and undiluted condensed clear chicken broth. Add the contents of one 18-ounce can tomato juice and cook for

10 minutes. While soup is cooking, season with 1 teaspoon each onion salt, celery salt, celery seed, and salt and ½ teaspoon coarse-ground black pepper. When bubbling, remove pot to a damp cloth or put in sink surrounded by sponges to prevent spilling. It will stay hot until ready to serve.

Vienna Sausages and Sauerkraut

Drain well three 4-ounce cans Vienna sausages and put over a low flame a deep saucepan or pot of at least 2½-quart capacity with 2 tablespoons bacon fat or any other kind of fat or shortening in it. Put sausages into pot and cook, stirring, until they take on color. While they are cooking, core and cut up 2 tart apples and chop coarsely 1 medium-sized onion, and add to sausages. When sausages are done, empty over them one 29-ounce can sauerkraut, undrained. Season with salt and pepper, stir well, and cook for 20 minutes.

Fixed-Up Rice Pudding

Over a low flame, put a deep saucepan or pot of at least 3-quart capacity, and empty into it two 15-ounce cans prepared rice pudding. Stir in ¼ teaspoon almond or vanilla extract, if you can, the contents of half an 8-ounce can or one 4-ounce can mincemeat, ¼ cup raisins, and 5 tablespoons apricot or gooseberry jam. Heat to bubbling and serve with assorted fancy cookies.

CLAM BROTH
ANNETT'S ENRICHED CHICKEN STEW
DRIED FRUITS AND RAISINS
HOT CHOCOLATE WITH RUM

Clam Broth

This can be purchased ready to serve, and 32 ounces will serve four. Puncture cans with beer-can opener, set into a deep large saucepan or pot over a high-medium flame, and pour in immediately enough water to reach two-thirds of the way up the sides of cans. When water boils, remove cans to a damp cloth to prevent spilling or, if circumstances permit, empty into a wide-mouthed thermos, discarding water. Set flame low and return empty pot to stove.

Annett's Enriched Chicken Stew

Into the deep saucepan in which the broth was heated, empty two 13-ounce cans chicken stew, one 13-ounce can boned chicken, and one 10½-ounce can undiluted condensed cream of chicken soup. Add 2 pinches each dried leaves of thyme and marjoram, 1 teaspoon celery seed, ¼ cup white wine or dry vermouth, and salt and white pepper to taste. Stir well, then stir in one 3½-ounce can French-fried onion rings and heat until bubbling. Serve in deep bowls, with buttered bread for the fist.

Dried Fruits and Raisins

Into four deep bowls put an assortment of uncooked dried fruit and a liberal amount of raisins. Serve with hot chocolate, as "fist food".

Hot Chocolate with Rum

Over a low flame, put a deep saucepan of at least 3-quart capacity, containing 2 squares bitter chocolate and ⅓ cup water. When chocolate has melted, add ½ cup sugar, a few good shakes of salt, and 2 tablespoons cocoa powder. Cook, stirring, until sugar has melted and mixture is smooth. Stir in ½ teaspoon vanilla extract, add 3 pints any kind of liquid milk, and heat just to the boiling point, stirring to keep milk from burning. Just before serving, stir in 5 tablespoons (three 1½-ounce jiggers) dark rum.

CANNED LASAGNE

ON FLATBREAD

HILLARY'S BUTTERSCOTCH PUDDING

ASSORTED COOKIES

Canned Lasagne

This can be bought ready to heat and serve, and two 15-ounce cans will serve four. Heat as directed on the can, remembering to use a receptacle at least twice as large and deep as necessary for the amount of food.

Flatbread

This interesting and filling bread is imported from Norway, keeps very well, and is to be found in many gourmet delicacy stores and departments.

Hillary's Butterscotch Pudding

The recipe for this dessert is given on page 264.

SYRIAN LENTIL STEW

RAW APPLES AND CHEESE CHUNKS

Syrian Lentil Stew

Over a low flame, in a deep saucepan or pot of 3 or more quarts in capacity, put one large onion, coarsely chopped, and 4 slices canned prefried bacon. While onion and bacon are cooking, drain well two 20-ounce cans lentil soup and one 1-pound can whole tomatoes, leaving vegetables in their cans. Stir ½ teaspoon dehydrated minced garlic into the onion and bacon, and then stir in tomatoes. Simmer for 10 minutes, then add the lentils and mix well. Next, stir in contents of one 1⅝-ounce jar imitation bacon bits and ¼ teaspoon ground coriander. Heat mixture until bubbling. Just before serving, drain well one 8-ounce can pineapple chunks and stir fruit into stew.

EMILIE'S MONGOLE SOUP

HOT CANNED CHERRY CAKE

Emilie's Mongole Soup

Over a low flame, put a deep saucepan or pot of at least 3-quart capacity, and empty into it two 10½-ounce cans undiluted green pea soup, one 10½-ounce can undiluted condensed consommé, and one 1-pound can whole tomatoes. While soup is heating, mash tomatoes while stirring, then add contents of one 8-ounce can peas with liquid, 1 teaspoon dehydrated minced onion, 1 teaspoon sugar, 1 tablespoon parsley flakes, ½ teaspoon ground nutmeg, and salt and pepper to taste. When soup boils, pour in two 5⅓-ounce cans undiluted evaporated milk, stir well, and serve in deep bowls. Since this is the main dish for this luncheon, the recipe provides for plenty of soup. Pass around croutons of any kind to sprinkle over soup.

Hot Canned Cherry Cake

Open a 1½-pound can cherry cake, cut into wedges in can, put can into a deep saucepan or pot, and add water to come two-thirds of the way up the sides of the can. Put pot over a low flame, cover, and heat for 25 minutes or until ready to serve.

DINNERS

(No preprandial appetizers are included, for the simple reason that we doubt anybody will have the time, or be in the mood, for anything like the usual cocktail hour.)

BRUNSWICK STEW

MASHED PUMPKIN

INDIVIDUAL PLUM PUDDINGS

Brunswick Stew

Slice 2 large yellow onions. Over a low flame, put a deep pot or kettle of at least 6-quart capacity with a cover that can be anchored securely (but do not cover), and put sliced onions in the pot. Drain over the onions one 1-pound can corn kernels, leaving corn in can and placing can where it cannot spill.

Simmer onions and corn liquid for 15 minutes, uncovered, then add one 29-ounce can stewed tomatoes, one 13¾-ounce can undiluted condensed clear chicken broth, and one 1-pound can butter beans or large yellow lima beans. Season with ¼ teaspoon dried minced garlic, ½ teaspoon ground cloves, 2 good pinches cayenne or ½ teaspoon crushed dried red pepper, and salt and coarse-ground black pepper to taste. Mix well, cover, and bring to a boil. Thicken with ½ cup uncooked dehydrated mashed potatoes and cook, stirring, for 5 minutes.

Add contents of three 5-ounce cans boned chicken and the re-served corn, re-cover, and heat through. Just before serving, stir into stew 2 teaspoons Worcestershire sauce.

Mashed Pumpkin

Over a low flame put a saucepan deep enough to hold one 29-ounce can mashed pumpkin. Place pumpkin in pan unopened, puncture the top of the can three or four times with an ice pick to allow steam to escape, add water to come two-thirds of the way up the sides of the can, raise flame to medium, and heat, un-covered, until water boils. Then lower flame and cook 15 minutes.

Individual Plum Puddings

These are made in England and imported by gourmet spe-cialty shops. They are excellent in flavor, rich and filling, and are small enough to fit into the cups of an egg poacher for heating, if desired. They are equally good cold, with or without bottled hard sauce.

BOILED BEEF

WITH VEGETABLES AND POTATOES

CANNED RUM AND PECAN CAKE

Boiled Beef with Vegetables and Potatoes

Even when bad weather hits, the energy that comes only from fresh beef makes it worth having aboard if the meat is brought on frozen and the icebox is operating, or if there are places cool enough to keep it for two or three days before cooking, and if the fuel supply is not yet getting too low.

A good piece of boiled beef does take a long time to cook, but it needs no watching, once it's off to a good start. Use a lean and solid piece of beef rump or top or bottom round weighing be-tween 4 and 5 pounds, and a kettle deep enough to allow the meat to be covered with water, with at least 2 inches to spare.

Put the meat into the kettle, cover with cold water, and add 1 bay leaf, 6 peppercorns, 1 tablespoon salt, and 1 onion stick with 4 whole cloves. Cover securely, anchor the kettle to the stove, start a low flame, and bring to a boil. When you can hear the water bubbling, move the kettle to the free burner, put two asbestos pads over the flame, return kettle to lighted burner, re-anchor securely, and simmer, allowing 1 hour a pound for cooking, by which time it should be spoon tender.

An hour before serving, scrape 8 raw carrots and add to kettle. If they bring the water too high, ladle some out. Re-cover and continue cooking.

Fifteen minutes before serving, peel and cut into quarters 8 medium-sized potatoes, add to kettle, and then add, without draining, the contents of one 14-ounce can celery stalks. Again, ladle out some liquid if needed, and re-cover.

When ready to serve, lift meat out of kettle and put into any fairly deep receptacle, well secured against spilling. Prise the meat apart with a large fork or cut roughly into chunks. With a slotted spoon, remove vegetables to deep serving bowls in even proportions, put meat over them, and ladle a little broth into each bowl.

Any meat left over makes great sandwiches, or can be reheated in canned mushroom gravy enriched with dehydrated beef broth and served over rice. The cooking liquid makes a fine broth to serve hot, perhaps during a long night watch.

Canned Rum and Pecan Cake

This hearty cake, already restoratively well-enhanced with rich dark rum, can be ordered by mail, and one cake will serve four handsomely. It arrives in a vacuum-sealed tin and, of course, will keep indefinitely until opened, and as long as any fruitcake after opening if protected from dampness.

To serve hot, put unopened can into a deep saucepan or pot, surround with water to come two-thirds of the way up the can, puncture can three or four times with an ice pick to allow steam to escape, bring water to a boil, and steam 20 minutes. The cake is, however, also very good cold.

MUSCOVY MEAT BALLS
MASHED POTATOES III — CANNED BRUSSELS SPROUTS
CANNED ORANGES WITH GOOSEBERRY JAM

Muscovy Meat Balls

Over a low flame put a pot or saucepan twice too deep for the amount of food and empty into it four 8-ounce cans or two 1-pound cans cocktail meat balls. Stir in contents of 2 envelopes dehydrated beef broth, ½ teaspoon each ground nutmeg and cloves, and salt and coarse-ground black pepper to taste. Raise flame to medium, heat to a boil, and cook 10 minutes. Stir in 1 cup fresh or canned sour cream, heat to boiling point but do not boil, and serve over mashed potatoes and brussels sprouts.

Canned Brussels Sprouts

While meat balls are cooking, over a low flame put a large saucepan or pot deep enough and large enough to hold two 15-ounce cans brussels sprouts. Put unopened cans into pot, puncture each can top three or four times with an ice pick, and surround with water to come two-thirds of the way up the sides of the cans. Raise flame to medium, bring to a boil, and cook for 10 minutes. Remove cans to a nonspill surface, discard water in pot, and, after opening, lift out brussels sprouts with a slotted spoon to serve, then discard liquid in cans.

Mashed Potatoes III

On the free burner, prepare four servings of dehydrated mashed potatoes according to the directions on the package, using half again as much butter as called for.

Canned Oranges with Gooseberry Jam

Open one 29-ounce can mandarin oranges or orange sections, and with slotted spoon distribute fruit evenly among four deep bowls, leaving syrup in the can. Spoon over each portion 1 heaping tablespoon gooseberry jam, and with same spoon, add to each 3 tablespoons orange syrup, then discard the balance.

Individual Canned Steak and Mushroom Pies

These are to be found in the better supermarkets and in gourmet specialty shops. They are imported from England and, though directions call for heating in an oven, they can be steamed till hot. One pie will serve one person generously.

Over a low flame, put a very large pot or kettle, deep enough to hold four pie cans stacked up, or wide enough to hold two stacks of two cans each.

Puncture each can three or four times with an ice pick, arrange in kettle with any suitable device between each can to allow steam to escape, and add enough water to come just below the top of the bottom can. Cover securely, heat to a boil, and steam 15 minutes. Open cans as directed on package, but don't be unhappy if the piecrust is not as crisp as you would like—the flavor will be unchanged.

Hot Mincemeat on Pound Cake

Over a low flame, put a saucepan or pot twice too deep for the amount of food, and in it put one 8-ounce jar or can moist mincemeat. Stir in ½ cup sour cream, canned or fresh, and serve in bowls over broken-up raisin pound cake.

Bradley "Toast"

Over a low flame, empty into a saucepan twice too deep for the amount of food one 10½-ounce can undiluted condensed cream of potato soup, 1 cup undiluted evaporated milk, and one 29-ounce can whole tomatoes. Season with salt and coarse-ground black pepper. Raise flame to medium and, stirring constantly, bring to a boil. Turn flame as low as possible, break up the contents of one 12-ounce can corned beef, drain well one 8-ounce can green peas, and add both to pot. Heat through, and serve over broken-up hardtack.

CANNED CHICKEN MACÉDOINE

HOT CANNED PUMPERNICKEL

STEWED DRIED APRICOTS

TOPPED WITH VANILLA PUDDING

Canned Chicken Macédoine

Over a low flame, put a large saucepan twice too deep for the amount of food. Empty into it one 10½-ounce can undiluted condensed cream of celery soup and ⅓ soup can any kind of liquid milk or cream (except sour), and then mix well. Season with ½ teaspoon oregano and salt and coarse-ground black pepper to taste. While soup is heating, drain well one 1-pound can cut green beans, one small bottle pimiento-stuffed green olives, and one small can water chestnuts (slice the latter, if not already sliced). Add all to soup and stir well, whether or not the soup has yet heated. Add contents of two 5-ounce cans boned chicken, with jelly surrounding it, and stir well again. Bring to a boil and serve in deep bowls, over plenty of any kind of croutons.

Stewed Dried Apricots with Vanilla Pudding

Cook instant dried apricots as directed on package and drain, reserving apricot liquid. Over a medium flame, into a big, deep saucepan, empty one package vanilla pudding and cook as directed on package, substituting ⅓ cup apricot liquid for ⅓ cup of the milk called for, and discarding the rest of the apricot liquid.

Put apricots into deep bowls, dividing portions evenly, and top with hot vanilla pudding, also divided evenly. As a grace note, if feasible, strew a few slivered almonds on top of each portion.

CANNED ROAST BEEF WITH RED WINE
AND VEGETABLES
POTATO SALAD VII, CANNED, HOT
CANNED GREEN GRAPES

Canned Roast Beef with Red Wine and Vegetables

Drain over a large, deep saucepan or pot three 7½-ounce cans roast beef slices, one 1-pound can whole baby carrots, and one 3-ounce can sliced broiled-in-butter mushrooms, leaving all solids in cans and placing cans on counter onto a damp towel, or in the galley sink, to keep them upright. Add to liquid 1 teaspoon salt, coarse-ground black pepper, 2 teaspoons dried minced onions, ¼ teaspoon dried minced garlic, and 1 bay leaf. Bring to a boil, uncovered, add ½ cup red wine, and cook until reduced by half (about 20 minutes). Stir in meat and vegetables, heat through, and serve over hot canned potato salad.

Potato Salad VII, Canned, Hot

Over a low flame, put a saucepan deep enough and large enough to hold two 14-ounce cans potato salad. Puncture the top of each can three or four times with an ice pick, place cans in pot, and surround with enough water to come two-thirds of the way up the sides of the cans. Bring water to a boil and heat, uncovered, for 15 minutes.

Canned Green Grapes

Drain, discarding the syrup, three 8¼-ounce cans green grapes. Divide into four equal portions, sprinkle ground ginger over each portion, and serve with cake or any kind of cookies.

SPANISH RICE OVER CANNED KALE
APPLES OVER BROKEN-UP OATMEAL COOKIES

Spanish Rice

In a pot twice too large and deep for the rice and liquid, cook enough instant rice for four servings, as directed on the package. While rice is cooking, open one 10½-ounce can chicken livers in mushroom gravy and one 3-ounce can broiled-in-butter sliced mushrooms; drain off mushroom liquid, leaving mushrooms in can. When rice has cooked and been drained, return rice to pot, stir in chicken livers and mushrooms, and cook uncovered for 7 minutes. Drain well one 1-pound can whole tomatoes, stir into rice mixture, then add one 3½-ounce can French-fried onion rings and stir well again. Just before serving, stir into mixture 1½ cups grated sharp cheddar cheese.

Canned Kale

Over a low flame, set a deep saucepan or pot large enough and deep enough to hold two unopened 14-ounce cans kale. Puncture each can on top three or four times with an ice pick to allow steam to escape, set cans in pot, add water to come two-thirds of the way up the sides of the cans, raise flame to medium, bring water to a boil, and cook for 15 minutes. When ready to serve, lift cans out of water, leaving water on stove over a low flame; wrap a towel around each can, open, and drain well. Put into the bottom of four deep bowls and ladle Spanish Rice on top.

Apples over Broken-Up Oatmeal Cookies

Into the same pot in which the kale was heated, set two unopened 1-pound cans sliced pie apples, puncture the top of each can three or four times with an ice pick, and heat as kale was heated, using the same timing. Break up 12 crisp (not chewy) oatmeal cookies and distribute evenly among four deep bowls. Lift cans of apples from pot, open, drain well, and divide fruit among the four bowls. Lastly, over each portion, dribble honey generously, if you can.

Dishes You Cook Ashore, Then Bring on Board

APPETIZERS

Liz's Liverwurst

In a commodious bowl, mash ¼ pound sliced and skinned liverwurst. Grate into it one golf-ball–sized white onion and stir well. Add 1½ teaspoons dehydrated parsley flakes or chopped fresh parsley and salt and coarse-ground black pepper to taste, and stir well again. Add enough mayonnaise to bind well, and stir once more.

This will keep a week to 10 days in the refrigerator.

Shrimp Spread

Into a bowl of suitable size, empty one well-drained 4½-ounce can any kind of shrimp, and squeeze ½ lemon over shrimp. Add salt and coarse-ground black pepper, mash shrimp thoroughly, stir in enough mayonnaise to moisten, and add 2 tablespoons curry powder. Blend thoroughly, cover well, and refrigerate.

This will keep a week to 10 days in the refrigerator.

Camembert Marinée

In a largish bowl, soak overnight 1 whole ripe Camembert cheese, from 4 to 5 inches in diameter, in dry white wine to cover.

In the morning, soften 1/4 pound butter. When butter is soft, drain the cheese and scrape off any discolored portions, but do not remove all crust. Work butter well into cheese, until mixture is perfectly smooth, then chill for 30 minutes in refrigerator.

Meanwhile, put a 5-inch heavy skillet with 1 tablespoon butter in it over a low flame, and, when butter has melted, toast 2/3 cup slivered almonds until nicely tan. Remove from skillet to drain on paper towels, newspaper, or brown paper bag. When cool, chop finely with a sharp knife.

Remove cheese from refrigerator, re-form into its original shape, and cover top and sides thickly with chopped almonds. Return to refrigerator until 1/2 hour before serving.

MEATS

Roast Beef

As a practiced cook, you need no instructions for cooking this. For galley purposes, use a solid cut without bones and with very little fat around it. Undercook it a little, unless your gang likes all meat well done.

Special Pot Roast

Use a lean and solid piece of top or bottom or eye round weighing 4 to 5 pounds. Trim off any excess fat, and make two rows of inch-deep incisions at frequent intervals around all four sides. Into each incision, poke 1 pimiento-stuffed olive cut in half lengthwise, leaving four slits unfilled. Into each of these, insert 1/2 clove garlic.

Slice thinly 2 large white onions, put a large heavy skillet with 3 tablespoons butter, or drippings, or any other kind of fat in it over a medium flame, and when fat is melted, stir in onion. While onion is cooking, dice 1/2 pound uncooked bacon; when onion begins to take on a little color, add bacon. When fat from bacon begins to run, add meat, and brown a little on all sides.

While meat is browning, peel, seed, and chop coarsely 7 medium-sized tomatoes. Into a soup ladle or small saucepan, put two 1 1/2-ounce jiggers of rum. Heat rum, set a light to it, and pour, flaming, over the meat. When flame has gone out, add tomatoes, 1 bay leaf, ½ teaspoon each dried leaves of thyme and basil, and salt and coarse-ground black pepper to taste.

Remove everything to a deep, heavy stew pot or casserole, cover with foil, then put on lid and cook in a slow oven for 4 hours.

Cold Fried Chicken I

Multiple as are the recipes for this comestible, I prefer this method (origin unknown), whose keynotes are plenty of butter, a very low flame, and special seasoning. I have brought it aboard on many a cruise, after cooking and chilling ashore. It never fails to please and, after the first meal, suffices for sandwiches and/or salads as well.

For four persons, I use 1 quartered fryer and 1 extra breast. Spread chicken pieces on wax paper, after removing all loose fat and the "bishop's nose". Sprinkle each piece generously on both sides with salt, coarse-ground black pepper, garlic salt, onion salt, celery seed, and dried thyme leaves.

Set a heavy 12-inch skillet over a low flame, put ½ stick (4 tablespoons) butter in it, and, when butter has melted, arrange chicken pieces in skillet, skin side down. Cook each piece slowly until golden brown on one side, turn, and cook slowly on the other side until the same color. When done, pour 3 tablespoons (one 1½-ounce jigger) bourbon over chicken, raise flame high briefly, and remove chicken from skillet, to drain on paper towels or newspaper or brown paper. Scrape up all the bits and juices in the pan and dribble over the chicken pieces. Let cool. When cool, put into any airtight container and chill in refrigerator.

My Favorite Ragoût

What makes this ragoût distinctive is, first of all, that the meat is cut into *small* cubes, not the usual 1- to 2-inch size stipulated for most stews, ragoûts, and so on. Secondly, the seasonings are interesting and different.

Remove all fat and gristle from a 2½ pound piece of top round of beef, and cut into ¾-inch cubes. Measure out separately 1 tablespoon brandy or dark rum and 3 tablespoons flour. Scrub and stem 16 small mushrooms, cut in half crosswise the contents of 1 small jar pimiento-stuffed olives, and peel 16 small white onions.

You will also need two 10½-ounce cans undiluted condensed beef broth, black currant jelly, tomato paste, ½ cup red wine (claret for preference), and 1 bay leaf.

Over a high flame, put 4 tablespoons (½ stick) butter in a heavy skillet 10 inches wide or larger. When butter is sizzling, add cubed meat and brown quickly on all sides without lowering flame. As meat is about to finish browning, pour the spirits into a soup ladle, heat over a very low flame and, when meat is done, pour the spirits on it. Stir rapidly to bring up all the browning residue in the pan and, with a slotted spoon, remove meat and set aside. Lower flame to medium, put 2 more tablespoons butter in skillet, and, when it has melted, add mushrooms and onions, brown quickly, stirring and shaking the pan, and remove from skillet.

Remove pan from flame and stir in 1 soupspoon tomato paste and the flour. When smooth, add 2 cups (about 1½ cans) undiluted condensed beef bouillon. Return to a medium flame, stirring until sauce comes to a boil; then set flame low. Add wine and 1 tablespoon currant jelly, stir until jelly has melted, then stir in olives. Return meat, mushrooms, and onions to pan, stir well, put two asbestos pads or a flame-tamer under the pan, cover, and simmer slowly until meat is tender—about 45 minutes to 1 hour.

My Own Meat Loaf

This is a stand-by for every cruise we undertake, because it keeps so well (up to 2 weeks in the icebox), stores readily in a plastic bag, and seems to be unaffected by some leakage into the bag from melted ice, if not left that way for more than a day.

Best of all, there are so many hot and cold ways to serve it; à la Fermière (see page 76), cubed in an Empanada (see page 99), sliced and lightly sautéed, in a salad, and in sandwiches, to name a few. Some cooks, cleverer than I, or having an oven aboard, even make meat loaf in the galley.

For a 3-pound meat loaf, put 1½ pounds each ground chuck

and ground round into a very large receptacle, chop coarsely 4 large yellow onions, and fry them over a medium flame in any kind of fat or shortening, or combination of fats, stirring from time to time, until so dark a brown that they are almost burnt.

Over the meat, pour 1 cup fine bread crumbs (flavored or plain), ¼ cup (4 tablespoons) dehydrated parsley flakes or finely chopped fresh parsley, 1½ tablespoons salt, 1 teaspoon each coarse-ground black pepper and celery salt, and ½ teaspoon each dried leaves of thyme and marjoram. In a separate receptacle, beat 3 eggs and 1 cup any kind of liquid milk together until blended.

When onions are done, drain on paper towels, brown paper, or newspaper and set to cool. With both hands (there is no substitute that I've found) thoroughly mix all the dry ingredients into the meat, then pour in the egg and milk mixture and, with both hands again, mix thoroughly. Add the onions, which need only be cool enough to handle readily, and mix again to distribute them well.

Transfer the mixture to a medium-sized shallow ovenproof dish or heavy pan (oval, oblong, or round) and shape into a loaf. Pour over the loaf enough hot tap water to come a third of the way up the sides of the loaf, smooth top of loaf with your hands, and bake at 350° for 2 hours.

VEGETABLES

Potatoes Hashed in Cream

The night or day before preparing, bake 4 good-sized baking potatoes in the usual way, let cool, and then put in refrigerator overnight.

When ready to prepare, peel potatoes with a sharp knife and cut into ¼-inch squares. Over a low flame, put a large heavy skillet, add potatoes, and pour over them enough heavy sweet cream just to cover potatoes. Bring to a simmer and cook, uncovered, until most of the cream has been absorbed. Season with salt and coarse-ground black pepper, raise flame high, and cook until just beginning to brown. Remove skillet from stove, let cool, and store in refrigerator in any airtight container.

To reheat on board, follow instructions given on pages 141 and 144.

Green Beans à la Façon de Chez Moi

Wash well 1¼ pounds fresh green beans, and snip off their ends. Put in a large skillet, add ½ inch water, and set over a high flame. When water boils, turn flame as low as possible and cook beans for no more than 5 minutes, then drain and set aside. Meanwhile, chop finely 1 small white onion.

Return skillet to stove over a low flame, put 2 tablespoons bacon fat into it, and, when fat has melted, add 2 teaspoons soy sauce, ¼ teaspoon grated lemon rind, ½ teaspoon oregano, and the onion. When onion begins to take on color, stir in ¼ teaspoon dry mustard and the beans and cook, covered, 5 minutes more.

To finish preparation on board at serving time, follow instructions given on page 141.

SALADS

Potato Salad III

Peel and cube 6 medium-sized raw baking potatoes, put into a saucepan, cover with undiluted condensed canned consommé, add 1 whole clove garlic, cover, and cook until potatoes are barely tender (about 10 minutes). Drain well, discard garlic, and save soup for use on another occasion.

While potatoes are cooking, drain 1 jar or can pimientos and cut pimientos into strips; open, but do not drain, two 2-ounce cans flat anchovy fillets, remove fillets from can (leaving oil), and dice; and chop finely 1 small white onion.

Put potatoes into a large bowl. While still warm, add pimientos, anchovies, onion, and 2 tablespoons dehydrated parsley flakes or minced fresh parsley, and stir well. In a separate receptacle, put anchovy oil, the juice of ½ lemon or 1 tablespoon bottled lemon juice, 1 teaspoon celery seed, 3 tablespoons chopped fresh basil, salt and coarse-ground black pepper to taste, 3 tablespoons tarragon vinegar, and 2 tablespoons olive oil. Shake or beat well, stir into potatoes, and let cool.

Peel, seed, and dice 1 medium-sized cucumber, and thin ½ cup mayonnaise with heavy cream. Stir cucumber into cooled potatoes and bind with thinned mayonnaise. Chill thoroughly.

DESSERTS

Peppermint Chocolate Ice Cream

Over a low flame, in the top of a double boiler melt, with 2 tablespoons heavy cream, 6 medium-sized peppermint patties, or the equivalent in large ones.

Prepare chocolate ice cream mix as directed on package, using light cream, then stir in melted peppermint-patty mixture, remove to any suitable container, and freeze hard.

Maple Wafers

Sift together ¼ teaspoon baking soda, ¾ cup flour, ⅓ teaspoon baking powder, ¼ teaspoon salt. In a large saucepan, bring to a boil, stirring constantly ¾ cup maple or maple-flavored syrup and ⅓ cup butter or margarine. Boil for 30 seconds, remove from fire and stir in dry ingredients. Batter will be lumpy. By teaspoonfuls, place 8 dabs of batter on a greased cooky sheet, well apart. Bake at 350° for 6 to 8 minutes or until golden-tan. Take each cooky carefully from sheet, roll around handle of a wooden spoon, place on a rack to cool. Repeat cooking, rolling and cooling process until all batter is used.

Oatmeal Wafers

In any container big enough for all the batter, cream together ½ cup softened butter and 1 cup sugar, then add 2 whole eggs and stir well. Next: 4 tablespoons flour, 2 teaspoons baking powder, 2 cups quick-cooking oats, and blend well.

Grease, then flour, a cooky sheet. By soupspoonfuls, drop batter onto sheet, well apart. Bake at 350°, watching constantly. When cookies go flat, after first puffing up, and are no longer shiny, take out and let cool. Repeat until all batter is used.

Smooth Trade-Off Ideas

~ If there's no egg for cooking a baked dish, increase baking powder by one teaspoon per egg or add the equivalent to prepared mix.

~ Use honey or syrup instead of sugar. Reduce liquid called for in recipe by 1/4 cup for each cup honey or syrup.

~ Three tablespoons powdered cocoa and 2 teaspoons any shortening, oil, or fat equals 1 ounce baking chocolate.

~ Many fats can replace butter if you remember to use a third again as much other fat as the amount of butter called for.

~ Soda bicarb and cream of tartar can replace baking powder; 1/4 teaspoon bicarb and 1/2 teaspoon cream of tartar equalling 1 teaspoon baking powder.

~ Lemon juice or vinegar stirred into soured canned cream or undiluted evaporated milk makes a good jury-rig sour cream. Taste before using.

~ Exchange brown sugar for white, cup for cup, any time.

~ To turn powdered egg into its fresh equivalent, add 2 table-spoon water to 1 tablespoon powder.

~ Celery seed and celery salt, combined, can substitute for fresh celery; 1/4 teaspoon celery seed plus 1/2 teaspoon celery salt gives the same flavor as 1/2 cup fresh chopped celery.

~ Whipped cream is the sine qua non for some cooks, who won't truck with the pressure-canned kind. Trade-offs: equal parts of powdered milk and water plus 3/4 teaspoon lemon juice per 1/3 cup; 1 unopened can evaporated milk heated in boiling water 10 minutes, cooled at least 1/2 hour, then whipped; 1 cup thin cream mixed with 1/2 teaspoon gelatin powder, 3 to 4 drops lemon juice added, then whipped.

~ Volume for volume, green olives, sliced, substitute for green peppers; black pitted sliced olives substitute for mushrooms.

Resources for Gourmet
Canned Foods

To keep up with the wants of an ever-more-sophisticated eating public, the producers, distributors and importers of unusual, fascinating and delectable food in packages or cans are offering a greater and greater variety all the time. None need refrigeration— a big boon to any galley executive. Pacing these efforts, gourmet food shelves in supermarkets, shops devoted to fine foods, and specialty food outlets of all kinds are growing at a great clip.

To be sure, distribution has not yet fully caught up with demand so far, and as a result some of the specialties mentioned in this book may not be ready at hand in your own particular area. To offset this possibility, this chapter comprises a list of the suppliers of a number of canned gourmet foods that are sometimes hard to find easily. Addresses are included, and, where possible, the name of an executive to whom to write, some of whom, we acknowledge may, by the time you read this, have moved onward to other spots in other firms. Yet someone has taken each one's place, receives and answers the predecessor's mail, and will respond to any inquiry of yours, as a matter of courtesy. Write to the executive listed and you will surely get an answer from someone; it doesn't much matter who, so long as your query is answered fully and to your satisfaction.

Any of the listed firms will be glad to honor your written query about an outlet near you, and many will send you goods by mail order. A few have mail order catalogs as well.

And—in the spirit of sharing secrets with like-minded cooks—
you might be doing your own favorite food shop a favor by asking
the manager to stock the things that especially appeal to you.

Product	*Manufacturer or Distributor*

APPETIZERS

Powdered Quiche (France)	A. & A. Food Products Corp. 135 East 144th Street Bronx, N.Y. 10451 *write to:* Mr. Frankel
Twiglets (Peek, Frean—England)	A. B. (America) Ltd. 201 East 42nd Street New York, N.Y. 10017 *write to:* Mr. Stanley Moss
Roland Skewers	American Roland Corp. 22 Hudson Street New York, N.Y. 10013 *write to:* Mr. C. J. Winkel
Stuffed Vine Leaves	Arista Oil Co. 143 Franklin Street New York, N.Y. 10013 *write to:* Mr. John Mashahladius
Southern Country Ham Spread	Beaumont Inn Foods, Inc. Harrodsburg, Ky. 40330
Chopped Chicken Livers (Baldinger Brand)	Cresca Company, Inc. 2500 83rd Street North Bergen, N.J. 07047 *write to:* Mr. Walter M. Levi
Shrimp-Cheese Waffles (F.A.B. Foods, London)	Lemberger Food Co., Inc. 129 Fair Street Palisades Park, N.J. 07650

BREADS AND CRACKERS

Tortillas, Taco Shells (Ashley Brand)

A. & A. Food Products Corp.
135 East 144th Street
Bronx, N.Y. 10451
write to: Mr. Frankel

Brenmer Wafers
Brenmer Oval Oat Crackers

Brenmer Biscuit Co.
727 North Kedzie Ave.
Chicago, Illinois 60612

Sliced Pumpernickel (Soekeland Brand, Germany)

T. G. Koryn, Inc.
66 Broad Street
Carlstadt, N.J. 07022
write to: Mr. T. G. Koryn

Finn Crisp (Flatbread)

A. V. Olsson Trade Co.
1 Pondfield Road
Bronxville, N.Y. 10708

DAIRY

Butter (Darigold Brand)

Consolidated Dairy Products
1474 North Indiana
Los Angeles, Calif. 90063

Brie—Camembert—Goat Cheeses (France)

Europa Foods, Ltd.
1 Lexington Avenue
Bethpage, N.Y. 11714
write to: Ruth Berger

"Fol Amour" Cheese (France)

T. G. Koryn, Inc.
66 Broad Street
Carlstadt, N.J. 07022
write to: Mr. T. G. Koryn

Whole Fresh Milk
Sour Cream
Heavy Cream
Half-and-Half
Butter

Real-Fresh Co.
P. O. Box 1551
Visalia, Calif. 93277

Six de Savoie Cheese (France)
Petit Münster de France

Otto Roth & Co., Inc.
177 Duane Street
New York, N.Y. 10013
write to: Mr. Ed Crimmins

DESSERTS

Powdered Flan (Cup Custard—France)

American Roland Corp.
22 Hudson Street
New York, N.Y. 10013
write to: Mr. G. J. Winkel

Mincemeat, Flavored with Scotch
   Whiskey (Scotland)

H. L. Bendorf Corp.
111–50 76th Road
Forest Hills, N.Y. 11375

Baba au Rhum

M. Bertauche
San Rafael, Calif.

Individual Plum Puddings (England)

Cowan & Fransman
325 Spring Street
New York, N.Y. 10013
write to: Mr. Julian Cowan

Chocolate Nut Roll
Fruit Nut Roll

Crosse & Blackwell, Inc.
100 Bloomingdale Road
White Plains, N.Y. 10603
write to: Mrs. H. J. Britt

Rice Pudding

S. S. Pierce & Co.
133 Brookline Avenue
Boston, Mass.

Rum and Pecan Cake

Stern's
1248 West Paces Ferry Road
   at 1–75
Atlanta, Ga. 30327

FISH

Iceland Brook Trout (Ora Brand,
   Reykjavik, Iceland)

Liberty Import Corp.
66 Broad Street

Carlstadt, N.J. 07022
write to: Mr. Louis L. Barth

Finnan Haddie (Maine, AM Look Co. Brand)

The H. G. Norton Co., Inc.
Drawer 269
New Milford, Conn. 06776
write to: Mr. H. G. Norton

Oysters, Whole

S and W Fine Foods, Inc.
333 Scherwin Street
San Francisco, Calif. 94134
write to: Customer Relations

FREEZE-DRIED FOODS

The firms listed at the right all carry an assortment of freeze-dried and instant foods; all are happy to fill mail orders. Some have catalogs, some do not, but nothing holding with this type of edible, we have never tried any of their products, but do consider a selection to be an important component of your emergency food locker. Choose the one closest to your home grounds as the first one to get in touch with.

Alpine Hut, Inc.
4725 30th Avenue, N.E
Seattle, Washington 98105

Bernard Food Industries, Inc.
1125 Hartrey Avenue
Evanston, Ill. 60204

Canoe Country Outfitter
629 East Sheridan Street
Ely, Minn. 55731

Chuck Wagon Foods
176 Oak Street
Newton, Mass. 02164

Greenman, Leon R.
132 Spring Street
New York, N.Y. 10012

Oregon Freeze-Dry Foods, Inc.
Albany, Oregon 97321

Remington's
11230 Georgia Avenue
Wheaton, Maryland 20902

Tex's Sporting Goods
910 Wilshire Boulevard
Santa Monica, Calif. 90401

FRUITS

Sliced Mangoes White Peaches		American Roland Corp. 22 Hudson Street New York, N.Y. 10013 *write to:* Mr. G. J. Winkel
Gooseberries in Syrup Raspberries in Syrup Strawberries in Syrup	Baxter Brand Fochabers, Scotland	The British Trade Development Office 150 East 58th Street New York, N.Y. 10022 *write to:* Mr. Allen C. Bryson
Baked Apples Petit Pickled Pears	Harry and David Brand	DiStanislao-Calkins Co. P.O. Box 712 Medford, Oregon 97501 *write to:* Mr. Jos. DiStanislao

JAMS

Scotch Whiskey Flavored Orange Marmalade
Armagnac Brandy Flavored Apricot Jam

H. L. Bendorf Corp.
111–50 76th Road
Forest Hills, N.Y. 11375

MEATS

Salami (Denmark)
Beef Enchiladas (Texas)

A. & A. Food Products Corp.
135 East 144th Street
Bronx, N.Y. 10451
write to: Mr. Frankel

Chicken Livers in Mushroom Gravy

Brandywyne Mushroom Co.
West Chester, Pa.

Pre-Fried Bacon (Swift & Co.)

Brown & Sharp Co.
P.O. Box 4220
Downey, Calif. 90241

Whole Chicken

Dennis Food Co.
Augusta, Illinois

Sauerbraten
Sherry Cured Smoked Ham

Hickory Valley Farm, Inc.
Little Kunkletown
Stroudsburg, Pa. 18360
write to: Miss Millie Howe

Meat Balls in Sour Cream (Kottbüller)
Chicken Cacciatore (Famous Foods of
  the World)
Beef Stroganoff (Famous Foods of the
  World)

George A. Hormel & Co.
General Office
Austin, Minn.

Sauerkraut and Sausages
Cassoulet de Toulouse

T. G. Koryn, Inc.
66 Broad Street
Carlstadt, N.J. 07022
write to: Mr. T. G. Koryn

Sliced Roast Beef with Gravy
Beef and Mushroom Pie
Beef and Kidney Pie

Liberty Import Corp.
66 Broad Street
Carlstadt, N.J. 07022
write to: Mr. Louis Barth

Stuffed Cabbage
Beef Stroganoff
Lamb Stew
Boiled New England Dinner
Pot Roast
Chicken Stew

S. S. Pierce & Co.
133 Brookline Avenue
Boston, Mass.

Sliced Bacon (Danefoods, Denmark)

Plumrose, Inc.
66 Fadem Road
Springfield, N.J.

Smoked Corned Beef
  Tongue
Boeuf Bourguignon
Corned Beef and Cabbage
} Westzstein Brand

Premier Smoked Meats
89 North 6th
Brooklyn, N.Y.

Smoked Cervelat
  Sausage
Westphalian Ham
} Koopman Brand, Germany

C. & J. Willenborg, Inc.
1237 Park Avenue
Hoboken, N.J. 07030

SALADS

Beetroot Salad
Potato Salad

A. & A. Food Products Corp.
135 East 144th Street
Bronx, N.Y. 10451
write to: Mr. Frankel

Celery Salad (West Germany)

C. & J. Willenborg, Inc.
1237 Park Avenue
Hobeken, N.J. 07030
write to: Mr. John Willenborg

SAUCES

Bourbon Dessert Sauce

Beaumont Inn Foods, Inc.
Harrodsburg, Ky. 40330

Green Basil Sauce (Tigullio, Italy)
Béarnaise Sauce (Belgium)

Cowan & Fransman
325 Spring Street
New York, N.Y. 10013
write to: Mr. Julian Cowan

Polynesian Sauce
Bolognese Sauce
Newburg Sauce
Champignon Sauce

Crosse & Blackwell, Inc.
100 Bloomingdale Road
White Plains, N.Y. 10603
write to: Mrs. H. J. Britt

SOUPS

Cream of Broccoli
Cream of Cucumber
Cream of Romaine

Chalet Suzanne Food Co.
Lake Wales, Florida

Gazpacho

Crosse & Blackwell, Inc.
10 Bloomingdale Road
White Plains, N.Y. 10603
write to: Mrs. H. J. Britt

Thin Oxtail Soup (Australia)

Europa Foods Ltd.
1 Lexington Avenue
Bethpage, N.Y. 11714
write to: Ruth Berger

Pennsylvania Dutch Pea Soup with Ham
  Chunks
Lentil Soup with Keilbasi Sausage

Hickory Valley Farm, Inc.
Little Kuilkletown
Stroudsburg, Pa. 18360
write to: Miss Millie Howe

Garbanzo (Famous Foods of the World)

George A. Hormel & Co.
Austin, Minn.

Venison Soup with
  Vegetables
Hunter Soup with
  Vegetables
Oyster Soup with   Frank Cooper, Ltd.
  Guiness Stout   Oxford, England
Wild Duck and
  Orange Soup
Cream of Scampi
Cream of Pheasant

House of Lawrence, Inc.
30 East 42nd Street
New York, N.Y. 10017
write to: Mrs. E. G. Orsenigo

Thick Oxtail (Bender & Casells, England)
Bouillabaisse   Morvandelles,
Potage St. Germain   France

Liberty Import Corp.
66 Broad Street
Carlstadt, N.J. 07072
write to: Mr. Louis Barth

VEGETABLES

Red Cabbage with   Felix Brand,
  Apples   Sweden
Baby Dill Potatoes
Stuffed Eggplant   Castle Village
            Brand
Ratatouille   Conserves Héro,
Potato Pancakes   Switzerland

A. & A. Foods, Inc.
135 East 144th Street
Bronx, N.Y. 10451
write to: Mr. Frankel

Celery Stalks
Endives

Imported Directly from
   France by B. Altman & Co.
361 Fifth Avenue
New York, N.Y. 10016
write to: Mr. James Cappiello

Wheat Pilaf (cracked wheat—bulgur) — Old World Brand, Fisher Flouring Mills, Seattle, Wash. — T. G. Koryn, Inc. 66 Broad Street Carlstadt, N.J. 07022 *write to:* Mr. T. G. Koryn

Whole Chestnuts (Clément Faugier, France)

Brussels Sprouts
Flageolets
Leeks
} Le Semeur, Belgium — Liberty Import Corp. 66 Broad Street Carlstadt, N.J. 07072 *write to:* Mr. Louis Barth

Celery Knobs
Kale
} Basserman Brand, West Germany

Pinto Beans

Frijoles Refritos with Chili
Garbanzos
Tomatoes and Jalapenes
} El Paso Brand — Mountain Pass Canning Co. Anthony, Texas 88021

Wine Sauerkraut
Red Cabbage
Kale
Celery Stalks
Broad Beans
} West Germany — C. J. Willenborg, Inc. 1237 Park Avenue Hoboken, N.J. 07030 *write to:* Mr. John Willenborg

MISCELLANEOUS

Coffee-pot Holder — Pat Baird's Ship's Wheel 1516 West 55th Street LaGrange, Ill. 60525

3-qt. Aluminum Double Boiler — Chilton Aluminum Aluminum Specialty Co. Manitowoc, Wis.

Non-Skid Dinnerware — Yachting Tableware Box 546 Wilmington, Delaware 19899

Servespoon — Ace Mfg. Co. Chalfont, Pa.

Index

To make this index as useful as possible, certain types of page entries are specially marked. Numbers in *italic* type refer to the <u>menu</u> pages on which the dishes are listed. Words in *italic* are recipe titles in a foreign language. Bold figures following each recipe title indicate the page on which the recipe appears.